I0792925

# MASSACHUSETTS CORRECTIONAL INSTITUTION Bridgewater

# MASSACHUSETTS CORRECTIONAL INSTITUTION Bridgewater

## *A Troubled Past*

MICHAEL J. MADDIGAN

THE History PRESS

Published by The History Press
Charleston, SC
www.historypress.net



First published 2018

Manufactured in the United States

ISBN 9781467139137

Library of Congress Control Number: 2017958382

*The moral test of Government is how that Government treats those who are in the dawn of life, the children; those who are in the twilight of life, the elderly; and those who are in the shadows of life, the sick, the needy and the handicapped.*
*—Hubert H. Humphrey (1911–1978)*

# Contents

# Preface

Conceived in 1854 in a spirit of altruistic social reform at a time when Massachusetts was a world leader in the provision of charitable services to its citizens, the Massachusetts State Almshouse at Bridgewater was intended as a model of state-sponsored welfare. Its role and the public attitude toward it changed so drastically, however, that just over one hundred years later, its successor institution, the Massachusetts Correctional Institution (MCI)–Bridgewater, was seen as epitomizing the nation's failed social policies and was considered one of the worst prisons in the country. Today, the institution's legatee, the Bridgewater Correctional Complex, continues to draw scrutiny as it grapples with century-old issues, and its most visible unit, Bridgewater State Hospital, remains controversial for its treatment of patients.

Massachusetts's correctional complex at Bridgewater evolved from a single almshouse and later penal institution housing alcoholics, vagrants, "defective delinquents" and the criminally insane to its present arrangement of four individually administered units with specialized roles: Bridgewater State Hospital (a forensic psychiatric facility housing mentally ill criminals and pre-trial detainees undergoing evaluation), Old Colony Correctional Center (a medium-security prison), Massachusetts Alcohol and Substance Abuse Center (a minimum-security detoxification and substance abuse treatment unit for civilly committed males) and the Massachusetts Treatment Center (a medium-security facility housing criminally sentenced male sex offenders and civilly committed individuals considered sexually dangerous persons).

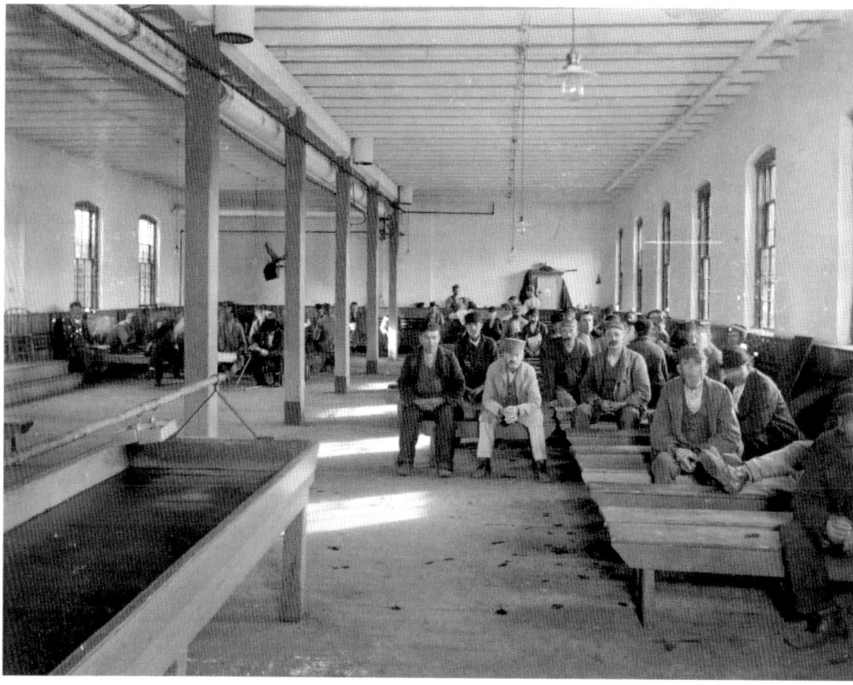

Bridgewater State Farm, prison department, recreation room, circa 1900. *Harvard Art Museums/Fogg Museum, Transfer from the Carpenter Center for the Visual Arts, Social Museum Collection, 3.2002.270.3. Unidentified Artist. Imaging Department © President and Fellows of Harvard College.*

Historically, Bridgewater has been troubled in part by an ever-changing and frequently unclear mandate that resulted in the historic commingling of the criminal, the poor, the mentally disturbed, the aged, the ill and the infirm, making it a challenge to administer the institution effectively or to rehabilitate its residents. Over the years, many inmates and patients have been illegally confined, committed without due process or without having been convicted of a crime. Understaffing, the absence of professional staff, deteriorating facilities, periodic abuse and violence and the tendency to use Bridgewater as a repository for individuals not wanted elsewhere contributed in the past to degrading conditions and an entrenchment of custodial rather than rehabilitative care. Given this dark history, it is not surprising that Bridgewater has a record of escapes and suicides, as many have sought to leave it by any means possible.

While class action suits since the 1970s have brought drastic improvement in both the administration of and conditions existing at

Bridgewater, the very public challenges regarding the care and treatment of patients and inmates that persist today are not new; there is remarkable continuity between contemporary issues and those present nearly from the institution's founding. In 1987, a report by the Massachusetts senate attributed Bridgewater's problems to "130 years of unplanned and haphazard evolution." It is the purpose of this volume to examine that evolution and specifically those issues that have tested the institution from the outset. The focus is on the years prior to 1990, when administration of MCI-Bridgewater as a single institution was ended and its several units came to be known as the Massachusetts Correctional Complex at Bridgewater, with an emphasis on the institution's first century.

It is suggested that a historical perspective should necessarily inform current discussions about the future of Bridgewater and how that institution should meet the needs of its patients, inmates, officers and administrators, as well as the expectations of the commonwealth. It is hoped that a better understanding of Bridgewater's troubled past may contribute to it becoming the model institution it once aspired to be.

# Acknowledgements

Uncovering the past of the Bridgewater correctional complex has been a rewarding and sometimes daunting task made easier by the assistance of several individuals whom the author wishes to gratefully acknowledge. Isabella Donadio, image research and permissions coordinator, Harvard Art Museums, Cambridge, was most helpful in securing permission to publish images from Harvard's extensive collections. Caitlin Jones, reference archivist, and John Hannigan, head of reference services, at the Massachusetts State Archives were kind and supportive during the research process. Their knowledge of and passion for the archives' extensive holdings is both apparent and appreciated. The commonwealth is fortunate to have such caretakers for its archival resources. Bob Cullum and Monica Shin, digital projects librarian, at the Boston Public Library are thanked for permission to print images from the Leslie Jones Collection. Finally, thanks to the acquisitions and editorial teams at The History Press who helped guide this work to completion.

# Introduction

As early as 1639, residents of Massachusetts recognized a communal responsibility for care of the poor, the insane and the criminal. Precedent had been set earlier in England, where the task of caring for poor individuals fell to the community in which they resided with a 1572 parliamentary act establishing the office of overseer of the poor. A subsequent 1601 law providing for compulsory employment of poor able-bodied children and adults and "the necessary relief of the lame, impotent, old, blind, and such other among them being poor and not able to work" became the foundation for poor law administration in Massachusetts, laying the legal basis for both the almshouse and the workhouse. A string of laws further codified the manner in which poor persons in colonial Massachusetts were to be treated with a 1692 law providing for the compulsory employment of idle persons and loiterers.[1]

Until 1854, responsibility for the commonwealth's poor fell on each community individually and responses varied greatly, dependent as they were on a community's willingness to assist as well as its financial ability to do so. In the earliest days, the poor were boarded out to families, with their expenses being paid by the town. In time, however, institutions variably called poorhouses or almshouses were established as homes for the community's poor. Often these institutions were known as poor farms, as able-bodied residents were put to work at farming. Yet communities could not and sometimes would not bear financial responsibility for caring for the "unsettled poor," transient individuals who could not claim legal residence in any town

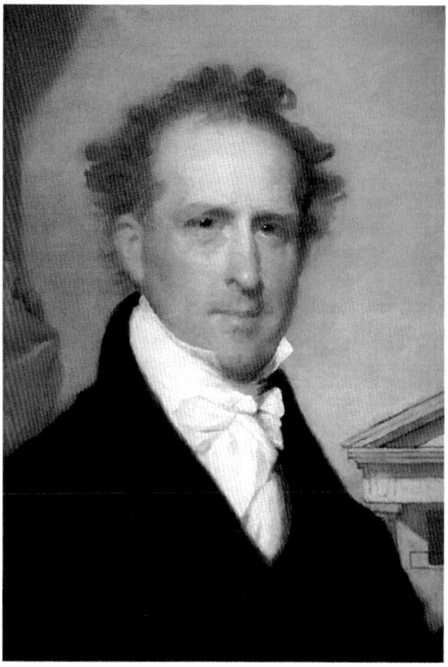

Josiah Quincy (1772–1864), oil on canvas, by John Gilbert Stuart, 1824 (detail). *Courtesy of Museum of Fine Arts, Boston.*

and therefore had no demand to any community's poor relief. These became the responsibility of the commonwealth.

In 1821, politician and educator Josiah Quincy recognized the drastic post-Revolutionary increase of the commonwealth's unsettled poor. The solution, Quincy believed, was greater state involvement in poor-law administration, including its direct supervision of pauperism, a recommendation he made before the state legislature. Quincy argued that the most economical means of caring for the poor was "*that of Almshouses, having the character of Workhouses*, or Houses of Industry, in which work is provided for every degree of ability in the pauper, and thus the able poor made to provide, partially at least, for their own support; and also to the support, or at least the comfort of the impotent poor."[2] Until establishment of the three state almshouses, paupers deemed fully chargeable to the commonwealth were housed in municipal almshouses, with the various towns and cities reimbursed by the state.

Concurrent with and connected to pauperism was the issue of the commonwealth's "insane and furiously mad." Many of these mentally ill individuals were also poor and so found themselves institutionalized in community almshouses as well as jails. Though a number of state asylums were established beginning with Worcester in 1833, the poor, the insane and the criminal continued to be institutionalized in common facilities, as noted by Dorothea Dix, an advocate for the indigent insane, in 1843. Ultimately, in an effort to provide the stricter classification urged by Dix and others like Horace Mann, Massachusetts in 1852 authorized three almshouses to be located at Bridgewater, Tewksbury and Monson for accommodation of the commonwealth's unsettled poor.[3] At the time, Massachusetts was a world leader in social reform, and the related issues of poverty and homelessness were believed by reformers, social thinkers and politicians alike to be soluble.

Chapter 1

# "A Partial If Not an Entire Failure"

## Bridgewater State Almshouse, 1854–66

### The Physical Complex

The site selected for the Bridgewater almshouse was the former homestead farm of Deacon Asael Shaw in the South Bridgewater (Titicut) section of Bridgewater, which was situated between the town center and the Taunton River. The commission established to implement the almshouse plan, in selecting locations for the commonwealth's three proposed almshouses, indicated that it would "have regard to the centres of the several pauper districts and to the general salubrity and health of the section."[4] In part, Bridgewater, situated in southeastern Massachusetts on the railroad line between Boston and Fall River, was settled upon as early as November 1852 "as a matter of convenience, and economy in transporting paupers."[5] Others later maintained that because of the prevailing public wish to segregate undesirable elements from population centers, "the institution was established 'a two day horse ride' from nineteenth century society."[6] For these commentators and others, Bridgewater, thirty miles south of Boston, was perceived from its very foundation as a place apart, not only geographically but morally and sociologically as well.

Built on a slight hill in 1853, the Bridgewater almshouse shared a common design with those built at Tewksbury and Monson. Except for the slate roof, construction of the three almshouses was wood frame throughout, material not considered ideal particularly in respect to fire prevention,

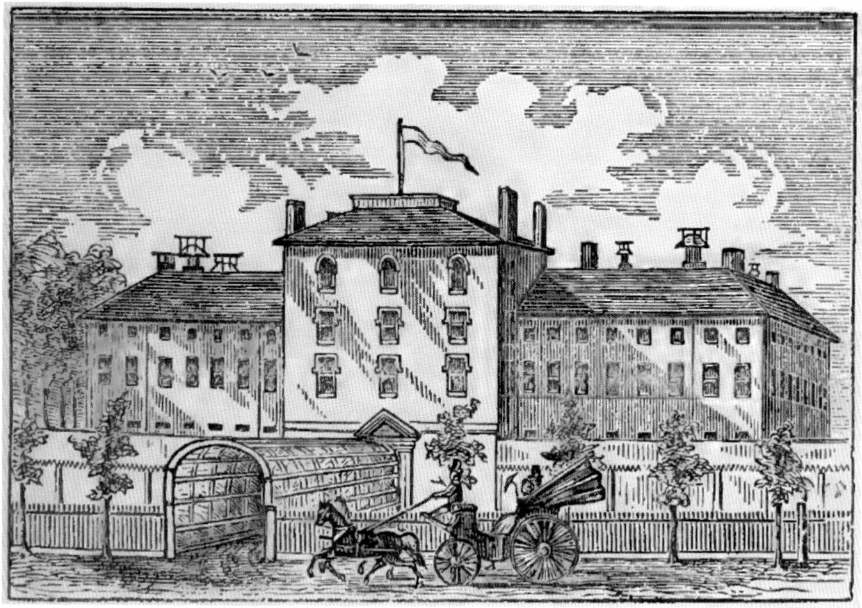

Bridgewater State Almshouse, October 1862. The image first appeared in the *Ninth Annual Report of the Inspectors of the State Almshouse, at Bridgewater.*

and the inspectors at Monson complained about it from the start. Their counterparts at Tewksbury concurred, writing of their building, which was identical to that at Bridgewater: "This immense pile, constructed of wood, without the protection of even a single brick or stone partition throughout its whole extent, is peculiarly liable to conflagration."[7] Future Bridgewater superintendent Hollis M. Blackstone was less restrained, retrospectively labeling Bridgewater a "cheaply conceived, poorly constructed old wooden fire-trap."[8] The sole masonry building was a combined baking and laundry house of stone built in 1855.

From the outset, the Bridgewater complex was physically challenged, and not due merely to its wooden construction. In 1859, the buildings were described as "but imperfectly constructed and finished originally, without sufficient regard to economy or comfort."[9] Slates on the roof of the main building were found to be of cheap quality and "miserably done" after many blew off during a windstorm and had to be replaced or re-secured. As late as 1859, the roof was still causing problems, and the issue seems never to have been satisfactorily resolved.[10] The cellar regularly filled with water, requiring installation of a drain. Most troubling, there was no potable water on site;

instead, water had to be drawn from the Taunton River. Even the look of the building was open to criticism. Sited on a rise in the land, it was described in August 1855 as "looming up like a field of boards."[11] Painted lightly with two coats, the building's exterior was so mottled it required thorough repainting to correct its shoddy-looking appearance.

## Administration

Initially, the Bridgewater almshouse was administered by three inspectors and a superintendent appointed by the governor and council. Levi L. Goodspeed (1822–1879) of Barnstable, an officer of the City Reform School at South Boston, was named the institution's first superintendent and was succeeded in 1870 by Captain Nahum K. Leonard (1825–1891) of West Bridgewater, who served until his resignation in July 1883. Oversight was provided by the Massachusetts State Board of Charities, established in 1863 to supervise the commonwealth's almshouses, lunatic hospitals and prisons. That board merged in 1879 with the State Board of Health to form the Massachusetts Board of Health, Lunacy and Charity. This body functioned until 1886, when an independent Board of Health was reestablished and oversight devolved to a truncated Board of Lunacy and Charity, which operated until 1898, when the administrative divisions were again separated. At this time, Bridgewater was placed under the jurisdiction of the Board of Charity, where it remained until 1919.[12]

The Bridgewater almshouse was officially opened on May 1, 1854, by proclamation of Governor Emory Washburn. Eligibility for admittance was certified by local overseers of the poor in towns in Norfolk, Bristol, Plymouth, Barnstable, Duke's and Nantucket Counties. Inmates represented a mix of classifications and included the young, old, aged, infirm, mentally disturbed, homeless, pauper and criminal.

## The Poor and Foreign Pauperism

The almshouse census was subject to economic fluctuations, and the depression of 1857 brought a great increase in the number seeking admission, so much so that the facility became "crowded with inmates, a large portion of who were [described at the time as] of the lowest, most degraded, worn-out, idiotic classes of human beings." Numbers beyond what were considered desirable were packed into rooms. The institution, capable of supporting 800 inmates, was during late 1857 and 1858 crowded with over 1,100. Economic downturns would long have such consequences. Superintendent Blackstone attributed the 1908 increase in the institution's population to the previous year's financial panic and the ensuing industrial depression.[13]

Inspectors also attributed early crowding to negligence among the commonwealth's poor law administrators, and they criticized communities that failed to properly investigate claims to state support. Eager to rid themselves of persons they deemed undesirable and lessen the financial burden on their towns, some Massachusetts overseers sent individuals to Bridgewater who were not fully eligible for admission. The situation was aggravated by worse overcrowding at the Tewksbury almshouse. In order to alleviate that problem, inmates were transferred from there to Bridgewater, with two hundred being received in May 1854 and an additional seventy-nine in November.[14]

From the beginning, a large percentage of inmates were foreign born, with the vast majority being Irish. When Superintendent Blackstone later blamed almshouse crowding on foreigners "who found almshouse conditions in this country luxury as compared with home life in the Old World," he disclosed much about his own prejudices, providing little true insight into the economic plight of immigrants, most of whom regarded Bridgewater as a place of last resort. Irish immigrants, in fact, held a strongly prejudicial view of the workhouse, and only the horrors of the Great Famine overcame their aversion to entering such institutions in Ireland.[15] Unable to secure work or barred from employment by nativist sentiments in Massachusetts, many Irish immigrants were left with no alternative but to seek the shelter of the state almshouse. Tellingly, Blackstone's comment reveals that from the very start of public welfare assistance in the commonwealth, distinctions between presumed "deserving" and "undeserving" recipients were made by social conservatives who classed the foreign born of the 1850s in the latter category.

The earliest extant list of Bridgewater's inmates records that 531 of the 860 admitted were Irish-born, a number that does not include American-born children of Irish immigrants.[16] Rather than reflecting the appeal of the almshouse among the Irish, the figure is indicative of the difficulty many Irish immigrants had in achieving financial stability and hints that

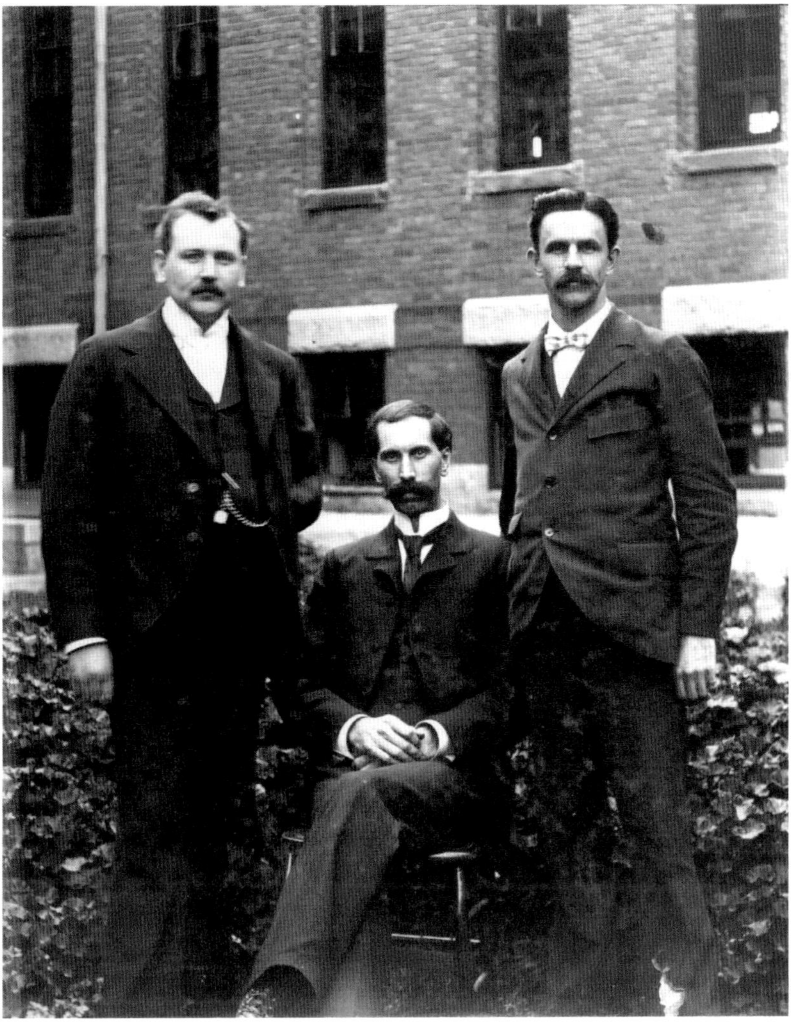

Bridgewater State Farm, Superintendent Hollis M. Blackstone (*seated*), circa 1900. *Massachusetts State Archives, State Farm (Bridgewater, Mass.), Photographs of facilities and activities [ca. 1900–ca. 1910], HS9.10/973X.*

it was the lowest social classes that found their way into such institutions, regardless of ethnicity. Another notable group of foreign-born almshouse inmates were the "Kanakas," South Pacific islanders engaged in the whaling trade out of southeastern Massachusetts, many of whom were afflicted with consumption. As late as 1905, consumptive "Western Islanders," largely from New Bedford and vicinity, were still being admitted to the institution.[17]

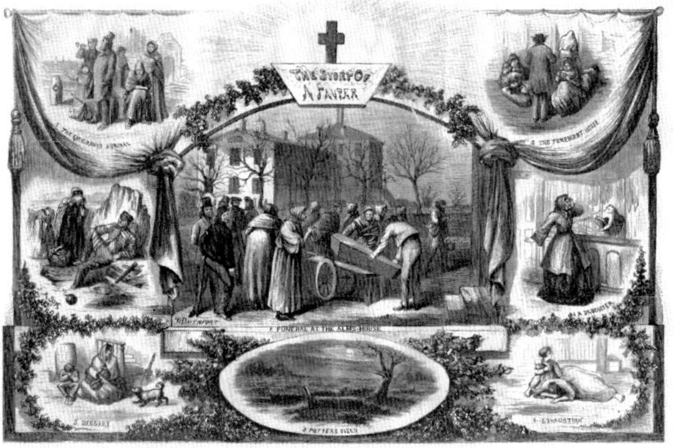

"Story of a Pauper" depicts the immigrants' plight, including, in the central motif, the "Funeral at the Alms-House." *Harper's Weekly*, February 8, 1868.

Not all citizens were disparaging of the foreigners, however, and some understood the plight of Massachusetts's newly arrived immigrants. In a debate over enfranchisement of naturalized voters on February 4, 1859, Alderman John C. Tucker of Boston encapsulated the immigrant experience for his listeners: "They had to do the drudgery, and by hard labor have broken down their constitutions, so that as a last resort after a weary life of ill requited toil for the public benefit, they must go to the almshouse to die."[18]

## THE INSANE

Classifications were not mutually exclusive, and among the poor entering the Bridgewater almshouse were the "insane poor." While the "*dangerously* insane" were barred from admission to the state almshouses, patients who were mentally disturbed to a lesser degree, the so-called harmless insane, continued to find their way there. In 1855, "nearly one hundred insane and idiotic poor" were admitted to Bridgewater, and this class quickly began to tax the resources of the institution, with continual calls being made for separate facilities for the "insane" and "demented." Though asylums for the insane existed at Worcester (1833), Taunton (1854) and Northampton (1858), both the Bridgewater and Tewksbury almshouses accommodated mentally ill inmates based in part on their classification firstly as paupers. The State Board of Charities acknowledged the commonwealth's lack of coordinated policy regarding the insane poor in 1864, writing that "the Bridgewater Almshouse seems to have been early selected for the experiment of supporting the harmless insane at such institutions; but when the first removals were made I have not learned. From the first, insane persons were occasionally admitted."[19] Inspectors of the Tewksbury almshouse recognized this practice in 1856 when they wrote that "it appears to be the policy of the State to make the State almshouses receptacles for a certain class of the insane paupers, such as are demented and harmlessly insane, who are regarded as incurables." But in the commonwealth's eagerness to alleviate the burden on its various mental institutions, less harmless individuals invariably were transferred to the almshouses, including Bridgewater.[20]

By October 1859, there were some 150 mentally ill lodged at Bridgewater (over a quarter of the almshouse population), and while some of these inmates were "demure and harmless, others are turbulent, noisy and quarrelsome."[21] The presence, particularly of the latter, proved disruptive and occasionally violent. The Bridgewater inspectors argued that such inmates should be sent to the commonwealth's asylums and should under no circumstances have contact with other classes but acknowledged that existing statutes permitted the transfer and committal of disturbed patients to what technically remained an almshouse. Despite an 1861 recommendation to the Governor's Council that these patients be relocated to the commonwealth's insane asylums, no action was taken to prevent further insane from being sent to Bridgewater, and in 1863, the inspectors there remarked that the "number of demented and partially insane in this institution is large, too large for their comfort or the comfort of those, who from necessity, are located near them."[22] Continuing failure to better classify and separate the inmates was acknowledged as problematic, undermining the ability of administrators to best care for each group at the institution.

Though the gradual increase in numbers of mentally disturbed individuals housed at the almshouse brought with it a rise in aggressive and self-destructive tendencies among inmates, administrators saw the presence of insane inmates as operationally beneficial. Many able-bodied poor entered the almshouse on the approach of winter but departed in the spring, leaving the mentally ill behind to shoulder a disproportionate share of the necessary farm labor in summer and fall. This seasonal fluctuation in the almshouse population was not unique to Bridgewater, and Tewksbury's census was noted in the early 1880s as varying from 800 inmates in summer to 1,200 in winter.[23] The tone of the 1857 Bridgewater report clearly displays the frustration felt regarding this situation:

> *During the winter season we have a large number of able-bodied men capable of performing much labor; but the season for labor is past, and their energies cannot be directed to any useful purpose. They are thus "help-eats," and not "help-meets" to the establishment; and when seed time arrives, and the earth invites the laborer to the toils of the fields, they quit our hospitalities, and go forth for the summer to work for themselves, leaving behind them but a small number of the feebler and more dependent portion of their company to toil for their next winter's support, when again many of them will return to share the bounty of the Commonwealth. Such are the difficulties under which we are obliged to labor, in the cultivation of our fields, producing our harvests, and in improving the condition and appearance of the estate belonging to the institution.*[24]

The following year's report was equally critical, lambasting those who "prefer to eat the bread of idleness furnished by other members of the Commonwealth who cannot live without work." In response to the situation of the transient poor, the commonwealth passed a law in March 1858 permitting the almshouse superintendents to subcontract inmates to outside persons. Should the inmate refuse, "he shall forfeit all claim to support as a state pauper."[25]

## DISEASED

Another classification of inmates was the diseased. Many inmates entered the almshouse with existing illnesses, and the hospital became an important adjunct to the almshouse, ministering to inmates as well as local residents admitted solely for medical care. The number of patients soon outgrew the available hospital accommodation, and in 1856, two additional wards were created.

The principal disease afflicting inmates was tuberculosis. During 1855, 94 of the 719 cases recorded at the almshouse hospital were diagnosed as tubercular.[26] Resident physician Charles A. Ruggles lamented that many almshouse patients were in the late stages of tuberculosis, "upon whom medicine has but slight effect, who are so much debilitated and enfeebled by disease, that it seems as though they came for the sole purpose to die… leaving us with but one course to pursue, to make their short stay on earth as comfortable, quiet, and as free from pain as possible."[27]

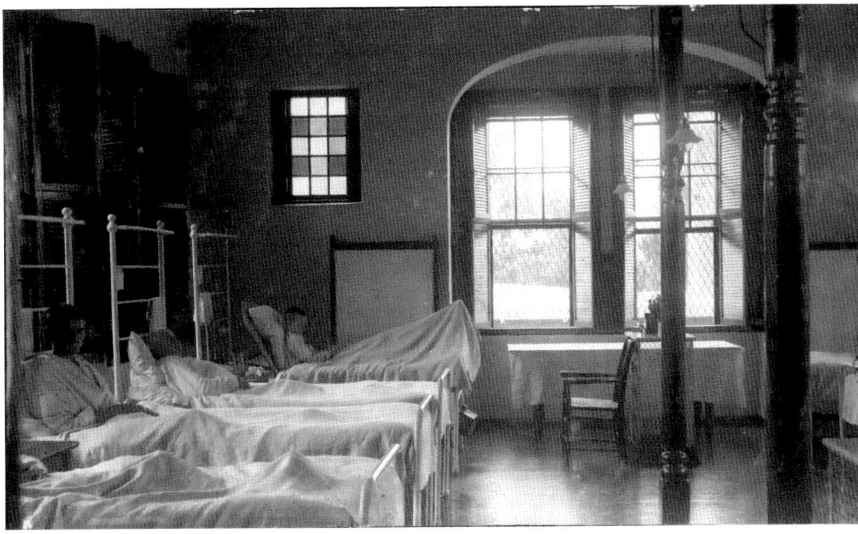

Bridgewater State Farm, hospital ward, circa 1910. *Massachusetts State Archives, State Farm (Bridgewater, Mass.), Photographs of facilities and activities [ca. 1900–ca. 1910], HS9.10/973X.*

These complementary though at times conflicting roles, as almshouse and hospital, fostered misperception among the public, which held a generally dim view of the institution, as acknowledged by Superintendent Goodspeed in 1857: "Viewed as a mere hospital for the suffering and the dying, our institution presents to the eye of the observer an appalling scene; but when viewed as the last and only refuge of the unfortunate, such institutions are indeed an honor to our Commonwealth."[28]

Perhaps the "appalling scene" envisioned by outsiders had to do with the institution's high mortality rate, which reached 12.5 percent in 1858 and attracted widespread comment. A subsequent legislative investigation determined the cause to be lack of attention to "*non naturals*, such as air, food, exercise and the like."[29] Such publicity did little to allay public fears of state-run institutions, which were increasingly perceived as places from which one did not return.

## Children

During its earliest years, the almshouse housed a large proportion of children under the age of sixteen, their numbers constantly fluctuating due to ongoing legislative efforts to properly classify paupers. Beginning in 1855, an effort to better provide for the commonwealth's orphaned pauper children by removing them from Bridgewater and segregating them at Monson, where a state primary school was temporarily established, became a source of tension.[30] Superintendent Goodspeed and the Bridgewater inspectors opposed this law, with the latter in 1856 urging its repeal. Goodspeed contended that children could be maintained at Bridgewater just as cost effectively as at Monson, though he conceded that they should be housed in a separate building. "The authorities at…Bridgewater view with no favor the continual removal of the orphan children to Monson; they submit, but it is with murmurs, to a policy which they disapprove."[31] Authorities at Monson, meanwhile, complained that Bridgewater was transferring its poorly clothed and diseased "idiots and invalids." Unsurprisingly, the commonwealth attributed its classification difficulties to a lack of cooperation among the three almshouses and recognized that conflict among the institutions undermined the effectiveness of the commonwealth's intentions. "The interests of the State must suffer if such establishments become centres of jealousy, cavil and intrigue, instead of harboring mutual respect and good-will," the Board of Charities chastised in 1864, having assumed jurisdiction of the almshouses just the previous year.[32]

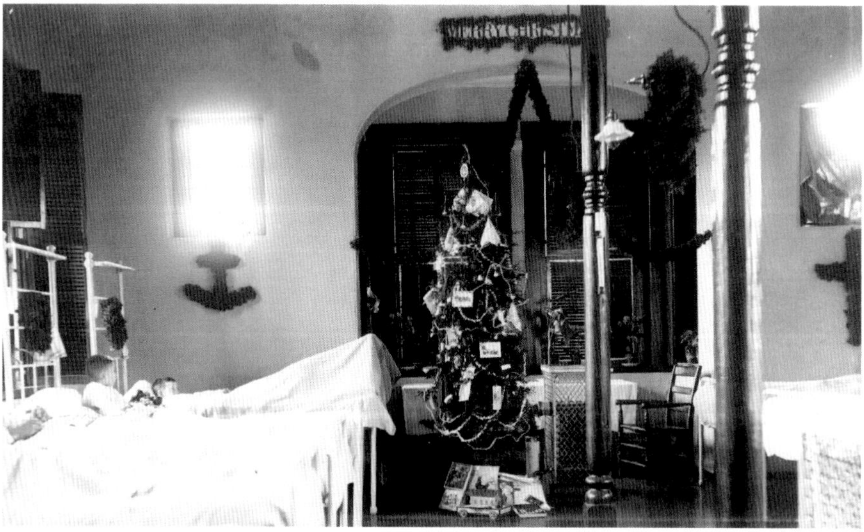

Bridgewater State Farm, children's hospital ward, Christmas, circa 1905. *Massachusetts State Archives, State Farm (Bridgewater, Mass.), Photographs of facilities and activities [ca. 1900–ca. 1910], HS9.10/973X.*

For children, life at Bridgewater was severe. In early 1855, the two almshouse schools (segregated by gender) were attended by over one hundred students, but the ongoing removal of children from Bridgewater compromised the educational quality such that by 1864, the State Board of Charities reported Bridgewater to have the worst schools of any of the state's three almshouses.[33]

The indenturing of children, thought to have a salutary effect on childhood development and favored by Superintendent Goodspeed, added to the severity of their lives. Many pauper orphans were placed with local families, where they were expected to earn their keep. Initially, the State Board of Charities appears to have held a naïvely wistful view of the lives of these children, but it soon realized the actuality of and potential for abuse and strongly recommended that care of indentured children be investigated regularly by a state agent.[34]

Acknowledging that "nearly all the influences of the adult population in an almshouse are opposed to developing the right character in children," in 1864, the State Board of Charities resumed transferring children to Monson, where a state primary school was permanently established in 1866.[35] At the time, adults were also better classified along disciplinary lines, with the "infirm and truly unfortunate" poor designated for Tewksbury and the voluntary poor and what Blackstone pejoratively termed "able-bodied rounders" destined for Bridgewater.

## THE FARM

From its establishment, the Bridgewater almshouse included a farm, though not until 1887 was the institution known officially as the "State Farm." The farm was an integral element of the almshouse, intended to occupy the able-bodied and instill the moral and material benefits of hard work. Given the role agricultural labor was to play at the almshouse, one qualification favoring Goodspeed's appointment as superintendent was his practical experience as a master farmer at West Barnstable. (He later served as president of the Barnstable Agricultural Society.) When acquired for the almshouse, the Shaw farm was "worn out, dilapidated and poor" and "little better than a barren waste," and Goodspeed was tasked with bringing it into productivity.[36]

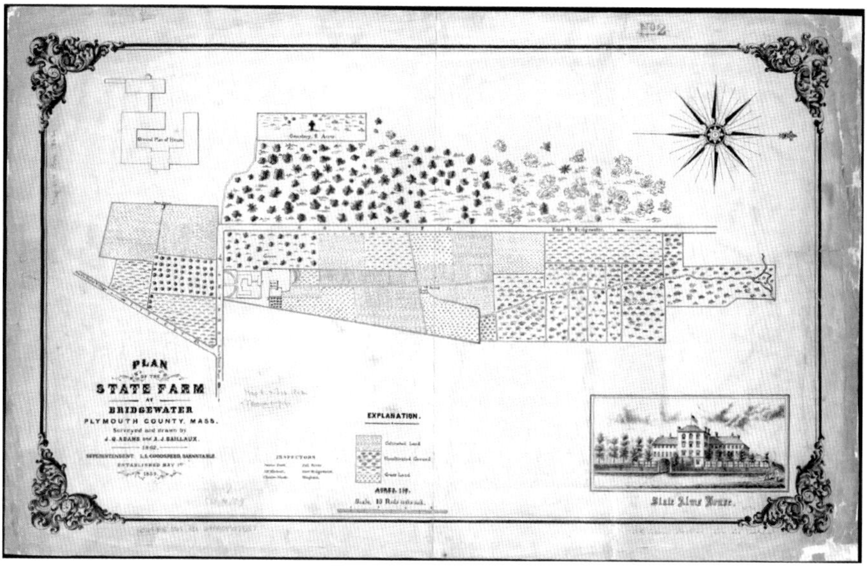


"Plan of the State Farm at Bridgewater, Plymouth County, Mass. Surveyed and drawn by J.Q. Adams and A.J. Caillaux, 1862." *Courtesy of the Boston Public Library.*

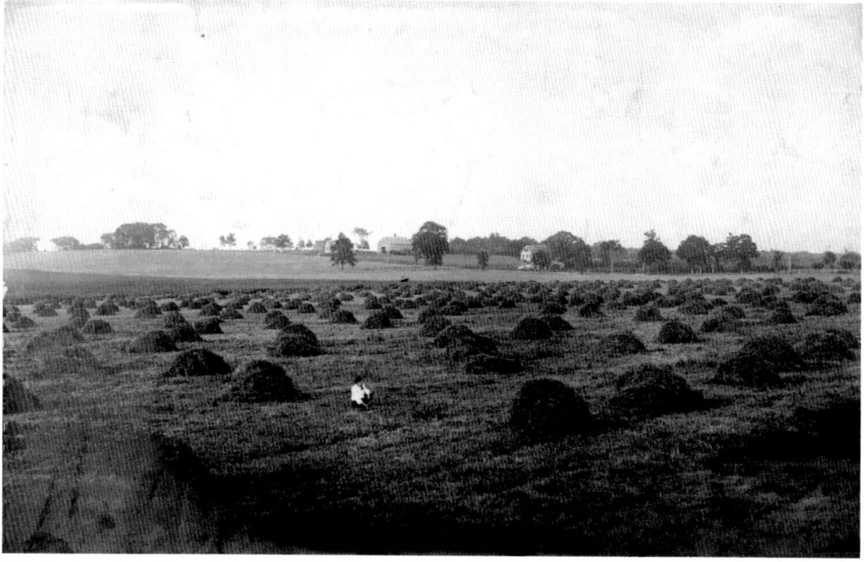

Bridgewater State Farm, cocked hay, circa 1900. *Massachusetts State Archives, State Farm (Bridgewater, Mass.), Photographs of facilities and activities [ca. 1900–ca. 1910], HS9.10/973X.*

Originally, the most extensively cultivated crops were hay, potatoes and root crops, including turnips, carrots, beets and parsnips. Hay soon became an important staple, and the farm's success with this crop necessitated construction of additional barns in order to keep it under cover, the first addition being made in 1863. In 1856, the beginnings of an apple orchard were established with the setting of one hundred trees on land immediately to the south of the institution. It began yielding in 1866.

## Inmate Life

While the lives of inmates at Bridgewater during its earliest years are not well chronicled, the inmates' experiences differed appreciably little from those of their counterparts at Monson, for which documentation does exist.

Among the most frequently discussed topics relating to the treatment of inmates in the commonwealth's charitable institutions was diet, and at Bridgewater the object was to provide "food of a plain, wholesome and substantial character, with a suitable variety through the week."[37] Beyond this, the specifics of meals at Bridgewater are not known, but the board provided by the Monson almshouse provides an indication. In 1854, breakfast each day consisted of bread, coffee and milk, while "those who labor" also received meat hash or pork and beans. Lunch was beef soup and potatoes on Mondays and Thursdays; fish, potatoes and gravy on Tuesdays and Fridays; pork, beans and potatoes on Wednesdays and Saturdays; and cold pork and beans and tea on Sundays. Supper each day consisted of bread, chocolate and milk. Separate meals were provided nursery children, infants and the sick.[38]

Again, Monson provides an indication as to what the daily routine at Bridgewater was like.[39] Though considered charitable institutions, the commonwealth's almshouses operated like prisons, with highly regimented activities and strict policies that limited movement and minimized fraternization. Public access to the almshouse was restricted, with visits prohibited on Sundays and permissible during non-visiting hours only by leave of the inspectors or superintendent. Visits were required to be conducted in the presence of an officer. Inmates were not allowed to leave the grounds without permission, to pass into any room other than their own without permission or to use tobacco without permission (in part due to fire safety concerns). A bell was rung daily at or before sunrise, fifteen minutes before breakfast, forty-five minutes before lunch, fifteen minutes before supper and at nine o'clock every night, at which time inmates were to extinguish all lights. Upon rising, inmates were expected to wash their faces and comb their hair. Baths, shaves and clothes changes were had at the discretion of the superintendent. Able-bodied inmates were expected to work for their keep. "Those who acquit themselves cheerfully and faithfully will receive proper encouragement; while the slothful and refractory shall receive exemplary punishment." "Exemplary punishment" was also prescribed for disobedience and, although not precisely defined, may have constituted confinement to cells on a diet of bread and water, as was resorted to at Tewksbury.[40] Attendance at Sunday worship services as well as daily prayer services at sundown was obligatory.

Cruelest of all was the fact that families sent to the almshouse were separated, which the State Board of Charities excused, helplessly arguing in 1864 that "it is hard to see what better mode could be adopted."[41] Yet there appears to have been some effort to provide a respite from all this. Thanksgiving 1855 was marked by a ball for the inmates.[42]

Given the restrictions placed on inmates, escapes (then euphemistically referred to as "elopements") were not uncommon. Among the earliest on record are those of fifty-year-old Mary Shay, suffering three years from phthisis; twenty-seven-year-old butcher Michael Canty, suffering from intermittent fever; Kanaka Dow, a Hawaiian seaman, suffering from pneumonia; and twenty-four-year-old William Nelson, a syphilitic seaman from New Brunswick, all of whom escaped from the almshouse hospital.

## "The Least Agreeable...of All Our Public Institutions"

Considerable emphasis was placed on the per capita cost of supporting inmates, and this became the yardstick by which success of the Bridgewater almshouse was measured, as well as the source of much criticism. As early as 1858, the Massachusetts almshouse system was judged a failure, largely due to its high operational cost. Governor Nathaniel P. Banks in his inaugural address of January 7, 1859, characterized the almshouse system as "a partial, if it [does] not prove an entire failure."[43] A subsequent legislative committee established to make recommendations for the economical and efficient administration of the commonwealth's charitable institutions was itself clearly dismayed at the occupants of the Bridgewater almshouse. "Such a motley collection of broken-backed, lame-legged, sore-eyed, helpless and infirm human beings, one would not have supposed it possible to get together in such numbers." Not only were many of the inmates infirm, but the large number of young children present led to the conclusion that it was unlikely that the almshouse population could ever be put to productive labor in numbers sufficient for the institution to be self-supporting. "Indeed, if it were not for the harmless insane, who are able-bodied, the most necessary operations of the farm could not be persistently maintained."[44] By 1864, the State Board of Charities was characterizing the commonwealth's three almshouses as "the most severely criticized, and the least agreeable to the philanthropist of all our public institutions."[45]

Chapter 2

# "The Name of Workhouse Was No Misnomer"

## Bridgewater State Almshouse and Workhouse for Vicious Paupers, 1866–72

Regarded as a failure as an almshouse, Bridgewater assumed new direction in 1866 when the commonwealth overhauled its almshouse system and improved inmate classifications. While Tewksbury was to remain an almshouse, Monson became an educational facility for pauper children and Bridgewater became a state workhouse where individuals convicted of vagrancy and petty vice crimes were to be sentenced, an action that was hoped would help offset the institution's expenses. Reformers believed that the workhouse would teach alcoholics, prostitutes, tramps, vagabonds, drug abusers and other misdemeanants the value of good, hard, honest labor.

Meanwhile, four inmate classifications were decreed, described by Governor Alexander H. Bullock in 1868 as the "chronic insane and the imbecile" destined for the commonwealth's various asylums, "those entering the Almshouses from poverty, induced by their own vicious indulgences, and sentenced to the State Workhouse" at Bridgewater, "the children at the Primary School" at Monson and "the paupers proper" at Tewksbury.[46] The intention was to segregate the virtuous or "honest poor" at Tewksbury from the so-called vicious poor, whose poverty was attributed to their criminality at Bridgewater.

Though Bullock in his legislative address of January 1867 termed the action "a measure of economy and humanity," it proved transformative. The addition of a workhouse (which served as the model for institutions elsewhere, including the 1869 Rhode Island state workhouse at Cranston) initiated Bridgewater's ultimate transition from an almshouse to a prison.[47] Laws surrounding vagrancy were tightened, and the increasing number of individuals convicted of misdemeanor offenses and sentenced to Bridgewater meant that by the time Nahum K. Leonard succeeded Goodspeed as superintendent in 1870, the combined almshouse and workhouse there had "become practically a penal institution."[48]

## Vagrancy and Drunkenness

The two primary areas with which the Bridgewater workhouse was concerned were homelessness and alcoholism, then criminalized by the commonwealth as vagrancy and drunkenness. Sentences were long. Typical were the cases of T.A. Peacock, who was sentenced for vagrancy by the Charlestown Police Court in September 1869 to an eighteen-month term in the workhouse; Catherine Lewis, convicted of being a vagabond, who was sentenced by the Boston Municipal Court on November 26, 1869, to two years at Bridgewater; and Mary McLaughlin, who received an identical sentence in Chelsea Police Court on November 29, 1869. McLaughlin, remarked one newspaper, "was complained of for being an idle and disorderly person….This was the thirty-sixth time that she was brought before a police justice on various charges, the most of them being for vagrancy. The good old town of Chelsea will not be troubled with this nuisance for at least two years to come, thanks to His Honor" Judge Bates.[49]

There was a lingering perception held by many that vagrants took advantage of the system, using the almshouse as a convenient shelter in winter before departing in spring. This was particularly galling for those who subscribed to this view, the first annual report of the Massachusetts Commissioners of Prisons remarking:

> *It has become a regular expectation, that is seldom disappointed…that in the fall certain vagrants will come in for winter quarters. Now we submit that when we learn, as we do from all over the State, that prison life is so little disagreeable, so little feared by certain tramps and vagrants, as to be regularly arranged for,—as on the whole, a desirable way to pass the winter,—it is time to make a change.*[50]

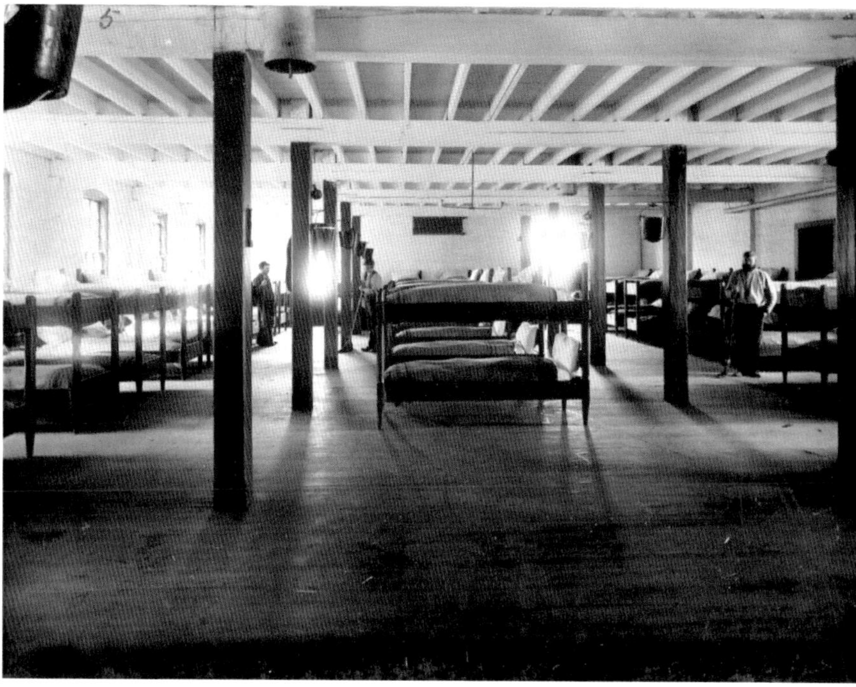

Bridgewater State Farm, loafing room, almshouse department, circa 1900. *Harvard Art Museums/Fogg Museum, Transfer from the Carpenter Center for the Visual Arts, Social Museum Collection, 3.2002.2712.5. Unidentified Artist. Imaging Department © President and Fellows of Harvard College.*

Though seemingly recognizing alcoholism as a disease and displaying greater sympathy for alcoholics than the homeless, the commissioners of prisons still argued for longer rehabilitative workhouse sentences for those sentenced for drunkenness rather than shorter retributive prison sentences in order to allow adequate time for their reformation. Among those deemed in need of reform were Brian Mullen, who was "convicted of being a common drunkard, and it being represented that he was very violent to his family when under the influence of liquor," who was sentenced by Boston Municipal Court on November 16, 1869, to eighteen months in the workhouse; and Nellie Bright, "a common drunkard," sentenced in November 1875 by the Superior Criminal Court to two years at the workhouse. That same month, Lavinia Robbins, also adjudged "a common drunkard," received a two-year sentence to Bridgewater from the Boston Municipal Court.

The sentences handed down to "drunkards" and "vagrants" were long, typically ranging from eighteen to twenty-four months, as the courts embarked upon a moral crusade to rid communities throughout the commonwealth of the presence of alcoholic and homeless persons. At the same time that these sentences were meted out, it is noteworthy that larcenists and those convicted of assault received sentences ranging from a mere sixty days to a year only.

## "Idle and Dissolute Lives"

An 1870 Massachusetts legislative report described the workhouse inmates: "A large majority of those confined in it come from the vicious classes of society. They are made up of the criminal poor—the lewd, the intemperate, and those suffering from a [presumably venereal] disease which is in itself a proof of their abandoned character."[51] Categorization of the workhouse as a prison by the State Board of Charities confirmed its role as a penal institution with little regard to the paupers or the insane who continued to reside there. Hollis Blackstone attributed the appointment of Leonard as superintendent in 1870 to Leonard's "judicial mind and calm self-possession," traits necessary in overseeing a prison.[52]

State officials were often excessive in their punishment of wrongdoers, fueling a public perception of the workhouse as a fearsome institution where even temporary indigence might lead to confinement. Illustrative was the tale of Ellen Connolly, a poor fisherman's wife who, in April 1872 while her husband was at sea, sought medical assistance for herself and her child at the Tewksbury Almshouse.

> *Shortly after her arrival at the Institution, as she alleges, Mrs. Connolly was brought before a Trial Justice on the charge of being idle and disorderly. The woman not knowing, as she expressed it, what it all meant, and being told to plead guilty, she did so, and was sentenced to six months' imprisonment in the Bridgewater Workhouse, but on the day of her trial the child died, and she was allowed the privilege of attending its interment, during which she managed to escape, and last night was arrested in this city* [Boston]...*on the charge of being an escaped convict. She was locked up in the Tombs, and will be returned to Bridgewater this morning. The woman states that her only crime is her poverty, and she does not wish to be imprisoned for being poor.*[53]

With the evolution of the almshouse into a place of confinement for the vicious poor, liberties there were still further curtailed, and indoor industrial employment was established to augment summer employment in the fields. Though the change was fraught with some obstacles and opposition, "a foundation of industry [was] so firmly laid that the changed name to workhouse was no misnomer."[54]

Chapter 3

# "To Reform, Restrain and Mitigate"

## Bridgewater State Workhouse, 1872–86

Bridgewater's role continued to evolve when, in 1872, the almshouse department was officially abolished and the complex put to use exclusively as a state workhouse, with all paupers being sent to Tewksbury.[55] Despite this rationalization of the commonwealth's charitable institutions, Bridgewater's mandate was muddied by the enabling legislation, which permitted paupers still to be sent to Bridgewater at the discretion of the State Board of Charities, particularly those "whose labor in domestic or other service...may contribute to the cost of their support," thereby ensuring the maintenance of a mixed classification institution.[56]

## "Mingling in Common"

Though Bridgewater's intended and official mandate following 1872 was strictly that of workhouse, the institution continued to serve a broad population described in 1876 as "an incongruous mass,—helpless children, tramps and vagrants, incorrigible drunkards, decrepit old women, harlots of the most abandoned character, paupers from the almshouse, graduates from our minor prisons, transfers from the state reformatories, petty criminals of every imaginable grade."[57] By 1878, the State Board of Charities, cognizant of the mixed populations that coexisted in the commonwealth's various charitable and penal institutions, was urging a stricter classification, a near impossible task given competing interests among these facilities as well as the actions of the courts.

The continuing presence of paupers at Bridgewater as well as Tewksbury's limitations as the commonwealth's sole remaining almshouse fueled calls in the 1870s that the state workhouse be abolished and Bridgewater revert to its former role. This proposal was opposed by the Bridgewater inspectors, who felt the transfer of paupers to penal institutions elsewhere would neither be beneficial to those affected nor cost-effective. Consequently, the poor, the criminal and the harmless insane remained in common confinement at Bridgewater, their numbers supplemented by newly arrived paupers who continued to be sent there largely due to overcrowding elsewhere. During one week in summer 1876, the Bridgewater workhouse saw one hundred committals, ninety-two of whom were transfers from Tewksbury.

Bridgewater officials were stymied in their own efforts to reduce the pauper population through out-transfers by the inmates' reluctance to

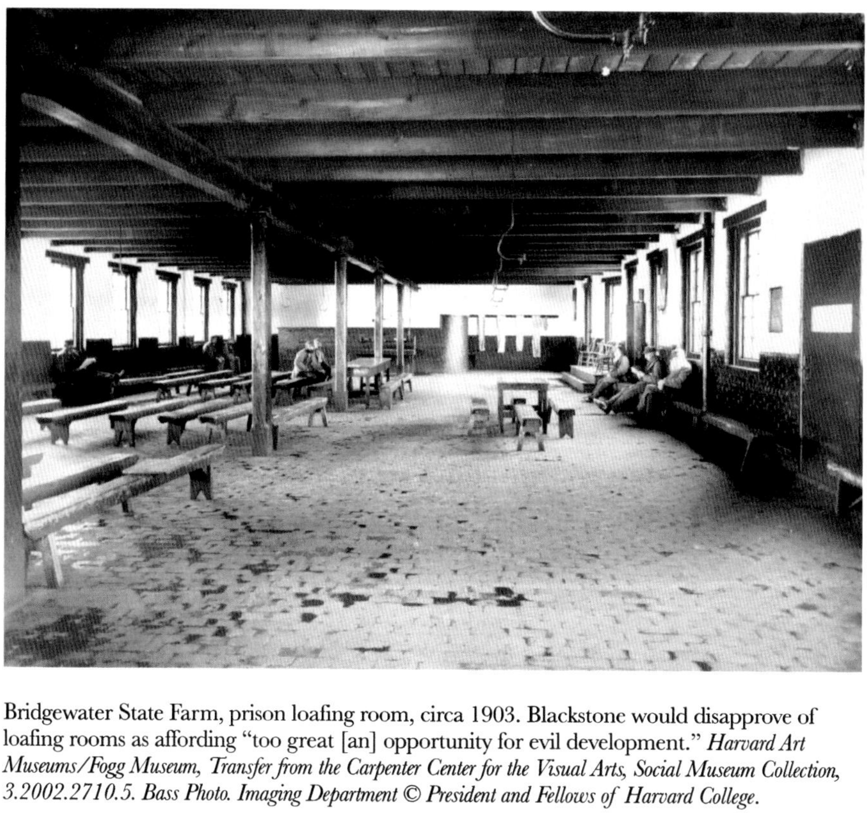

Bridgewater State Farm, prison loafing room, circa 1903. Blackstone would disapprove of loafing rooms as affording "too great [an] opportunity for evil development." *Harvard Art Museums/Fogg Museum, Transfer from the Carpenter Center for the Visual Arts, Social Museum Collection, 3.2002.2710.5. Bass Photo. Imaging Department © President and Fellows of Harvard College.*

relocate to other institutions. In 1883, the Plymouth *Old Colony Memorial* reported the example of one individual who, after twenty-seven years at Bridgewater, had become so "wonted to the situation he hated dreadfully to be transferred to Tewksbury."[58] Willard D. Tripp, general agent of the Massachusetts Board of Charities, in 1877 similarly noted many inmates' preference for Bridgewater over Tewksbury, though this inclination may have been motivated less by genuine enthusiasm for the former and more by fears concerning Tewksbury, the alarming conditions of which may have been known to Bridgewater inmates.

In addition to paupers, mentally disturbed individuals continued to be sentenced to the Bridgewater workhouse, an action the trustees disapproved of, as it had a tendency to be disruptive. "With this element mingling with the other prisoners, constant trouble is experienced. We question the wisdom of sending this class of people to a workhouse.…We trust the day is not far distant when the simple pauper, the insane, and the vilest of criminals will no longer be found mingling in common in any of our public institutions."[59] Yet even on this matter, Bridgewater administrators sent conflicting messages, with Superintendent Goodspeed having earlier expressed his view that Bridgewater *was* capable of housing mixed classifications. Court action affirmed this, as seen by the March 14, 1881 arraignment of Mary Gillett of Medford in Malden district court on a charge of vagrancy. Though "evidently deranged"—she thought herself to be President Garfield's daughter—she was sentenced to two years at the Bridgewater workhouse rather than being committed to one of the state mental hospitals.[60] In their defense, courts had few options. Though additional insane hospitals had opened in Danvers (1878) and Westborough (1884), the increase in the commonwealth's insane was outpacing overall population growth and crowding mental health facilities. Yet despite the increasing number of mentally disturbed patients being sent to Bridgewater, little in the way of medical care was provided, and if salaries are an indicator, treatment for the mentally ill was of low priority. In 1881, the engineer, chair shop overseer, head farmer, assistant farmer and kitchen overseer each received a higher salary than the institution's top medical professional, Dr. Edward A. Sawyer.

Helping ease the situation at Bridgewater was the process initiated in about 1878 of no longer sentencing women to the workhouse and transferring existing female inmates from Bridgewater to Sherborn, where a reformatory for women opened in 1877. By November 1878, the female population had been so reduced that only forty-three women remained, all, with the exception of those in the hospital, engaged in housekeeping. Nonetheless, even this success was problematic, and State Board of Charities secretary Sidney Andrews complained that "vagrant and imbecile" women sent to Sherborn were merely paupers who might be better and less expensively housed at Bridgewater.

While statutorily permissible, this mixed classification system was undesirable, creating difficulties in administering Bridgewater, as acknowledged by the 1878 report of the inspectors:

> *While this institution is numbered among the penal institutions of the Commonwealth, it is closely allied in its character and administration to the charitable institutions of the State. The class of persons sentenced here are, to a large extent, simply vagrants. There is another class that are of the more vicious and criminal character, that can only be kept here by the closest surveillance. This requires a larger number of officers that would seem necessary in all parts of the institution. The beneficence of the Commonwealth is signally illustrated in making provision for those who are incapable of caring for themselves, and in protecting society from those who, through vicious indulgence, have come to be a terror to the peaceful citizens, and a burden to the body politic. The aim of the management of this institution is, as far as possible, to reform the vicious, restrain the lawless, and mitigate the sufferings of those who have fallen prey to disease through vice and dissipation.*[61]

## "An Inquiry into Its Discipline and Management"

Difficulties in administering a mixed-class facility were reflected in growing criticisms of Bridgewater and the punishment imposed there during the latter half of the 1870s, which included confinement and the use of straitjackets. Responding to allegations of mistreatment of inmates by workhouse officers that appeared in the press in spring 1877 and particularly an article carried by the *Boston Pilot* reporting that an attendant had kicked and beaten an inmate, the Massachusetts legislature initiated an investigation into the conditions and management at Bridgewater.

Prior to 1877, Bridgewater had remained relatively untainted by allegations of brutality and was considered to be among the best managed of the commonwealth's several charitable institutions, with Superintendent Leonard being held in high regard. Nonetheless, reports of cruelty and excessive disciplinary force surfaced periodically. On March 12, 1874, steward Daniel Leary was alleged to have kicked elderly inmate Edward Dollard to death. Leary was temporarily suspended, and investigation by the State Board of Charities followed. Leary was said to have been provoked by discovery of a piece of bread concealed in sixty-year-old Dollard's sleeve, presumably "put away for a lunch between meals."[62] Three years later, in May 1877, the *Pilot* alleged that a Bridgewater attendant had kicked and severely beaten inmate John Sullivan. J.E. Crane, chairman of the inspectors of the State Workhouse, noting that the attendant had been dismissed following the incident, refuted allegations of mistreatment and maintained that "the 'unfortunate poor' are as comfortably clothed and better fed than the average citizens of the State." While this statement was intended to counter claims that inmates had been mistreated, it inadvertently fueled complaints that Bridgewater's inmates were unfairly taking advantage of the commonwealth's system of public welfare.[63]

During the 1877 legislative investigation, inmates testified to having been choked, strangled, beaten, kept on diets of bread and water and placed in close confinement. Two attendants admitted to the rough handling and striking of inmates, though only under extreme provocation and in order to bring inmates into subjection. Though unjustifiable, such behavior was perhaps understandable. Many inmates were repeat offenders, considered incorrigible and difficult to manage. Former officer Erastus B. Carl described them in 1877 as "a hard set of men to deal with."[64] (Contrarily, several inmates offered testimony indicating that they had been well treated, with one marveling that officers were not *more* severe.)

Taking several months to complete, the investigation became highly politicized, with the *Boston Globe* insisting that committee members were predetermined to find the institution guilty.[65] Superintendent Leonard saw the investigation as counterproductive, arguing that it undermined inmate discipline and materially interfered with operation of the workhouse. He blamed the whole episode on "the gossip of dismissed officers and the tales of scampish and vagrant inmates."[66] Not surprisingly, the final committee report was widely criticized. The State Board of Charities ultimately concluded that "in the management of the Workhouse, there has undoubtedly been in a few cases some abuse of its inmates by under-officers; but as a whole, it has been well managed, and the institution has been, and is, productive of much good."[67]

## "THE TRAMP NUISANCE"

In the wake of the 1877 legislative investigation came a new challenge, as heightened societal efforts to reduce growing homelessness filled the commonwealth's charitable and penal institutions with "tramps." In late July 1877, 25 vagrants were captured in empty ice cars at Cambridge and sentenced to Bridgewater on charges of vagrancy for thirteen months. At that same time, 6 others found in a lumberyard and abandoned houses also at Cambridge were sentenced to terms of ten months. As of January 1879, Bridgewater housed 355 male and 60 female inmates, of whom 260 had been sentenced as vagrants. In addition to targeting the genuinely homeless, Massachusetts's vagrancy statutes were often employed by communities to convict dubious characters when evidence of more serious crimes was lacking.

At the time, Massachusetts law defined vagrants as "all idle persons who, not having visible means of support, live without lawful employment; persons wandering abroad and visiting tippling shops or houses of ill-fame, or lodging in groceries, outhouses, market-places, sheds, barns, or in the open air, and not giving a good account of themselves; [and] all persons wandering abroad and begging, or who go about from door to door, or place themselves in the streets, highways, passages or other public places, to beg or receive alms."[68] Maximum sentences were set at six months.

Increased rates of vagrancy in the late 1870s fueled by economic dislocation following the so-called Long Depression of 1873–78, cyclical unemployment, minimal job security, untreated mental illness and physical disability, institutionalized racism, growing immigration and heightened job competition triggered demands for tougher vagrancy laws. The *Boston Globe* characterized vagrancy as a "business" engaged in by lazy individuals, and though it acknowledged that many genuinely came to homelessness through the loss of their livelihood, "after they have spent three or six months in idleness, and lost their pride by asking for and subsisting upon alms, they learn to prefer that mode of life to any other."[69] While harsh in its assessment, the newspaper was merely reflecting public attitudes dating back to pre-colonial days, when Cambridge College theologian William Perkins had branded English vagrants a social plague.

The *Globe* argued that punishment mandated by Massachusetts's existing vagrancy statute was not severe enough "to rid the country of these pests" and urged adoption of a law comparable to that enacted in neighboring New Hampshire, which established sentences of up to fifteen months' hard

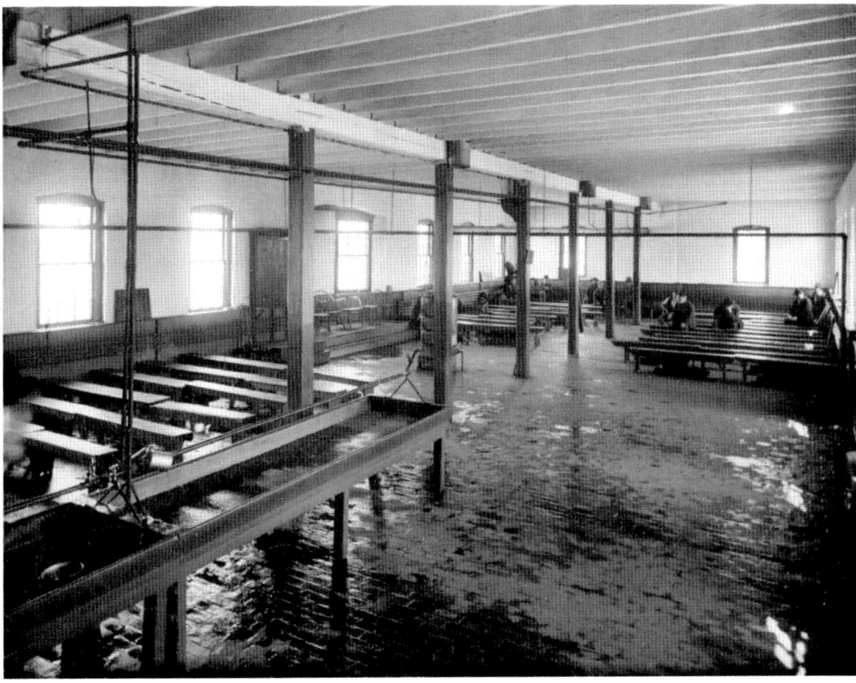

Bridgewater State Farm, dormitory building interior, first floor, circa 1900. *Harvard Art Museums/Fogg Museum, Transfer from the Carpenter Center for the Visual Arts, Social Museum Collection, 3.2002.2712.4. Unidentified Artist. Imaging Department © President and Fellows of Harvard College.*

labor for convicted vagrants. Given what it saw as the relative leniency of Massachusetts law, the *Globe* maintained that vagrants were "coming over from New Hampshire in swarms."[70] Editorials such as these fired readers who clamored for severer vagrancy laws, with the Massachusetts legislature responding in 1880 with new legislation that mandated stricter sentencing with workhouse terms of not less than six months and not more than two years. Though in Puritanical Massachusetts vagrancy had once been considered a sign of God's disfavor, Victorian Bay Staters saw vagrancy as a threat to civil society, as indicated by the law's very title: *An Act for the Protection of the People of the Commonwealth against Tramps.*[71]

Enforcement of the "Tramp Law" was unremitting. Though Bridgewater trustees regarded the new law as a powerful deterrent and attributed a reduction in admittances between 1879 and 1881 to it, the workhouse population soon exceeded pre-1879 levels. Aggressive police raids targeting locations where homeless individuals congregated (a practice known as the "hobo scoop") swelled the workhouse with convicted vagrants. The law's stringent application was not without flaw, and at least one individual was improperly incarcerated because of it. Having made a "comfortable fortune" in the West, Leonard Poole, on his return to Boston, was robbed and thrown from the train. Eventually, he made his way to Boston "in a dazed condition of mind" and without means. Under terms of the 1880 law, Poole's request for assistance and lack of residence in the commonwealth were considered *prima facie* evidence that he was a tramp. Poole was arrested and sent to the Bridgewater workhouse, where he was eventually located by his son-in-law and released in 1885.[72]

## "The Perils of Bridgewater"

For those who found themselves confined at Bridgewater, the workhouse was an unwelcoming place, and their testimonials fueled a liberal public perception of the institution as oppressive and relentless. In a letter to author and social reformer Annie Fields dated 1882, novelist Sarah Orne Jewett referred to the "perils of Bridgewater," which Mrs. Fields herself described as "a most unpalatable place."[73] (In contrast, John C. Alden of Bridgewater found that the workhouse was perceived in town as a well-managed institution devoid of cruel treatment.)

For the many inmates, whether pauper, criminal or insane, their initial experience was nearly identical. After answering questions regarding personal information and background,

> *the prisoner is bathed, and their clothing, if worth saving, is cleansed, bundled and labelled with the name of the owner and the time when it was received. Such things as are necessary for personal comfort or cleanliness, such as cutting the hair, shaving, etc., are performed, and then the prisoner is supplied with clothes furnished by the institution. These clothes are made in the work-house by the inmates; but are of no distinctive color or style. After the cleansing operation has been gone through with, the prisoner is sent into the receiving room, from which he is drafted to such work as he is most competent to perform. Of all the class of prisoners, the vagrants are the ones who give the most trouble, and it is against work that he struggles most strenuously. The inmates of the house sleep in dormitories, there being only about fifteen cells in the building, and these are used as places of punishment for the refractory or lazy ones.*[74]

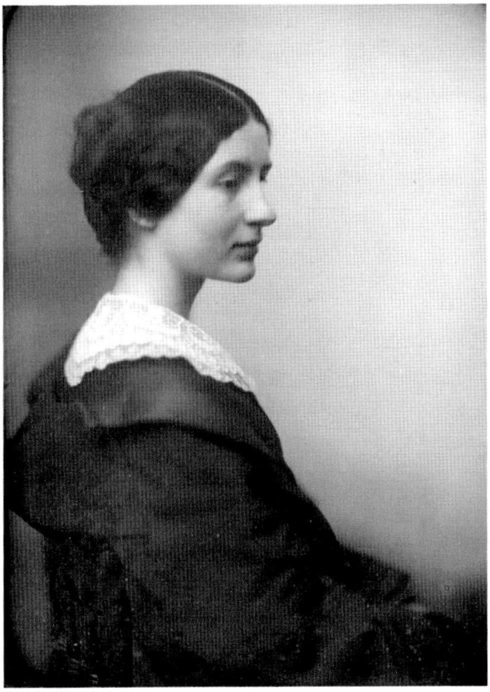

*Left*: Annie Adams Fields (1834–1915), author and social reformer. *Courtesy of Metropolitan Museum of Art.*

*Below*: Bridgewater State Farm, day room, west wing, second floor, circa 1900. *Harvard Art Museums/Fogg Museum, Transfer from the Carpenter Center for the Visual Arts, Social Museum Collection, 3.2002.2709.5. Bass Photo. Imaging Department © President and Fellows of Harvard College.*

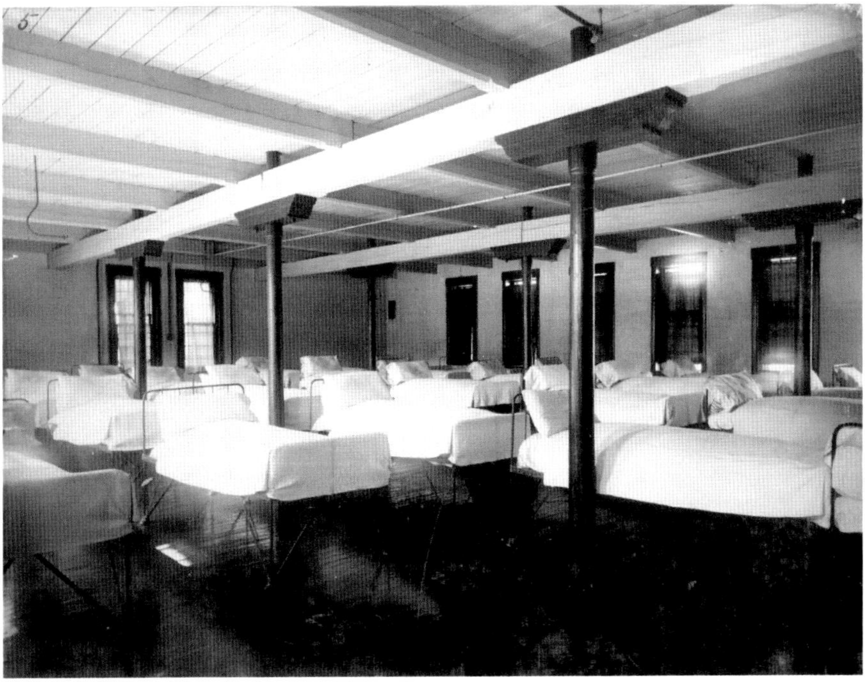

Beyond this, experiences varied greatly. Of the three classes housed at Bridgewater, paupers spoke most highly of the institution, perhaps recognizing the relief Bridgewater provided them from an alternative of poverty and want (although many seemed little perturbed when the complex was destroyed by fire in 1883). One elderly inmate told a Boston reporter in July 1883, "There wasn't a bad officer in the whole establishment, sir. We had food enough to eat and beer every Saturday, and our beds was as clean and comfortable as could be. We had fine ticks with elegant new straw and as clean sheets as there is in the city of London."[75]

Less inclined toward Bridgewater were criminals who were unwillingly incarcerated and refractory inmates who may at times have been subjected to excessive force by those attendants whose names recurred regularly in inmate testimonials. In 1885, an unnamed attendant was dismissed after having treated an inmate cruelly.[76] While not abused *per se*, alcoholics received no treatment at Bridgewater, as alcoholism was considered a crime and not a disease. Untreated, some alcoholics became desperate to satisfy their addiction, with sometimes tragic consequences. In July 1891, two inmates died after drinking wood alcohol used in the paint shop of the chair-making department, "which [deaths] the officers of the institution have kept very quiet."[77]

Other criminals chafed under the long sentences handed down by the municipal courts for drunkenness and vagrancy. For many, a sentence of two years' labor in the workhouse seemed interminable, and escapes occurred. In September 1875, Patrick Lane absconded from the workhouse and was captured at Boston. Anthony Dumas, sentenced to nine months in the workhouse for vagrancy, was so daunted by the prospect that in August 1875 he broke out of the lock-up in Wakefield, where he was confined prior to being transferred to Bridgewater, and escaped. Joseph Watson, sentenced to the workhouse for burglary, escaped and was captured at Charlestown in June 1877. Some escapees remained free for an extended period, such as Michael Sullivan, who escaped in March 1876 and remained at large for six months.

## The Work of the Workhouse

For those sentenced to the workhouse, idleness was not permitted, and inmates were set to labor. In January 1879, twelve to fifteen keepers maintained the discipline and order of the one hundred inmates employed in farm work as well as the thirty patients in the hospital, forty inmates in the sewing room making workhouse uniforms, twenty cleaning rooms and making beds, five whitewashing, five in the bake room, four in the boiler room, from ten to twenty in the carpenter and shoe shops, five to twenty breaking stone and five to twenty picking oakum. Though basket making had been introduced in 1875 to employ those inmates who could not be trusted to labor on the farm, this effort was soon abandoned as unprofitable.

Workhouse officials stressed the importance of labor, believing that it taught habits of industry to tramps who would otherwise remain idle while at the workhouse and become confirmed in their ways. Yet due to the scarcity of shop space, the financial failure of basket making and the lack of industrial skills on the part of many inmates, employment could be provided for only about half of Bridgewater's population. Additionally, both manufacturers and labor unions opposed the use of workhouse labor as competitively unfair and injurious to industrial workers. The commonwealth agreed but

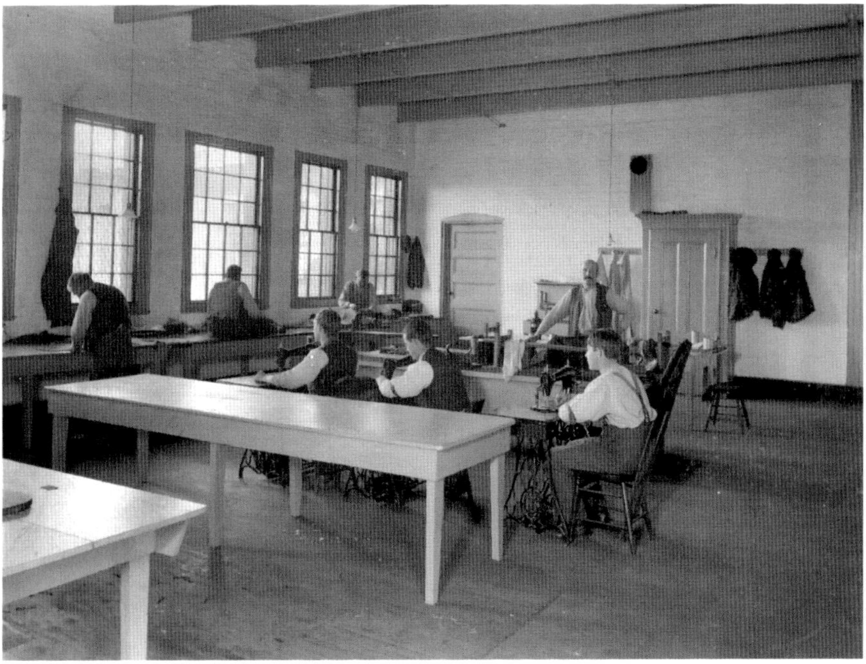

Bridgewater State Farm, prison department, tailor shop, circa 1900. *Harvard Art Museums/ Fogg Museum, Transfer from the Carpenter Center for the Visual Arts, Social Museum Collection, 3.2002.2707.1. Unidentified Artist. Imaging Department © President and Fellows of Harvard College.*

exempted the seating of chairs, which was introduced at Bridgewater in 1879 as a means to occupy those not engaged in farm work. Though an attempt was made in 1880 to introduce shoe making in such a manner that it did not compete with free labor, this experiment was unsuccessful and ultimately proved problematic.

The majority of inmates were assigned to outdoor work, and of the 249 residents housed at Bridgewater in September 1878, the bulk labored on the farm under guard. "They go out in companies of a dozen or more, in charge of an officer. This requires a larger number of officers than would otherwise seem necessary. Many of the men are former inmates of correctional institutions or the State Prison, and cannot be trusted beyond the limits of the yard."[78]

Some difference of opinion existed regarding the efficiency of the farm operation. Luther Glover, who served as assistant farmer for six months during 1873, considered the farm poorly managed, with hay put in the barn in poor condition and melons left to rot in the fields.[79] Glover criticized Superintendent Leonard's lack of farming experience and his over-reliance on subordinate officers on the farm. Erastus B. Carl, an officer at the workhouse in 1873, agreed. Assistant Superintendent William C. Howland, however, believed that the farm was well managed and had improved under Leonard's guidance. Jonathan L. Hall, who had been employed at the workhouse for five years, characterized it as the best farm in Bridgewater, as did Lafayette Keith, another Bridgewater farmer and secretary of the Plymouth County Agricultural Society.

Admittedly, though the farm played an important role in occupying otherwise idle inmates and contributed to their rehabilitation, this emphasis on Leonard's agricultural skills at first appears misplaced. The reason becomes apparent, however, when the value the commonwealth put on ensuring the self-sufficiency of its charitable institutions is recalled. If managed properly, the farm held the potential for substantially reducing the operating costs of the workhouse so that greater importance was placed on the qualifications of its superintendent to conduct the farm profitably rather than to rehabilitate the institution's inmates and prepare them for a return to society.

## "I Have Carried a Match One Year to Accomplish This"

Early in 1883, new allegations of mistreatment at Bridgewater were quickly overshadowed by developments surrounding the state almshouse at Tewksbury, which became the focus of an intensive investigation following charges made by Governor Benjamin Butler of abuses at that institution. While likely engrossed in following developments at Tewksbury, Bridgewater officials were forced to confront more immediate issues of their own. In late June 1883, Superintendent Leonard resigned and was succeeded by Hollis M. Blackstone (1848–1923), superintendent of the Marcella Street Home at Roxbury, an institution founded in 1877 for the care of pauper and neglected children. On the morning of July 7, within hours of Blackstone's appointment, virtually the entire Bridgewater complex was destroyed by fire after a disgruntled inmate, unhappy with the treatment he experienced there, set fire to the main workhouse building.

Since 1859, when Governor Banks had criticized the state almshouses as being "composed of materials so combustible that it would be difficult, in the event of conflagration, to avoid an appalling loss of life," the threat of fire had been a preoccupation of Bridgewater's annual reports.[80] Matches were banned, and smoking was closely supervised.

The July 1883 fire was discovered in the morning in the attic of the main almshouse building and "spread with inconceivable rapidity."[81]

> *In 15 minutes that portion of the building was all ablaze, and the fire was under full headway, creeping rapidly toward other portions of the structure. Between 150 and 200 inmates were in the Work-house, and Superintendent Blackstone, aided by a corps of assistants, did his utmost to remove everyone from the buildings. About 22 persons were confined in the hospital, but they were quickly conveyed to a place of safety. The inmates assisted the officers in removing the contents of the safe in the office, the record books, public documents, and other valuables, the loss of which would have been irreparable. Nearly all the bedding, furniture, &c., as well as all personal property of the prisoners were rescued from the flames.... The buildings are now a mass of ruins.*[82]

Though new, the institution's force pump failed to work, and telegrams were sent requesting outside help. The Old Colony Railroad assisted by transporting apparatus from Taunton and Brockton. The horse-drawn pumper *Ousamequin* was dispatched from the School Street firehouse at

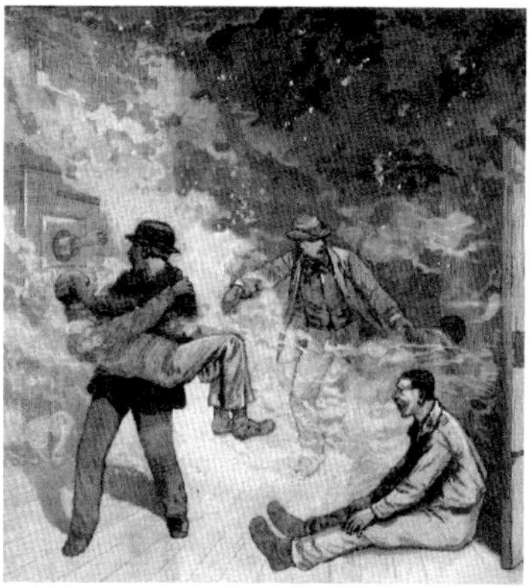

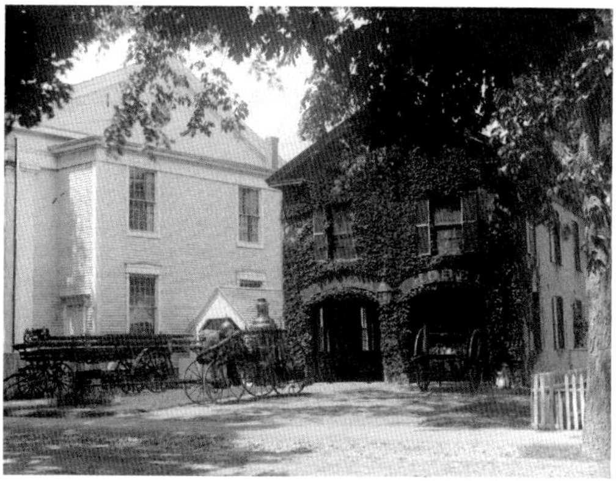

*Left*: Blockley Almshouse fire, Philadelphia, provides some idea of the similar 1883 Bridgewater fire, for which no images are extant. *Frank Leslie's Illustrated*, February 1885.

*Right*: School Street Firehouse, Bridgewater, circa 1883. *Author's collection.*

Bridgewater, but the horse died en route, and the engine had to be drawn by volunteer members of the Bridgewater Fire District the remainder of the way. Though some workhouse residents assisted with quelling the fire (at least two of whom were recommended for immediate release due to their good conduct during the fire), "most of the paupers who had been inmates of the institution sat upon the grass in a field close by and watched the flames reduce what had been their home to a heap of smoldering ruins."[83]

Destroyed in the blaze were the main workhouse building, the laundry building and the combined hospital and lock-up. Two barns survived. The fire proved a total loss, as at the time the commonwealth did not insure its property. Left homeless were 163 inmates, roughly equally divided among paupers and prisoners. Nearly immediately, accommodation was made for the paupers at the Tewksbury almshouse and the prisoners at the Westborough Reform School, which also was designated as the commonwealth's temporary workhouse.

In the confusion, a number of criminals escaped, and as late as July 10, Blackstone was unsure of how many were still free. Among the missing was James Gilmore, who was later captured and confessed to setting the fire. The *New York Times* described Gilmore as a "hardened prisoner" who was "very refractory" and whom it was frequently necessary to punish, a circumstance that appears to have fostered a vengeful attitude in him. At his trial, Gilmore stated that he had set the workhouse fire "because he was treated badly while living there," reinforcing previous allegations of institutional mistreatment at Bridgewater.[84] "I have carried a match one year to accomplish it. I shoved straw up the ventilator flue and disabled the steam pump, and I am glad the place is in ashes."[85] Gilmore was subsequently sentenced in October to twenty years' imprisonment for the crime.

## "Plain, Economical, Comfortable Houses"

The destruction of the workhouse combined with earlier proposals that the workhouse system be abolished raised questions concerning Bridgewater's future. Governor Butler, still preoccupied prosecuting the Tewksbury almshouse for gross mismanagement, was noncommittal. Though a number of factors favored rebuilding the workhouse at Bridgewater, where cultivable land and suitable agricultural buildings were already available, other alternatives were considered, including abandoning the workhouse system and transferring criminals to the county houses of correction and equipping the reform school at Westborough as a workhouse. To these, Butler added a fourth proposition: that the Bridgewater workhouse be rebuilt and to

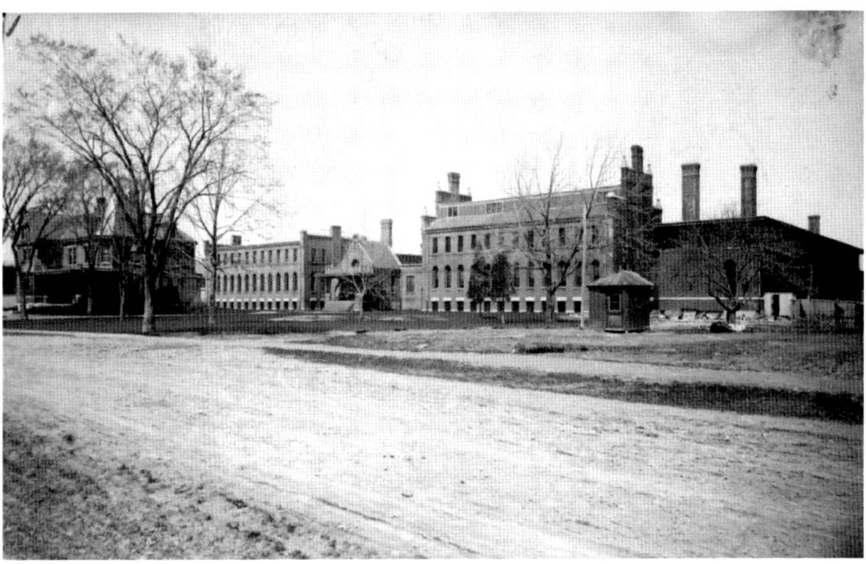

Bridgewater State Farm, view of buildings, east, circa 1900. *Harvard Art Museums/ Fogg Museum, Transfer from the Carpenter Center for the Visual Arts, Social Museum Collection, 3.2002.2712.1. Unidentified Artist. Imaging Department © President and Fellows of Harvard College.*

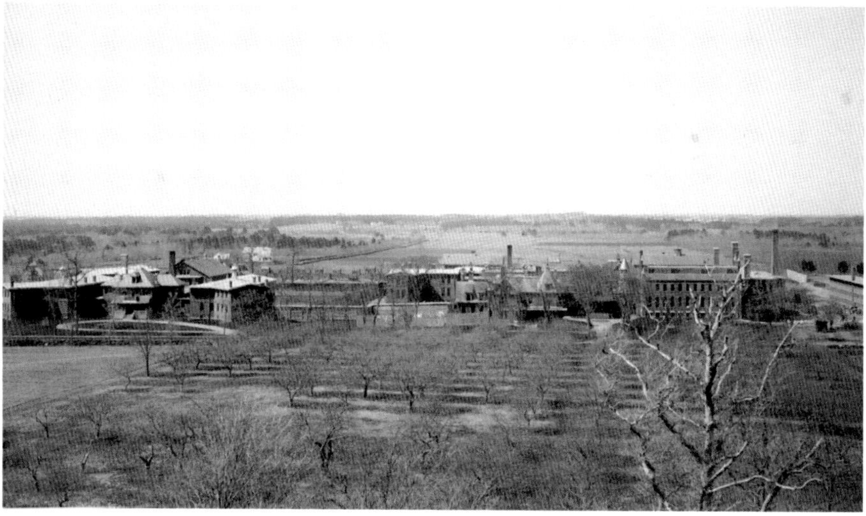

Bridgewater State Farm, bird's-eye view of institution, 1890s, with the Clough-designed almshouse-workhouse complex (*right*) and the later asylum buildings (*left*). *Harvard Art Museums/Fogg Museum, Transfer from the Carpenter Center for the Visual Arts, Social Museum Collection, 3.2002.882.3. Bass Photo. Imaging Department © President and Fellows of Harvard College.*

it added a new "insane hospital," a proposal that laid the foundation for Bridgewater's future formal role as a state forensic hospital.

Ultimately, reconstruction was authorized. Blackstone later joked that only the chimneystack remained after the fire, and the institution was rebuilt because a board member felt "it would be an extravagance to abandon such a valuable smoke-stack." In truth, frugality was the decisive factor, with rebuilding being deemed the most cost-effective solution.[86]

Boston architect George A. Clough prepared plans for the new facility and reduced the threat posed by fire by designing nine separate structures with sleeping, dining and hospital accommodations for 250 inmates in place of a single large structure. Clough, Boston's city architect between 1874 and 1883, planned a functional complex free of architectural adornment very much in accord with the legislature's wishes, as well as a later assessment of him as "competent but not very inspired."[87]

The buildings at Bridgewater were substantially completed by December 30, 1884, when 127 prisoners, 100 of whom were handcuffed in pairs, were transferred from Westborough to Bridgewater, brought to Titicut Station under armed guard of 8 policemen. At the time, Westborough's role as a workhouse was abolished and Bridgewater resumed its place among the commonwealth's charitable institutions.

Chapter 4

# "No Special Treatment Is Given"

## Bridgewater State Farm as Charitable Institution, 1886–1919

Likely in response to the suggestion made three years earlier by Governor Butler and with a view toward alleviating crowding in the commonwealth's lunatic asylums, in 1886 the Bridgewater almshouse became subject to taking "chronic insane" from the so-called pauper and harmless class. An asylum building accommodating 125 persons was opened the following year on the west side of the complex and placed under administration of the State Board of Lunacy and Charity.[88] The intention was to employ asylum patients on the farm, thereby reducing the cost of their care. Mentally disturbed individuals were initially welcomed at Bridgewater as a dependable source of farm labor, as they typically were able bodied, more so than paupers, who tended to be elderly, while criminals couldn't always be trusted not to escape while laboring outdoors.

Patients were transferred from the commonwealth's existing asylums at Worcester, Taunton, Danvers, Northampton and Westborough, which began to see in Bridgewater a means of off-loading more troublesome individuals, and these institutions consequently began sending their violent and criminally insane to Bridgewater. Though the earliest patients were considered harmless, escapes increased, and Bridgewater officials recommended construction of stronger facilities to keep patients secured. The state lunatic asylums supported an allocation of funds for this purpose in order that Bridgewater might be required to receive transfers entirely from the convict and criminal class, thereby easing their own burden. A close board fence fifteen feet high to enclose the buildings was raised in mid-1887,

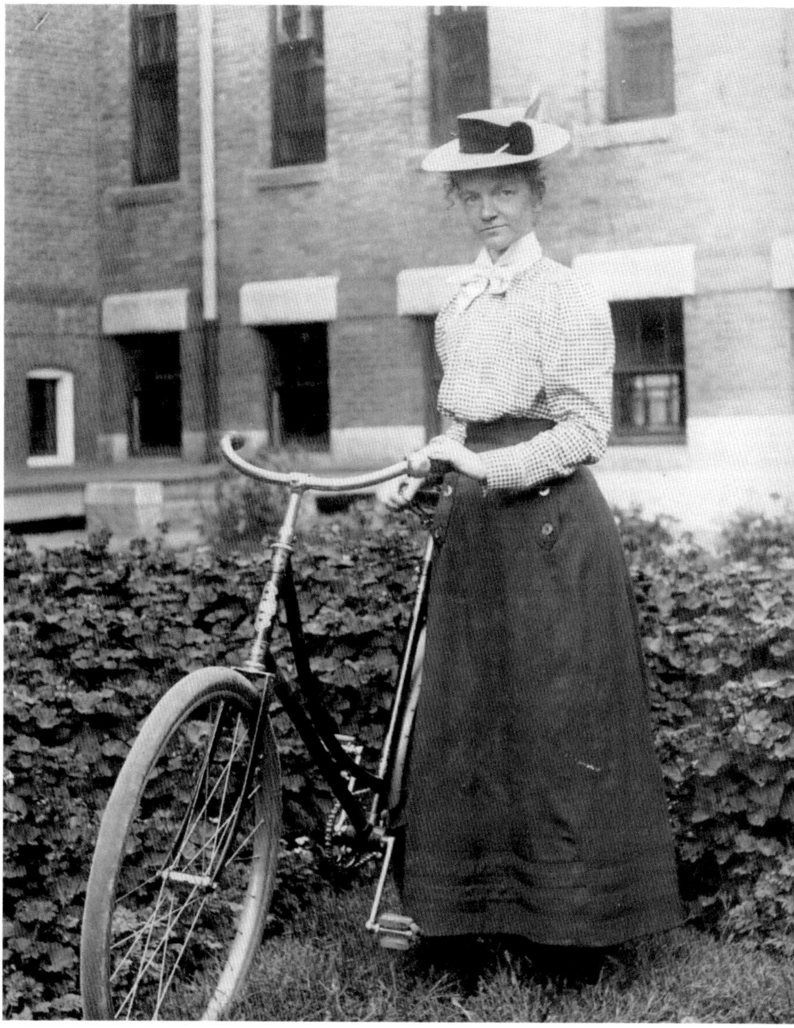

Bridgewater State Farm, bookkeeper Alice M. Nash, circa 1905. *Massachusetts State Archives, State Farm (Bridgewater, Mass.), Photographs of facilities and activities [ca. 1900–ca. 1910], HS9.10/973X.*

and work was begun on so-called strong buildings in which to confine these "active violent types" in 1888.[89] In 1890, transfer of aged inmates who were infirm or mentally ill from the state prison at Charlestown to Bridgewater was also permitted.[90]

Superintendent Blackstone writes that in deference to the presence of insane paupers (who were considered individuals largely not responsible

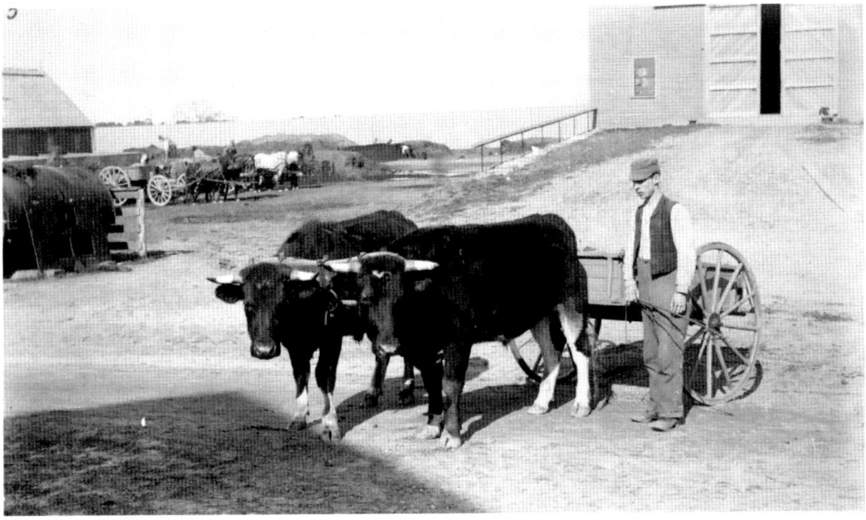

Bridgewater State Farm, pet steers, circa 1903. *Harvard Art Museums/Fogg Museum, Transfer from the Carpenter Center for the Visual Arts, Social Museum Collection, 3.2002.882.5. Bass Photo. Imaging Department © President and Fellows of Harvard College.*

for their circumstances) and to avoid the stigma of the workhouse label, the institution was renamed the Bridgewater State Farm in 1887, a change suggested by the trustees the previous year. "If some name were adopted as 'State Farm' it would appear more mild, and would not carry with it that terror to certain persons which is now sometimes the case."[91]

Though the renaming was successful in fostering a more favorable public perception of the institution, Blackstone would later write in 1899 that the rechristened State Farm was "not fully shown in character, purpose, or extent by the name given....The variety of duties required and offices performed in the medical, charitable, and penal directions, precludes for a name any convenient and euphonious word or phrase which would designate clearly the several interests committed by law to its care."[92]

The multiplicity of roles that Blackstone noted fostered a haphazard physical expansion as new structures were added to accommodate a growing and ever-changing population. Though Blackstone publicly stated that this ad hoc growth gave flexibility to the institution and was fiscally sound, it also was limiting and failed to adequately fulfill the needs of the population it served. In private, Blackstone recognized the institution's deficiencies, writing Massachusetts Prison Committee member F.B. Sanborn in 1889 of Bridgewater's inability to meet the needs of three recently admitted young men: "It seems to me they require two things which we cannot offer—greater security and educational opportunity." Blackstone requested that they be transferred to the state reformatory instead.[93]

The maintenance of Bridgewater as a mixed-classification institution also ensured that administrative problems continued.

> *The necessity for greater and closer classification of patients in the asylum has become strikingly apparent since the whole class of criminals have been collected into one institution. A percentage of the so-called criminals is not only of unsound mind, but incorrigible and dangerous. They should be allowed but limited liberty, and none whatever in common with the majority of the patients. Their presence on the open wards and yards is a constant menace to the good order and happiness of all concerned—an exposed danger not easily defended if attended with serious results.*[94]

It should be noted that such circumstances were not unique to Bridgewater. Communities operating comparable charitable institutions also confronted challenges with mixed classifications. In February 1897, New Bedford came under fire for its almshouse, where criminals freely mingled with paupers and where paupers were lodged with the mentally ill. "The spectacle of an

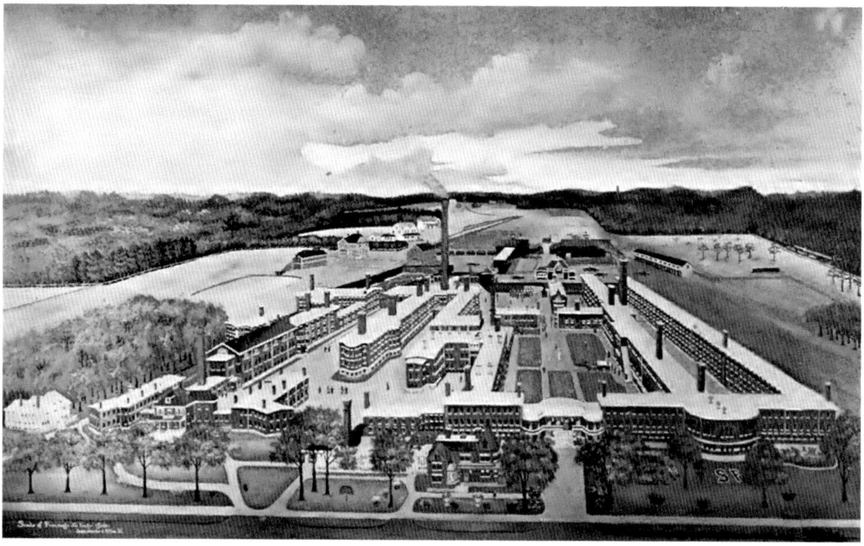

Bridgewater State Farm, circa 1896. The complex as it appeared before construction of the Tower Building on the east side of the prison in 1897. *Author's collection.*

old lady whose only offense is misfortune, and a child of 5 or 6 years old shut in a room with idiots and women committed from the slums…seems hideous to many people," remarked the *Boston Globe*.[95]

Bridgewater, like New Bedford and many of the commonwealth's cities, strove to better segregate its classes, and by 1899, the State Farm had progressed to serving three roles, each administered by a different department: the prison housing those convicted in criminal court of misdemeanor offenses, the almshouse and hospital accommodating state paupers from southeastern Massachusetts and the State Asylum for Insane Criminals.[96]

## "The Most Difficult Part of Our Complex Task"

Of the three State Farm departments, the most trouble-plagued was the Asylum for Insane Criminals, established in 1895 as the commonwealth's forensic psychiatric hospital and renamed Bridgewater State Hospital in 1909. In 1912, the trustees acknowledged that operation of the state hospital was "the most difficult part of our complex task."[97]

Criminally insane individuals for years had been sent to the State Lunatic Asylum at Worcester, which, like Bridgewater, struggled with the lack of a classification system, criminally insane being mingled with those who had been civilly committed. The result was disruptive and often violent behavior. Consequently, in an effort to reduce tensions at Worcester, criminally insane patients began being transferred to Bridgewater, and its role in this regard became formalized when the legislature authorized direct committals of male prisoners judged insane beginning in 1895. By 1896, all criminally insane patients had been transferred from the various state lunatic asylums and segregated at Bridgewater and were housed either in one of the 185 single rooms or in common dormitories that accommodated another 140 patients. Yet confined in the Bridgewater asylum with the 212 criminally insane were 88 non-criminal insane from the pauper class whose numbers were periodically augmented by transfers from the Almshouse Department of the State Farm. The asylum's first medical director, Arthur H. Harrington, recognized that this latter circumstance nullified the impact of efforts to restrict Bridgewater to those judged *criminally* insane. "It would be well if such inmates of the Almshouse Department as become insane were committed to the State Lunatic Hospitals, as the practice of

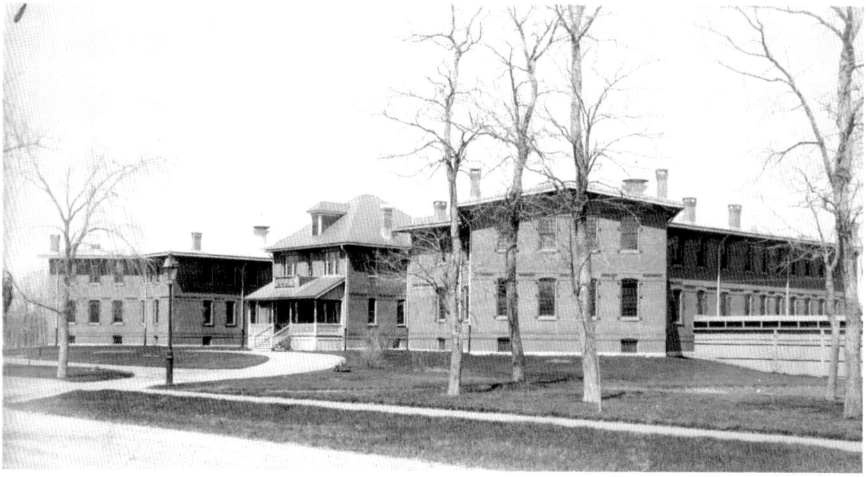

Bridgewater State Farm, asylum buildings, front, circa 1900. *Harvard Art Museums/Fogg Museum, Transfer from the Carpenter Center for the Visual Arts, Social Museum Collection, 3.2002.2709.1. Bass Photo. Imaging Department © President and Fellows of Harvard College.*

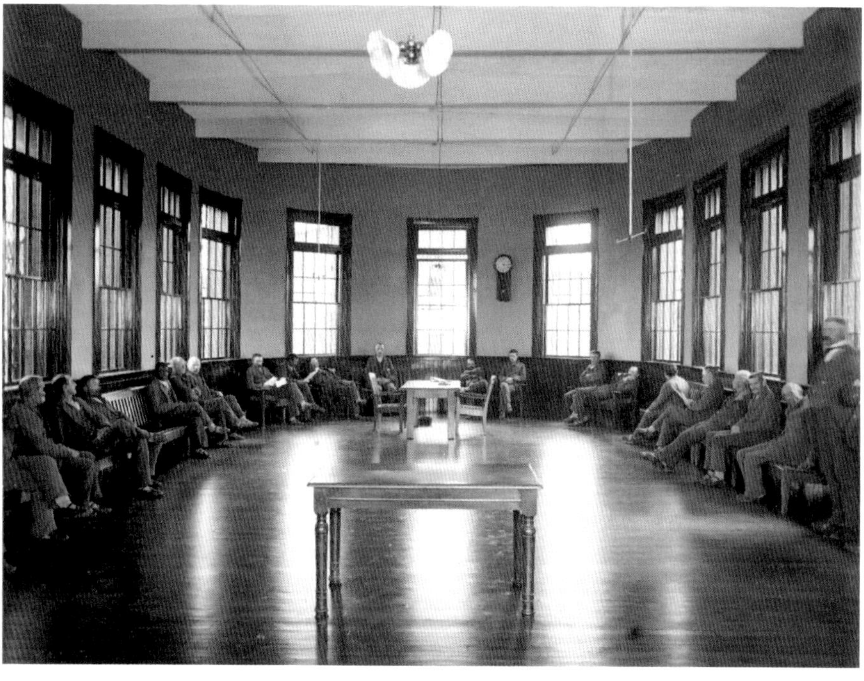

Bridgewater State Farm, asylum department, north day room, circa 1900. *Harvard Art Museums/Fogg Museum, Transfer from the Carpenter Center for the Visual Arts, Social Museum Collection, 3.2002.2708.2. Unidentified Artist. Imaging Department © President and Fellows of Harvard College.*

committing them to this asylum vitiates the legislation which aimed at a separation of the criminal and non-criminal insane."[98]

While Harrington advocated the removal of the non-criminal or harmless insane, the admission of criminally insane individuals saw no respite. The commonwealth's courts continued to commit insane males charged with or convicted of a crime to Bridgewater, while insane male convicts from Massachusetts's several other facilities found their way to Bridgewater, bloating the asylum's population and necessitating physical expansion, which was undertaken on an extensive scale between 1888 and 1912. Superintendent Blackstone suggested in 1897 that still further enlargement would be necessary were it not for the prospect of transferring some of the non-criminal cases to the Medfield Insane Asylum, opened in 1892. The practice of confining the criminally insane with those who had been civilly committed would have long-term repercussions.

The constant shuffling of inmates among the commonwealth's various charitable and penal institutions and the absence of professionally qualified

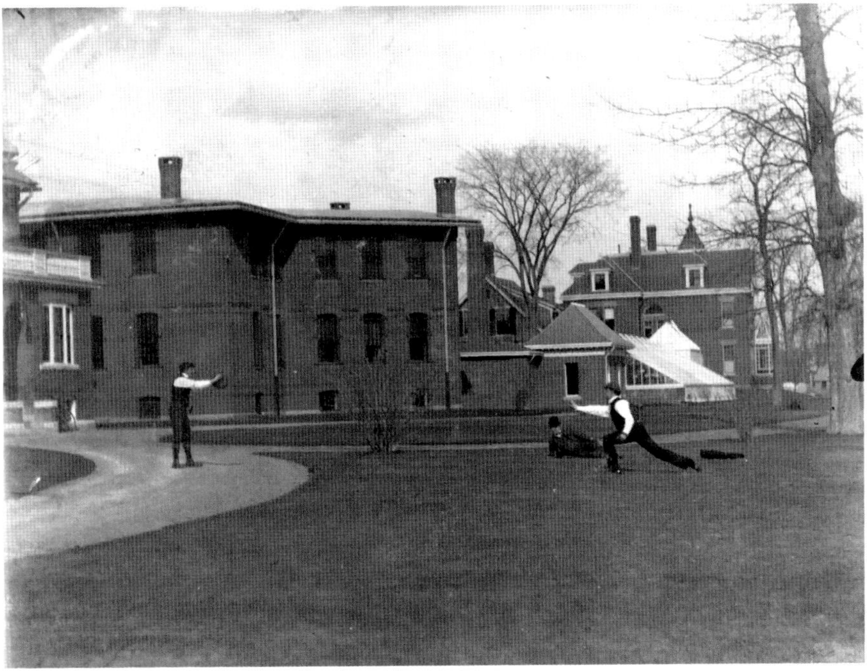

Bridgewater State Farm, impromptu catch in front of the hospital for the criminally insane, circa 1900. *Massachusetts State Archives, State Farm (Bridgewater, Mass.), Photographs of facilities and activities [ca. 1900–ca. 1910], HS9.10/973X.*

specialists created the potential for grievous mistakes, including wrongful incarceration. In 1892, Franklin C. Pratt of Weymouth was arrested on a charge of larceny for the theft of a horse and carriage. Judged an "incurable insane," he lingered in the Bridgewater asylum for eighteen months, despite his counsel's assertions that Pratt was sane. Finally, Pratt succeeded in securing a reexamination confirming his sanity. Reporting the incident, the *Boston Post* was blasé about the whole occurrence, which demonstrated "that sometimes a sane man can be detained in an insane asylum."[99] For his part, Superintendent Wrightington of the State Board of Lunacy and Charity denied that Pratt had been sane when committed, arguing that it was impossible for a sane man to be confined to an asylum.

Difficulties in clinically diagnosing mental illness also encouraged some inmates to "play" the system. In 1911, Bertram G. Spencer, who had been charged with the murder of Martha B. Blackstone at Springfield and remanded to the State Farm as insane, confessed to a fellow inmate that he was only feigning insanity, having "had to do queer things to fool the [Bridgewater] doctors" in order to avoid standing trial.[100] Ultimately,

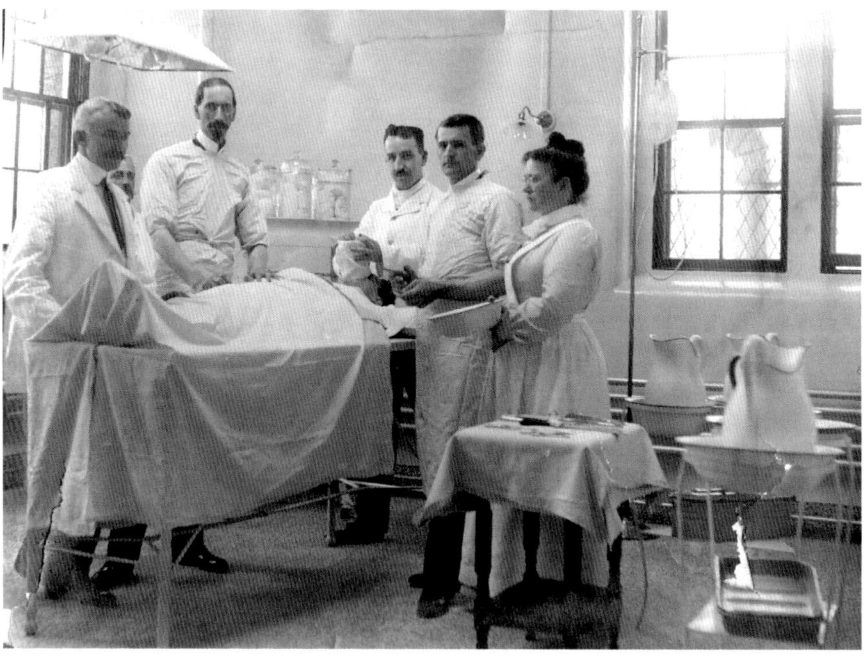

Bridgewater State Farm, operating room, circa 1910, with Superintendent Blackstone and Nurse Margaret Hamilton. *Massachusetts State Archives, State Farm (Bridgewater, Mass.), Photographs of facilities and activities [ca. 1900–ca. 1910], HS9.10/973X.*

he was determined competent, was tried and convicted and electrocuted in September 1912 at the Massachusetts State Prison. Ernest B. Emerson, medical director of the State Farm hospital, was understated when he spoke of the challenges in diagnosing mental illness in 1912, remarking that "the diagnosis between the criminal and malingerer, anxious to escape paying the price for his viciousness, and the insane man or defective, in trouble as a result of his mental disease, is at times most difficult."[101]

## "To Prevent, Check or Cure Intemperance Is the Same Old Problem"

Administration of Bridgewater's prison department was minimally less challenging. Overcrowding of inmates sentenced there for a variety of misdemeanor offenses remained one of the most serious issues but was a concern for the institution as a whole, with 1,200 inmates packed in Bridgewater's three departments in January 1894. Cots were required, and the chapel was pressed into service as a dormitory, in part to relieve the hospital, which was described as overflowing.[102] In the prison and workhouse plant, two-thirds of the inmates were cared for in dormitories, as there were only 225 rooms to house a prison population that fluctuated between 500 and 700. Superintendent Blackstone urged the construction of an additional 200 to 300 rooms or cells to ease conditions, arguing that rooms would be cheaper. By December 1897, the Tower Building with 300 additional "prison rooms" was under construction. It was quickly filled when, in 1898, the commonwealth enacted an indeterminate sentencing law for workhouse cases that set upward sentencing limits of a year for drunkenness and two years for all other offenses.

Bridgewater, in fact, maintained the highest average population of all the commonwealth's penal institutions, and numbers from the year ending September 30, 1910, may be cited as an example. Bridgewater housed an average population of 1,378 as contrasted with the Deer Island House of Correction (1,268), State Prison at Charlestown (855) and Massachusetts Reformatory at Concord (838).

Overcrowding at Bridgewater was exacerbated by the tendency of some judges to convict quickly and on the merest pretext. The Boston municipal court and the commonwealth's several police courts were the

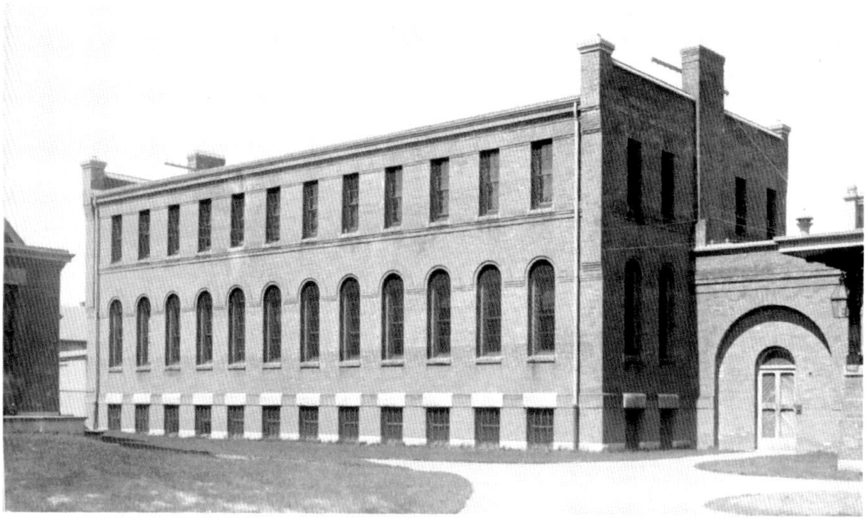

Bridgewater State Farm, dormitory building, circa 1900. *Harvard Art Museums/Fogg Museum, Transfer from the Carpenter Center for the Visual Arts, Social Museum Collection, 3.20022712.2. Unidentified Artist. Imaging Department © President and Fellows of Harvard College.*

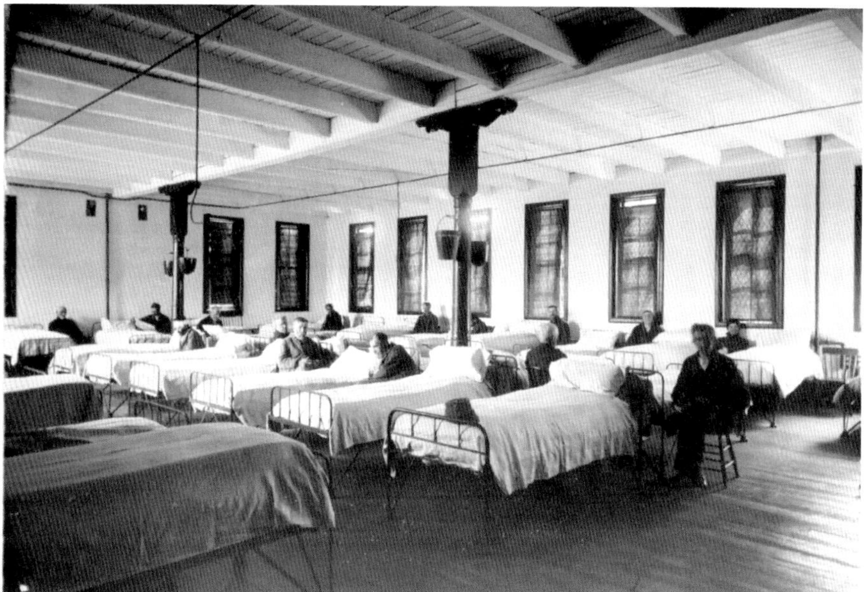

Bridgewater State Farm, dormitory building interior, second floor, circa 1900. *Harvard Art Museums/Fogg Museum, Transfer from the Carpenter Center for the Visual Arts, Social Museum Collection, 3.2002.2712.3. Unidentified Artist. Imaging Department © President and Fellows of Harvard College.*

most active in terms of sentencing convicts to Bridgewater. In the twelve months preceding September 30, 1904, the Boston municipal court sentenced 537 of the 1,980 individuals committed to Bridgewater, while the fifteen police courts added an additional 589. Throughout the period, a quarter or more of Bridgewater's commitments were processed through the municipal court at Boston, and in some years this number approached 40 percent. While these figures appear high, they pale in comparison to the actual number of arrests in Boston, which for drunkenness alone in the year ending September 30, 1902, reached 18,886, or nearly 52 a day. Clearly, most cases were disposed of without sentence, but this was of little consolation to Bridgewater officials, who had to contend with the number that ultimately were committed to the farm.[103]

By far, the greatest number of those sentenced were convicted of crimes against public order, with drunkenness attributing for 75 to 85 percent of committals between 1895 and 1919, with over three thousand individuals committed annually for the crime in peak years like 1911 and 1913. Next were the "vagrants, tramps and vagabonds." Beyond these offenses, a scattering of inmates were sentenced for being "idle and disorderly," for prostitution, non-support, attempted or successful escapes and lewd behavior. Each year, only a handful was sentenced for crimes against either persons or property, such as assault, larceny and breaking and entering.

The majority of those sentenced to Bridgewater were also male. While efforts had been made in the years surrounding 1880 to reduce the female population of Bridgewater, women, most of whom were convicted on charges of drunkenness, continued to be sentenced there largely in order to do housekeeping, "work which men cannot well do."[104] In 1898, forty to fifty females were housed at Bridgewater, and in the subsequent two decades, approximately 5 percent of those sentenced there each year were women. In 1906, a women's prison for Bridgewater was authorized, opening three years later in a newly constructed building. (It closed in 1930 when the remaining female inmates were transferred to Framingham.)

Among those sentenced were many who were considered insane and were more properly patients for one of the commonwealth's mental health facilities. The State Board of Insanity found in 1915 that of 793 Bridgewater prisoners surveyed, 262 had shown indications of mental disturbance, "which made the sentence an injustice," and estimated that 1 in every 14 vagrants was insane.[105] Incarceration of these individuals alongside alcoholics and the homeless served only to complicate administration.

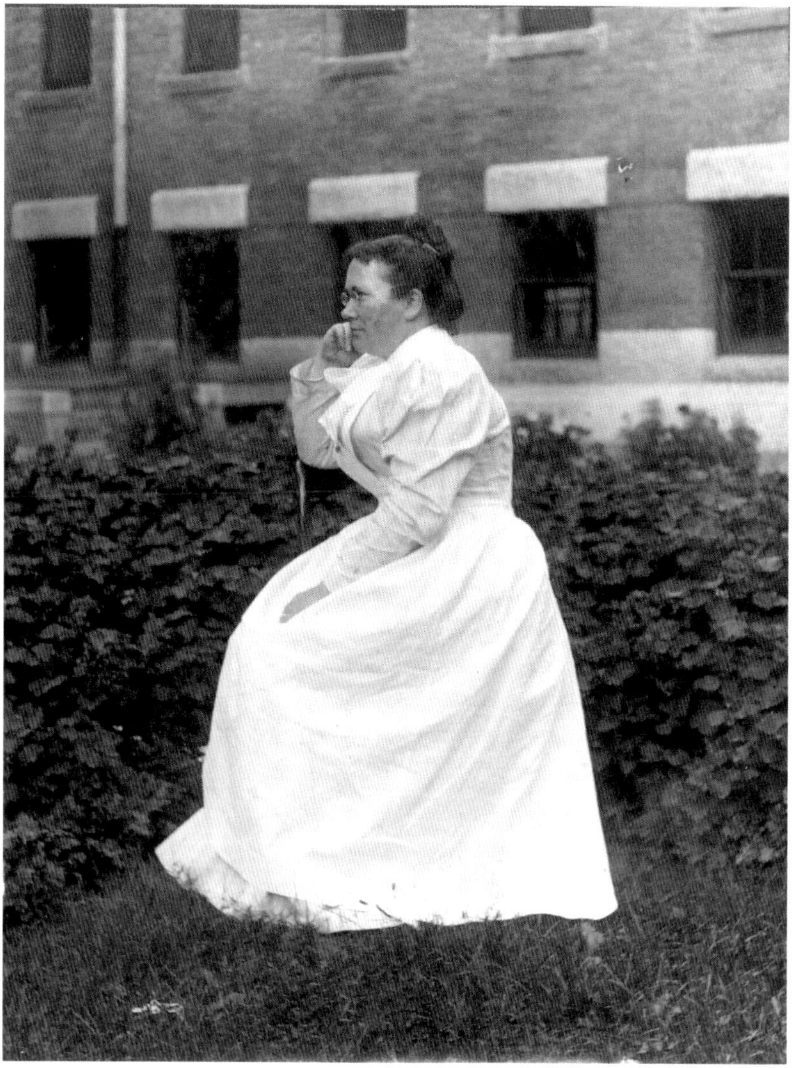

Bridgewater State Farm, Nurse (later Matron) Margaret Hamilton, circa 1900. *Massachusetts State Archives, State Farm (Bridgewater, Mass.), Photographs of facilities and activities [ca. 1900–ca. 1910], HS9.10/973X.*

In 1903, Governor John L. Bates appointed Judge William H.H. Emmons of the East Boston district court to the post of Boston police commissioner, an appointment that had ramifications for Bridgewater and highlighted the lack of coordination between the commonwealth's judiciary and its penal system. A noted teetotaler, Emmons sought to curb public drunkenness and was instrumental in passage of the police board's so-called drunk order, which called upon law enforcement to be more active in arresting intoxicated individuals who made themselves "obnoxious." "I think a man is drunk when he is out of his normal condition by the voluntary use of intoxicating liquor," opined Emmons. "The ordinary evidence I used to require when judge of the East Boston court was that, when a man's breath smelled of liquor and he staggered, or his speech was affected, he was drunk."[106]

Given the looseness of Emmons's definition and the avidity with which police and courts responded, overcrowding was again an issue at Bridgewater in late 1904, when Superintendent Blackstone urged the State Board of Charities to request the Boston courts to ease up on their sentencing. A large number of those sent to Bridgewater as "drunkards" were sentenced to terms of several months, which had the effect of filling the facility to overflowing, with 1,830 inmates reported there in December 1904. (The record was 1,850.) In response, ground was broken in summer 1905 for a new concrete prison building, with head farmer Bacon overseeing 30 prisoners doing the work.[107]

Whether a product of compassion or conditions in the prison, a new assessment of drunkenness and the penalties it should involve emerged about this time. Prison terms for drunkenness were reduced, which helped ease crowding, though drunkenness continued to be the principal crime for which individuals were sent to Bridgewater, accounting for 3,783 of 4,373 cases in 1910.[108] Additionally, the recidivism (re-offense) rate remained a concern, with nearly three-fifths of inmates being at least second offenders. (Two individuals had been incarcerated twenty-seven times.)[109] "To prevent, check or cure intemperance is the same old problem," remarked a weary Blackstone in 1911.[110] Recidivism likely remained high as little was done toward reforming chronic alcoholics confined at Bridgewater, for whom "a quart of whiskey daily for many years was a not infrequent history," as discovered by one clinical researcher in 1904.[111]

Those reformative efforts that were made to assist inmates incarcerated at Bridgewater and steer them toward a better life were undertaken by private charitable organizations rather than the commonwealth. Inmates convicted of drunkenness were often paroled after three months to the care of reform organizations such as the East End Christian Union at Cambridge, which received into its care 100 men in 1906, 117 in 1907 and 98 in 1909.[112] Similarly, the John Howard Industrial Home for Discharged Prisoners, founded in 1890, established a mission in the former Seth Washburn house at South Bridgewater to help discharged criminals

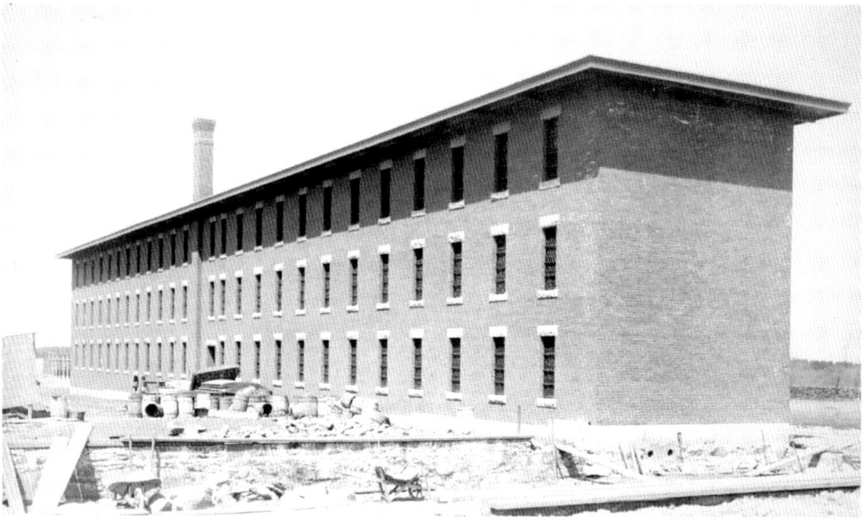

Bridgewater State Farm, new prison building, circa 1903. *Harvard Art Museums/Fogg Museum, Transfer from the Carpenter Center for the Visual Arts, Social Museum Collection, 3.2002.882.2. Bass Photo. Imaging Department © President and Fellows of Harvard College.*

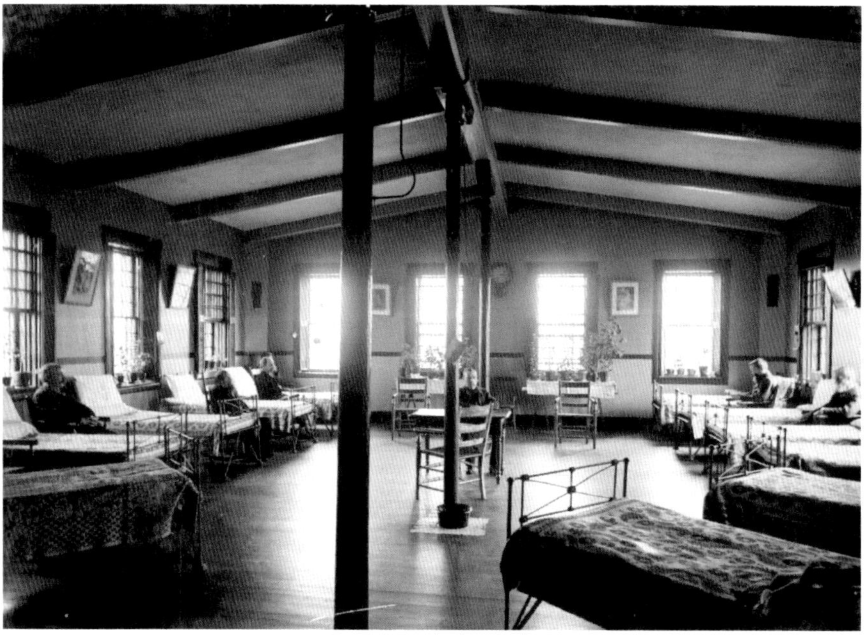

Bridgewater State Farm, dormitory building, west wing, circa 1900. *Harvard Art Museums/Fogg Museum, Transfer from the Carpenter Center for the Visual Arts, Social Museum Collection, 3.2002.2709/3. Bass Photo. Imaging Department © President and Fellows of Harvard College.*

"lead lives of honesty and thrift." Sadly, the home was destroyed by fire on November 25, 1899, just five weeks after opening. The Massachusetts Society for Aiding Discharged Convicts was also instrumental in providing assistance to former Bridgewater inmates.

Continued overcrowding at Bridgewater resulted in deteriorating conditions and the loosening of any classification system that existed. In 1905, an unnamed Boston minister visited the State Farm, following which he addressed an open letter to Governor William L. Douglas. While some of the minister's concerns were motivated by his strict morality (he challenged the propriety of furnishing a smoking room for inmates) or were relatively minor (he complained that beans were served without pork), other allegations were more substantial, including that "criminals and paupers got nothing but bread and water for supper, that the right of appeal to the superintendent was denied prisoners, [and] that the men were discharged in winter without suitable clothing." The *Middleboro Gazette* seemed dismissive of the charges, which Blackstone attributed to the growth of the institution. "The place is growing very rapidly," pointed out the newspaper, "and while such conditions as keeping the criminals and paupers together are not regarded as ideal, it is something for which the immediate management isn't responsible."[113]

Despite these challenges, Bridgewater State Farm maintained a high reputation and continued to be regarded as a model institution. A British delegation studying American institutions for the "feeble-minded" in November 1905 found Bridgewater to be a "well managed and highly interesting institution," though it criticized the employee inmate ratio of one to eighteen as "a very low figure considering the number of sick and insane."[114] Similarly, in 1908, when a legislative delegation arrived from Ohio to investigate the management of penitentiaries and the use of convict labor, it recorded its view that "in the North the oldest and best developed prison farm is the State Farm at Bridgewater, Mass."[115]

## FARM LABOR AND PRODUCTIVE INDUSTRY

The principal means of occupying inmates at Bridgewater remained the farm, which served as an example for other prisons and became even more closely identified with the institution following the 1887 name change. Although institutional farms existed elsewhere in the commonwealth, that at Bridgewater was the largest and most productive. By 1899, the farm comprised 716 acres and within six years had reached a full two square miles (1,280 acres). Of these, 60 acres alone were devoted to potato cultivation, including one single plot of over 50 acres.

Farm tasks occupying a large force of men and as many as seventeen horse teams and nine ox teams daily were meticulously recorded. Typically, twelve officers were supervising crews engaged in morning and afternoon work, though on holidays and rare days of inclement weather, no work was performed. "Rained all day. Nothing doing," was the terse entry in the farm ledger for January 3, 1911.[116] Haying was an enormous undertaking, and in 1905, three hundred inmates and twenty-five carts were required to mechanically mow 1,100 acres of standing grass. Following the harvest of 450 tons of hay, the gang was transferred to work in the potato fields, hoeing and destroying bugs.[117]

Despite the prioritization of farm work, indoor work or "productive industry" was still provided, though largely confined to the cane seating of chairs, which, along with umbrella making, was the sole industry permissible by law after 1897 in Massachusetts prisons. Blackstone called chair caning an "industry of last resort" but recognized its value in keeping inmates from idleness.[118] Originally conducted on a piece-price system through which contractors paid the commonwealth a set price for each piece completed

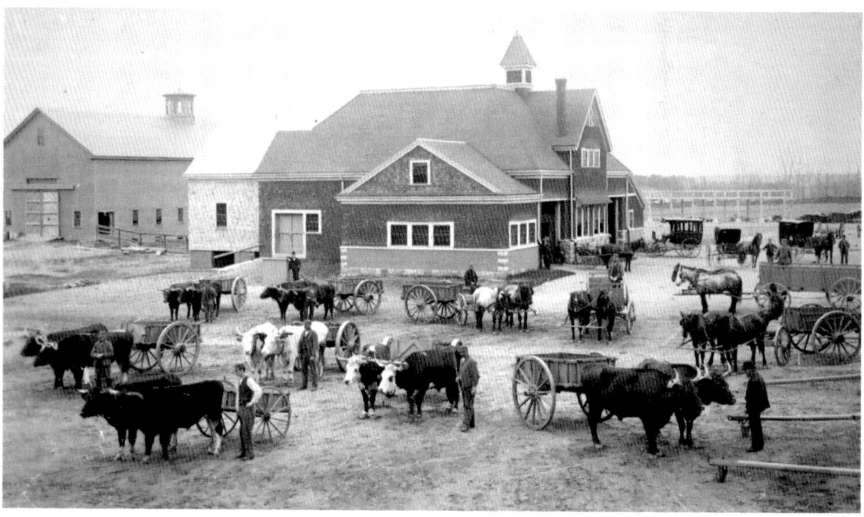

Bridgewater State Farm, stable and teams, circa 1903. *Harvard Art Museums/Fogg Museum, Transfer from the Carpenter Center for the Visual Arts, Social Museum Collection, 3.2002.882.1. Bass Photo. Imaging Department © President and Fellows of Harvard College.*

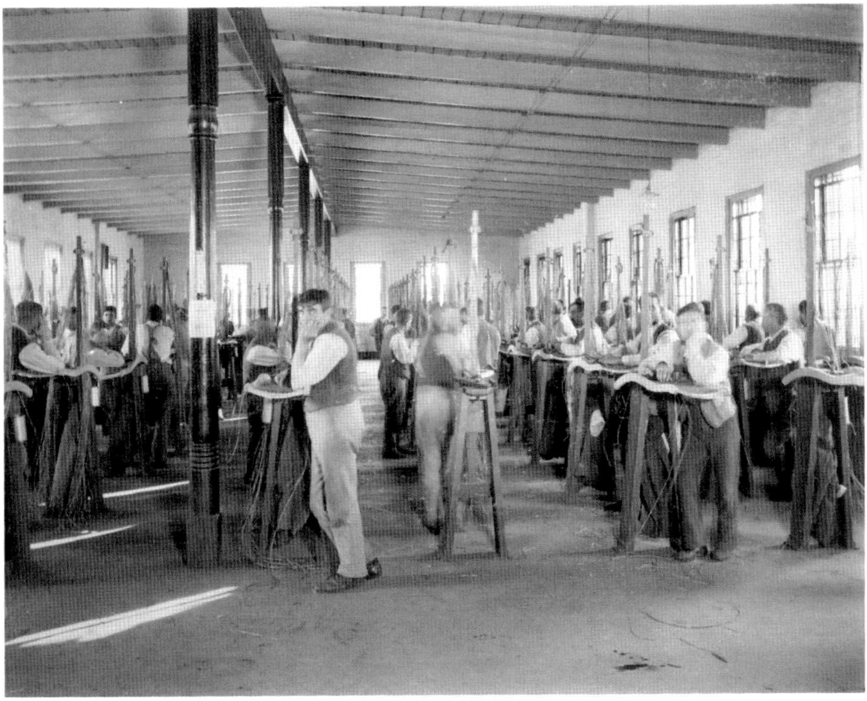

Bridgewater State Farm, prison department, chair shop, circa 1900. *Harvard Art Museums/ Fogg Museum, Transfer from the Carpenter Center for the Visual Arts, Social Museum Collection, 3.2002.2707.2. Unidentified Artist. Imaging Department © President and Fellows of Harvard College.*

by the inmates, in 1903, public-account cane seating was introduced experimentally, with the commonwealth purchasing raw materials and selling finished goods on the open market. On average, 150 inmates were occupied in cane seating each year, but due to opposition from organized labor, which challenged prison work as unfairly disadvantageous to free laborers, chair caning was suspended in August 1914, and idleness increased.

A small number of inmates also engaged in furniture making, producing pieces for the commonwealth, and about 1911, blanket weaving was introduced, though it never occupied a large number of inmates, with the maximum number employed in 1915 being twenty-six. Weavers were responsible not only for producing blanket cloth for finishing at the Concord reformatory but also weaving suitings, shirtings and toweling for use at the farm and the commonwealth's other public institutions. As industries, only chair caning was conducted on a consistently profitable basis, largely as there were no costs associated with it under the piece-price arrangement.

And while ostensibly undertaken in order to provide inmates with the opportunity to learn how to make a living, "the industries maintained [at Bridgewater] seem to be far more largely carried on as sentences" rather than as rehabilitative activities.[119]

Indoor work was done intermittently as needed, with other tasks often taking priority. World War I and a growing leniency within the municipal courts had the effect of reducing commitments to Bridgewater, as well as the institution's labor pool. In the late 1910s, work had to be suspended in the industrial shops so that insane inmates, many of whom had not been in the open for years, could be sent to the fields and the dairy. So desperate for agricultural labor was the State Farm that outside help had to be hired in 1919.

Those inmates not engaged in either agriculture or productive industry were put to work elsewhere in the facility. A November 30, 1917 census records 625 non-field workers occupied as house workers and sweepers, sewers, kitchen workers, hospital attendants, weavers, engineers, carpenters,

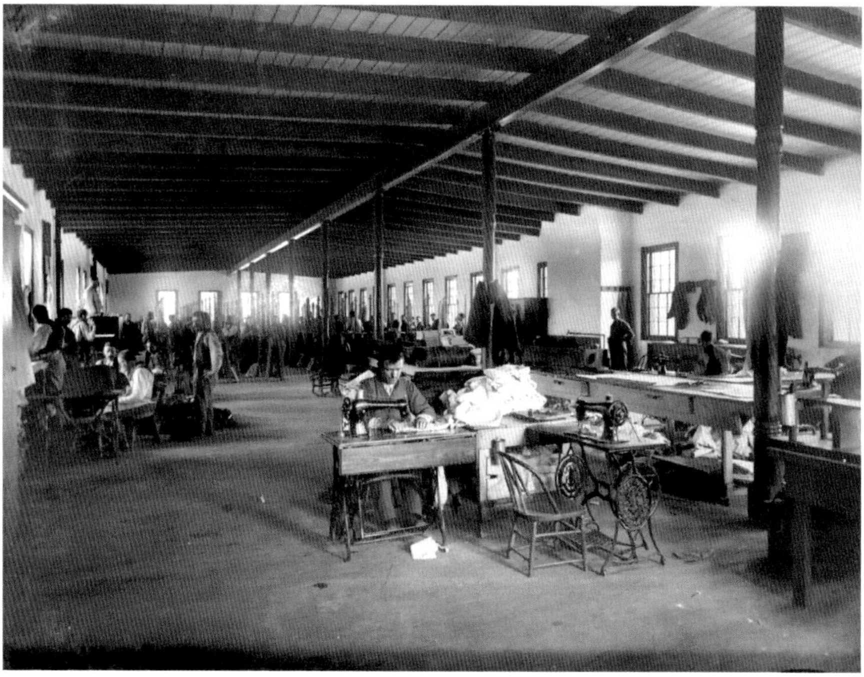

Bridgewater State Farm, prison workshop, circa 1903. *Harvard Art Museums/Fogg Museum, Transfer from the Carpenter Center for the Visual Arts, Social Museum Collection, 3.2002.2710.4. Bass Photo. Imaging Department © President and Fellows of Harvard College.*

masons, firemen, repairmen, gardeners, yard hands, dairymen, barbers, clerks, painters and whitewashers, blacksmiths, pipers, tinsmiths, storehouse workers, machinists and librarians. Not only did these men and women contribute to creating a well-maintained institution, but they also produced many of the goods necessary for its functioning, including in 1899 2,177 coats, 1,972 pairs of pants, 1,560 sheets, 1,397 bath towels, 814 pairs of Balmoral shoes, 550 pairs of brogans and innumerable other items of clothing, textiles and footwear.

In addition to inmate labor, considerable professional staff was needed to operate the farm, many of whom lived onsite in dormitories. Houses were furnished by the commonwealth for the superintendent and the farm's physician, while Blackstone (later Alden) Square immediately southeast of the prison was developed with privately owned homes for key farm personnel beginning in 1890. House lots there were sold to Henry J. Strann, clerk (1890); Benjamin F. Robinson, overseer of the chair shop (1891); Melvin Hatch, supervisor of the insane (1892); and Henry S. Keith, assistant farmer (1894). Head farmer G.E. Bacon constructed his own house on Conant Street in the fall of 1893.

The census of March 1900 records that in addition to Blackstone as superintendent, the staff included a medical director, two housekeepers, four physicians, four nurses, twelve officers, two gatemen, a matron, two

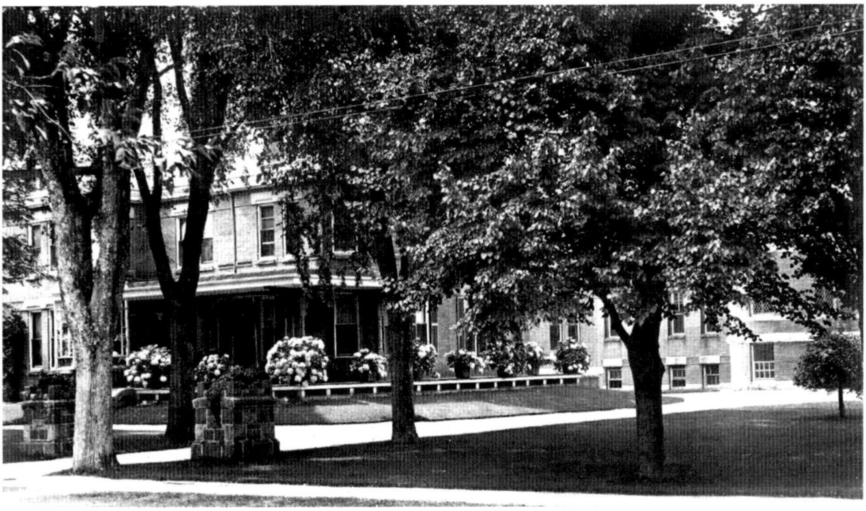

Bridgewater State Farm, entrance and superintendent's residence, circa 1910. *Author's collection.*

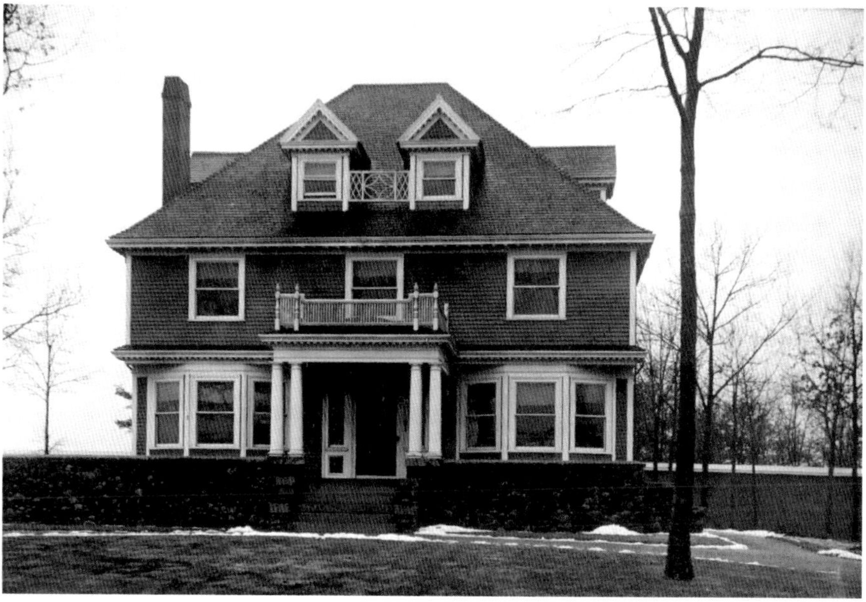

Bridgewater State Farm, residence of the medical director of asylum for insane criminals, circa 1900. *Harvard Art Museums/Fogg Museum, Transfer from the Carpenter Center for the Visual Arts, Social Museum Collection, 3.2002.2686.2. Unidentified Artist. Imaging Department © President and Fellows of Harvard College.*

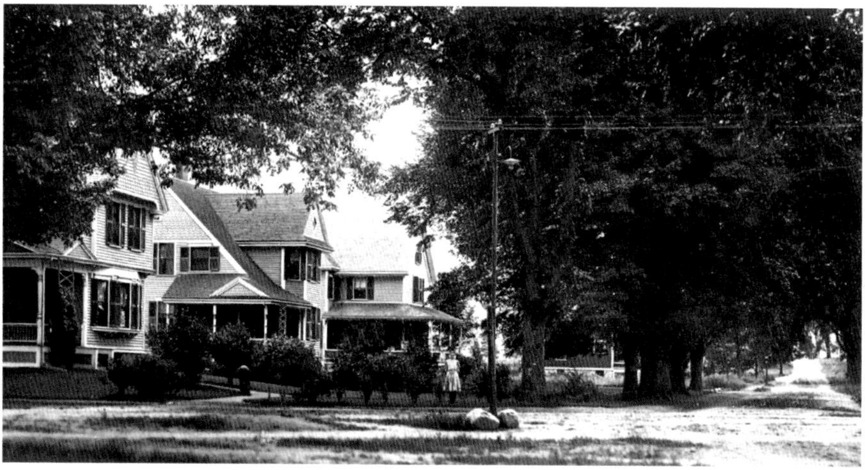

Blackstone (Alden) Square, Titicut Street, circa 1910, was developed following 1890 with houses built by state farm officers and administrators. *Author's collection.*

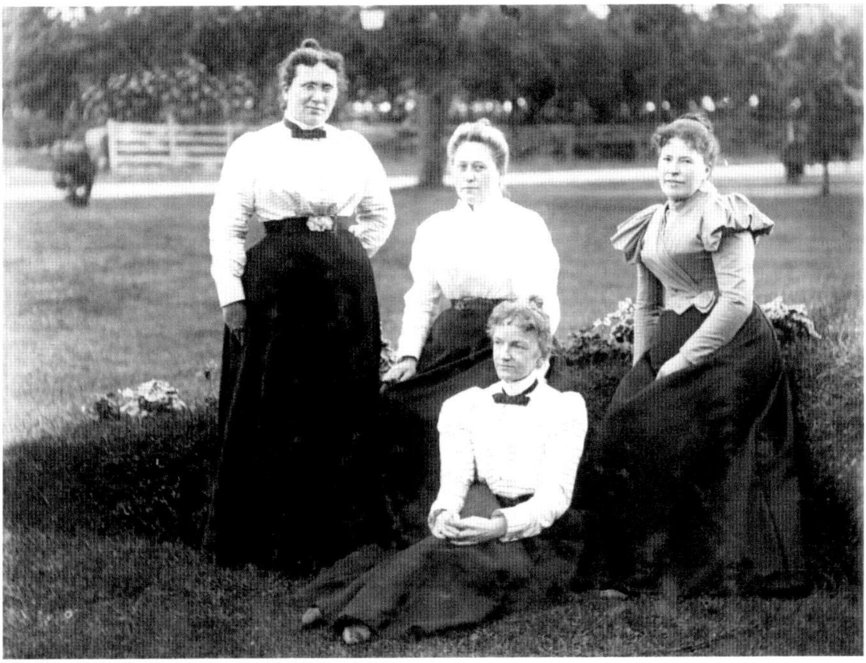

Bridgewater State Farm, Nurse Margaret Hamilton, bookkeeper Alice Nash and two others, circa 1905. *Massachusetts State Archives, State Farm (Bridgewater, Mass.), Photographs of facilities and activities [ca. 1900–ca. 1910], HS9.10/973X.*

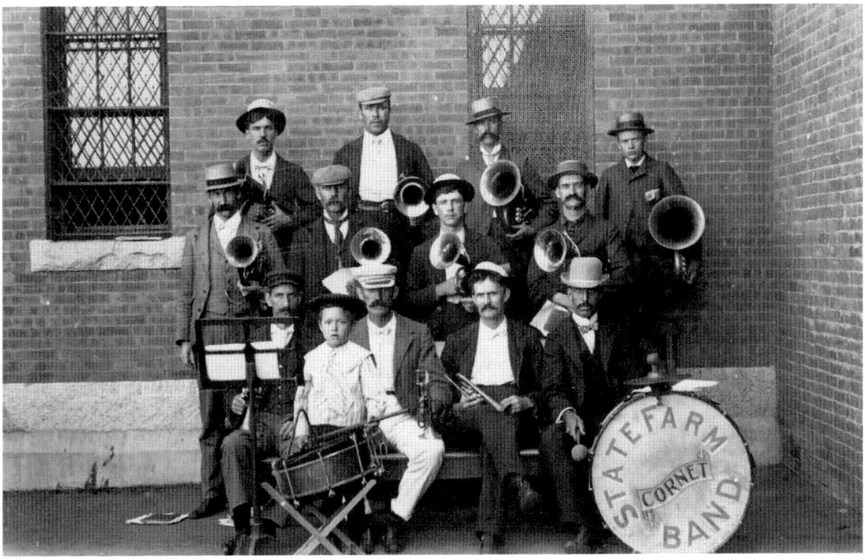


Bridgewater State Farm, cornet band, circa 1905. *Massachusetts State Archives, State Farm (Bridgewater, Mass.), Photographs of facilities and activities [ca. 1900–ca. 1910], HS9.10/973X.*

cooks, one baker, one stenographer, one plumber, a stationery engineer, a boiler foreman, a wheelwright, a herdsman and a day laborer. These officers and staff formed a closely knit community that relied on one another and shared a common aspiration to assist society's neglected and less fortunate individuals.

## MAINTAINING DISCIPLINE

While surviving correspondence from the period records the operational difficulties the State Farm faced, less well documented is the challenge the institution had maintaining discipline, a problem that accompanied the increased population. Though Bridgewater housed only a few criminals deemed truly dangerous (in the early 1900s only three inmates—one arsonist and two murderers—were held under life sentences), many inmates were former convicts hardened by successive terms in the commonwealth's penal institutions. During 1896, 395 of 1,332 inmates admitted to Bridgewater during the course of the year were repeat offenders, reflecting a recidivism rate of over 25 percent. In 1915, nearly 49 percent had been previously incarcerated. In 1917, the number reached 53 percent and in 1918 nearly 55 percent.

In order to minimize disorder, inmates were occupied as much as possible, primarily through work but also through diversion. Thanksgiving 1904 was celebrated with a meal, football and other outdoor sports, while residents of the insane department were engaged playing baseball the following year. "Every pleasant day they spend several hours at the fascinating game."[120] A library of several hundred volumes of donated and discarded books was available, and entertainments by outside organizations as well as internally organized events were held.

One of the most critical aspects of inmate morale was food. Though the State Farm's menu was comparable to the state prison at Charlestown and the reformatory at Concord, it appears Spartan compared to some of the commonwealth's other institutions, particularly considering the large proportion of inmates expected to perform physical labor. A sample menu for the week ending July 3, 1915, provides a record of the board furnished to State Farm inmates at the time:

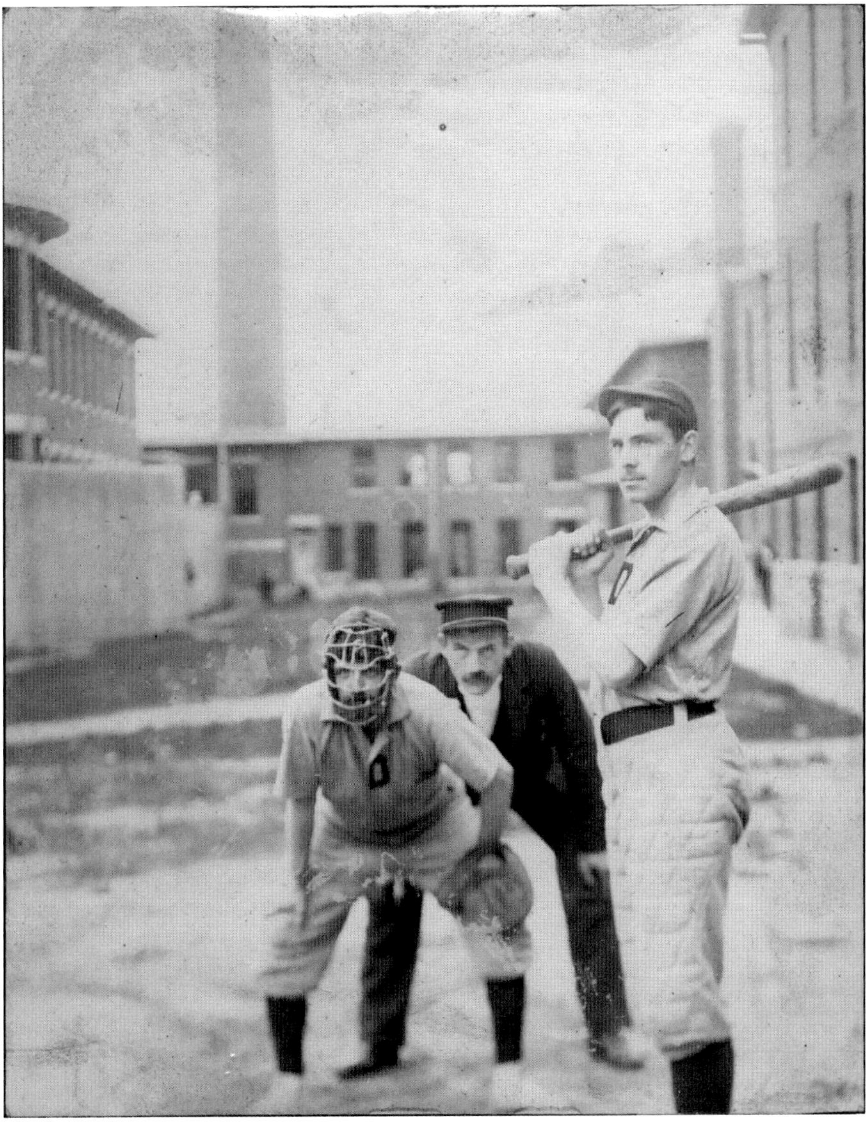

Bridgewater State Farm, prison baseball, circa 1900. *Massachusetts State Archives, State Farm (Bridgewater, Mass.), Photographs of facilities and activities [ca. 1900–ca. 1910], HS9.10/973X.*

*Sunday*
*boiled rice with sugar, bread, coffee (breakfast); baked beans, bread (dinner); bread, tea (supper)*

*Monday*
*oatmeal with sugar, bread, coffee (breakfast); beef soup, bread (dinner); corned beef hash, bread, tea (supper)*

*Tuesday*
*bean stew, bread, coffee (breakfast); corned beef, potatoes, bread (dinner); boiled rice with sugar, bread, tea (supper)*

*Wednesday*
*corned beef hash, bread, tea (breakfast); baked beans, bread (dinner); apple sauce, bread, tea (supper)*

*Thursday*
*oatmeal with sugar, bread, coffee (breakfast); corned beef, potatoes, beet greens, bread (dinner); strawberries with sugar, corn meal with sugar, bread, tea (supper)*

*Friday*
*pea soup, bread, tea (breakfast); fresh fish chowder, bread (dinner); gingerbread, white bread, tea (supper)*

*Saturday*
*canned corn beef, bread, coffee (breakfast); fresh beef, potatoes, brown gravy, bread (dinner); prune sauce, strawberries with sugar, bread, tea (supper)*

While the State Farm was generally acknowledged to be a well-run facility, efforts to minimize disorder were not always successful, and occasionally violence erupted. "There were lively times at the State farm one day of this week. A number of the paupers conceived a wild yearning for liberty before their necessary discharge papers were received, and because they couldn't get out, went on a strike, and refused to perform their regular duties. A taste of the irons and a few hours of cell confinement reduced them to proper order once more."[121]

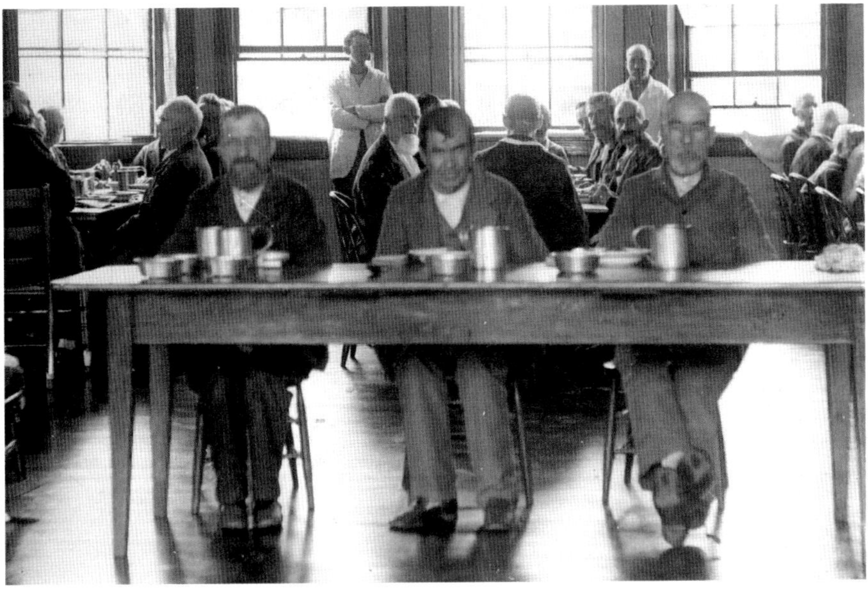

Bridgewater State Farm, inmates' dining hall, circa 1905. *Massachusetts State Archives, State Farm (Bridgewater, Mass.), Photographs of facilities and activities [ca. 1900–ca. 1910], HS9.10/973X.*

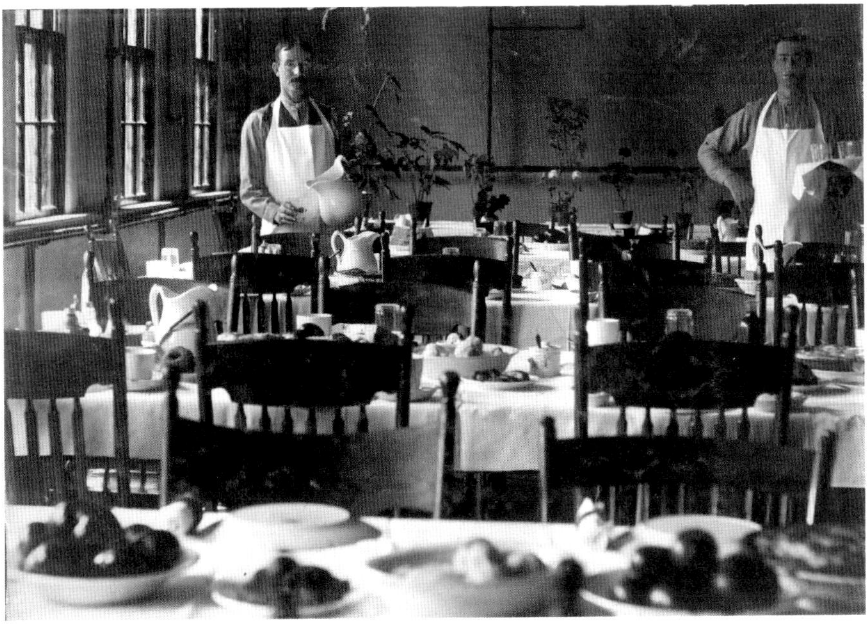

Bridgewater State Farm, staff dining room, circa 1905. *Massachusetts State Archives, State Farm (Bridgewater, Mass.), Photographs of facilities and activities [ca. 1900–ca. 1910], HS9.10/973X.*

As had been the case in the past, refractory inmates were on occasion handled roughly, sometimes with tragic consequences. In September 1912, hospital patient Charles B. Navers, who was disorderly and resisted being removed to another room, was assaulted by attendant Fred Sears and died of his injuries four days later. Sears was later convicted of manslaughter and sentenced to eighteen months' imprisonment.

The following year, Heber J. McLean, a former attendant with eight years' service at Bridgewater State Hospital, addressed a meeting of the Massachusetts Hospital Reform Society and offered shocking testimony that patients had been handled cruelly and that "wager on the probable time that patients will live...caused attendants in Massachusetts insane hospitals to hasten or retard their deaths."[122] While McLean acknowledged the difficulties faced by hospital attendants, whose duties were "at all times irksome, and often disgusting," and whose pay was paltry, hc argued that society's desire to imprison the mentally ill delivered them into the hands of "attendants, who as a class are inferior men—given to drunkenness, hardened by their environment, and often vicious and brutal—utterly unskilled, untrained and unqualified for the work they are called upon to do." While perhaps unduly unjust, McLean's allegations (which were subsequently dismissed by the Plymouth County Grand Jury but repeated nearly seventy years later by another state hospital officer) called into question the level of training and compensation provided to Bridgewater attendants. Much of the blame

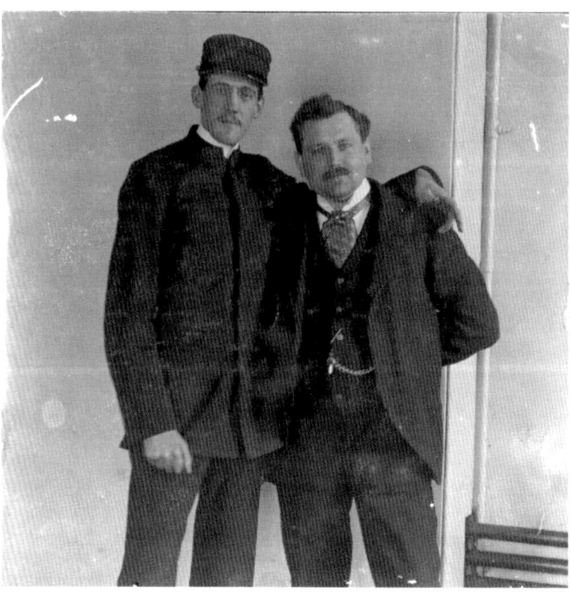

Bridgewater State Farm, unidentified attendant and officer, circa 1900. *Massachusetts State Archives, State Farm (Bridgewater, Mass.), Photographs of facilities and activities [ca. 1900–ca. 1910], HS9.10/973X.*

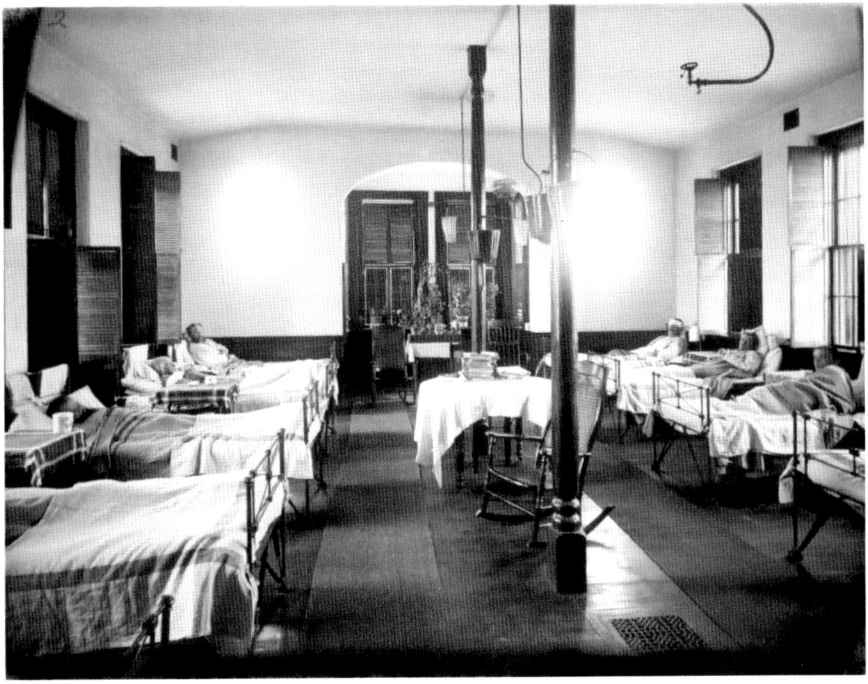

Bridgewater State Farm, short ward, ten beds, circa 1900. *Harvard Art Museums/Fogg Museum, Transfer from the Carpenter Center for the Visual Arts, Social Museum Collection, 3.2002.2711.2. Bass Photo. Imaging Department © President and Fellows of Harvard College.*

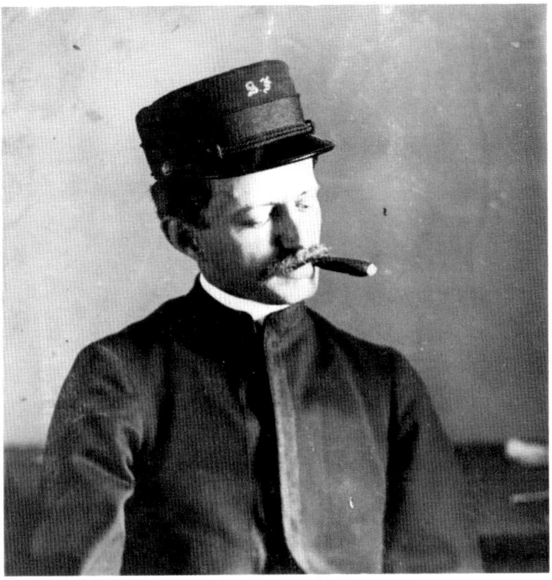

Bridgewater State Farm, attendant with "SF" monogrammed cap, circa 1900. *Massachusetts State Archives, State Farm (Bridgewater, Mass.), Photographs of facilities and activities [ca. 1900–ca. 1910], HS9.10/973X.*

for the situation McLean placed at the doorstep of legislators who failed to adequately address the situation. "You cannot legislate neglect, abuse and brutality out of our institutions," he admonished them.[123]

Violence also occurred between inmates. On February 25, 1918, during an altercation, Alexander Thompson fatally stabbed fellow inmate Charles Wood in the smoking room. Wood was serving a nine-month sentence for vagrancy and Thompson a four-month sentence for drunkenness.

Guards were also sometimes assaulted, as was the case of Francis Jenkins, "who was so terribly injured by a…crank [he] received $4500 from the state.…His injuries have made him a physical wreck."[124] Under such circumstances, retaining competent asylum attendants remained challenging, with an 1888 report acknowledging that these men were "as a whole, less constant in service." No doubt poor pay and the hazards of the position encouraged turnover.[125] Efforts were made to improve the quality of medical care, and following 1886, the farm strove to employ medical students and undergraduates as hospital stewards.[126]

## Taking "Leg Bail"

Despite claims that "all the crowd of bums…seem to take quite kindly to the prospect of being cared for through a promised hard winter, at the expense of the old Bay State," escapes from Bridgewater remained a near monthly occurrence. Many escapees simply wanted to return to their families so never left the commonwealth and were easily recaptured. Patrick Moore, an elderly man, escaped the workhouse in May 1889, fleeing to his home in Webster to see his wife, who was blind and feeble. Six months were added to his sentence, due originally to expire in August 1891. On May 8, 1890, Charles Williams, described as "wildly insane," escaped and was believed to have hidden in the thick woods about Titicut or Middleborough. James McDonald, Joseph McAdams and George Egot escaped on July 25, 1890, each dressed in the easily identifiable prison uniform of light gray pants and striped hickory shirts. On August 30, 1893, an unnamed prisoner who had served the first of ten months' imprisonment for drunkenness took what was euphemistically referred to as "leg bail." In October 1893, twenty-two-year-old Eli Longley escaped from the farm. Arsonist Lewis A. Wright, who as an eighteen-year-old office boy in 1893 had been convicted of crimes resulting in the loss of five lives and causing $5 million worth of property damage, escaped in July 1894 and was free for a period of days before being caught at Brockton. He was returned to Bridgewater. In late June 1896, Cornelius O'Hearn escaped and was recaptured on Common Street in Lowell on June 27 after a week's liberty. On July 26, 1900, five prisoners audaciously escaped and fled toward Boston. Two were caught in October and returned to the prison under an indefinite sentence. In early November 1902, John L. Duell and John B. Lavelle slipped away while at work in the fields but were soon afterward captured. In summer 1904, trusty Fred Stead of Worcester, sent to the farm for drunkenness, walked away from his job driving the express wagon between the farm and the rail depot. He was captured in Worcester in early February 1905. Fred Sturtevant, along with Joseph King, escaped by crawling through ventilation work and was captured at Middleborough days later on June 25, 1904, and returned to the institution. Henry Cannon escaped late on the night of August 16, 1904, though few details of how he did so were made known. Thirty-five-year-old John Dansereau—an inmate since 1898 when he was transferred from the state prison at Charlestown, where he was incarcerated for horse stealing—loosened the bars of his cell in the insane criminal department and escaped on October 9, 1904. On April 25, 1905, trusties Henry C. Godfrey and Peter Ferry, who had been working as nurses in the hospital ward, scaled the twelve-foot courtyard wall by means of a crate stacked on a handcart. John Stevens, also a trusty, committed from the Boston municipal court for drunkenness on July 14, 1905, escaped while haying on August 3 by making a run through the field. Perhaps taking his cue from Stevens, Edward Mooney, committed on March 29, 1905, on a charge of vagrancy from the Boston municipal court, escaped four days later while engaged in outside work. Less than three weeks later, trusty William Vincent of Brockton was similarly reported as missing. Ephraim Manney, sentenced on a charge of drunkenness, slipped away while on duty on the milking gang on February 26, 1906.[127]

While this litany of escapes (and there were more) demonstrates that the "elopement" of inmates may have been commonplace and represented little threat to public safety, escapes of a more serious nature occurred as well.

> *One of the boldest escapes ever attempted at the State farm, was that by two men confined in the insane wards, last Saturday noon* [July 22, 1893]. *One of the prisoners was a crank of the dangerous class, and the other was the notorious kleptomaniac, Francis J. Holland, who made good the threat recorded at the time of his recent recapture, following his Memorial Day break, that he would skip out whenever he saw fit. He ingeniously fashioned*

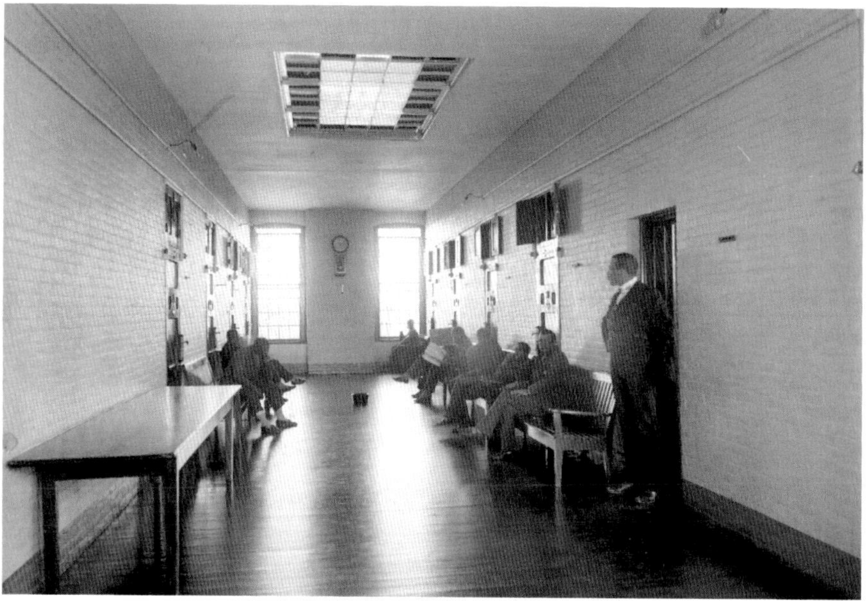

Bridgewater State Farm, asylum department, east day room, circa 1900. *Harvard Art Museums/Fogg Museum, Transfer from the Carpenter Center for the Visual Arts, Social Museum Collection, 3.2002.2708.3. Unidentified Artist. Imaging Department © President and Fellows of Harvard College.*

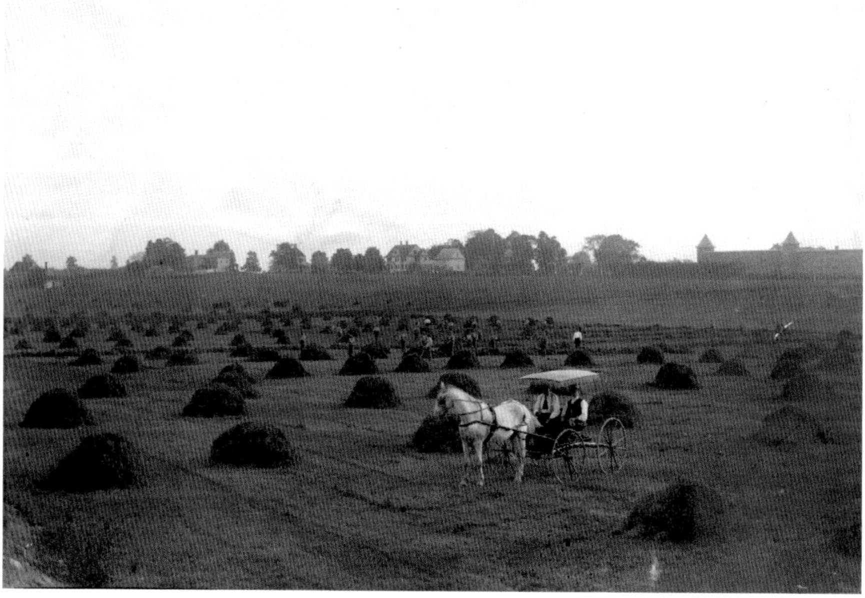

Bridgewater State Farm, circa 1900. *Massachusetts State Archives, State Farm (Bridgewater, Mass.), Photographs of facilities and activities [ca. 1900–ca. 1910], HS9.10/973X.*

> *a key out of bits of metal which he got hold of, and about 12 o'clock, Saturday, unlocked his cell door, and after liberating the occupant of a neighboring cell, both men walked daringly forth from the enclosed grounds, and succeeded in reaching the woods north of the institution.*

Holland was recaptured about a mile north of the depot despite offering fierce resistance, during which Officer Tibbetts "was obliged to use the stick upon him before reducing him to submission." The *Middleboro Gazette* understatedly remarked, "Altogether, it was a pretty exciting day at the farm."[128]

Another escape that had much greater fallout was that of Minot St. Clair Francis and Frank R. Wiley on September 17, 1905. Francis, described in one newspaper at the time as a "desperado, with a long criminal record," had attempted criminal assault on a woman at Swampscott and been incarcerated at Charlestown State Prison, where he had twice attempted suicide before being judged insane and transferred to Bridgewater in June 1905. Other prisoners abetted the escape:

> *A fake fight was started in the insane recreation yard, and when the attendants got busy in quelling the disturbance, two of the prisoners, Minot S. Francis and Frank R. Wiley, were seen making their way to the eaves of the insane department building. Wiley clambered to Francis' shoulders and*

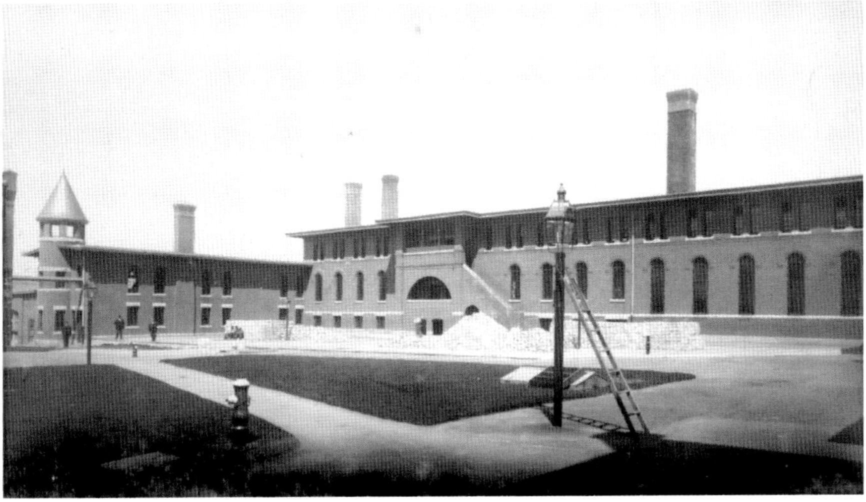

Bridgewater State Farm, prison building, circa 1903. *Harvard Art Museums/Fogg Museum, Transfer from the Carpenter Center for the Visual Arts, Social Museum Collection, 3.2002.2710.1. Bass Photo. Imaging Department © President and Fellows of Harvard College.*

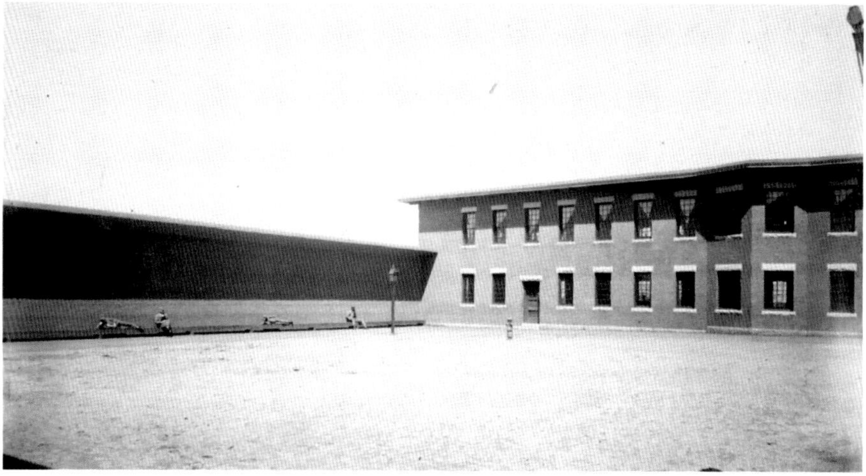

Bridgewater State Farm, prison yard, circa 1903. *Harvard Art Museums/Fogg Museum, Transfer from the Carpenter Center for the Visual Arts, Social Museum Collection, 3.2002.2710.2. Bass Photo. Imaging Department © President and Fellows of Harvard College.*

> *in this way reached the roof and clambered up, then he stooped over and assisted Francis to the roof. It was easy for them then to run across the roof to another building and then to the fence and from there to the ground. They were ordered by the officers to stop, but as the officers were without firearms the order could not be enforced.*[129]

Armed posses were dispatched to track the two, who were last seen fleeing through the fields toward Taunton before being lost in the dusk. Francis remained free until recaptured in Maine in November 1906.

In the wake of the Francis escape, reports appeared in some Boston newspapers that a riot among the two thousand inmates was imminent and guards had been withheld from pursuing the escapees and retained at the farm as a show of force. Though these stories were discounted, Superintendent Blackstone conceded that "it is a source of regret that the usual conditions of security felt to have hitherto offered sufficient restraint in the stronger wards for the insane have been recently disturbed by the escape of two clever convicts."[130] Despite Blackstone's contention regarding the security of the farm, escapes continued, with most prisoners simply going "over the wall," including inmates Alfred Girard, Louis D. Rogers and William Sullivan, who in October 1912 scaled a seventeen-foot wall and escaped from the criminal insane department.

## SUICIDES

While some prisoners contemplated physically absconding from Bridgewater, other inmates considered suicide their only means of escape, and numerous instances of what was termed "self-destruction" are recorded. In 1889, one inmate jumped to his drowning death in the Taunton River. John Kemmler, transferred from the Worcester House of Correction eight years earlier as an inmate of the criminal insane ward and considered harmless, hanged himself on July 1, 1897, with a noose improvised from a handkerchief and a piece of found rope. On November 16, 1898, John Murphy, who was between sixty and seventy and had been sentenced to Bridgewater several times, committed suicide in the insane ward by hanging himself with his bedsheet. "He has been mentally unbalanced for some little time in a mild sort of way."[131] On November 3, 1905, twenty-four-year-old inmate Frank B. Miller of Pennsylvania committed suicide. Sentenced in June for drunkenness, Miller, like Murphy

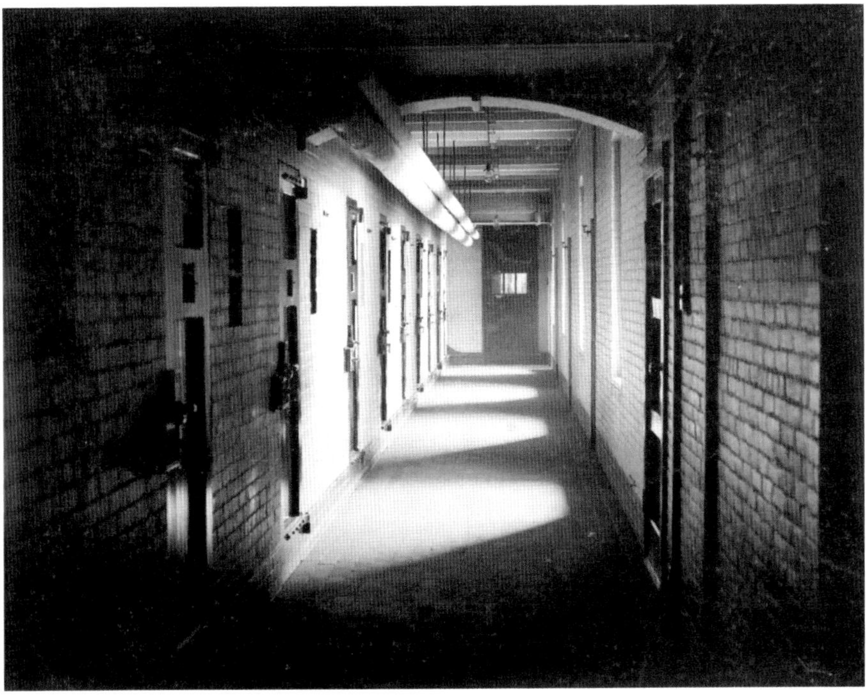

Bridgewater State Farm, asylum department, north corridor, circa 1900. *Harvard Art Museums/Fogg Museum, Transfer from the Carpenter Center for the Visual Arts, Social Museum Collection, 3.2002.2708.4. Unidentified Artist. Imaging Department © President and Fellows of Harvard College.*

before him, fashioned a rope from shredded bedsheets and hanged himself from his cell door.[132] Suicides remained high, with inmates most commonly hanging themselves, as was the case in 1909, 1911 and 1912.

Yet not all inmates held a negative view of the State Farm. In 1910, when sentenced to Bridgewater as a vagabond, John Shoulditz stated "something good, the farm," though this remark prompted authorities to question his sanity.[133] Other inmates found the State Farm safe and comforting as the only familiar place they knew after years of incarceration. In 1909, when seventy-six-year-old John Fean was pardoned after serving thirty-three years of a life sentence for murder, he was "aged, despondent and suffering from lung trouble…[and] without friends or relatives to care for him."[134] He chose to remain at the State Farm rather than be released into a world that had moved forward without him.

Chapter 5

# "A Conglomerate of Insane and Defectives and Drunks"

## Bridgewater State Farm as Prison, 1919–55

In 1919, supervision of the Bridgewater State Farm was transferred from the Massachusetts Board of Charity to the Bureau of Prisons (later the Department of Correction), an action that confirmed the drift of the institution since its founding from charitable institution to penal facility.[135] During the next four decades, a reassessment of criminality and insanity and the connection between the two informed changes within the institution, which was severely challenged by its dual roles as prison and hospital for the criminally insane. In addition to these roles, in 1922 a defective delinquent department was added for the confinement of developmentally disabled individuals convicted of non-capital offenses who were deemed mentally unfit for release into society, adding yet another classification to those already housed at Bridgewater. Dr. A. Warren Stearns—Massachusetts commissioner of correction from 1929 to 1933, dean of Tufts Medical School and later a psychiatrist at Bridgewater—was critical of the mixed classification system that persisted, and in 1932, he advocated that the institution be devoted strictly to vagrants and tramps. "But now it is a conglomerate of insane and defectives and drunks. Everything has been tacked on there that nobody else wanted."[136] Because of these stresses, the institution would begin to devolve during this era from a highly respected institution to one of the worst and most sharply criticized prisons in the nation.

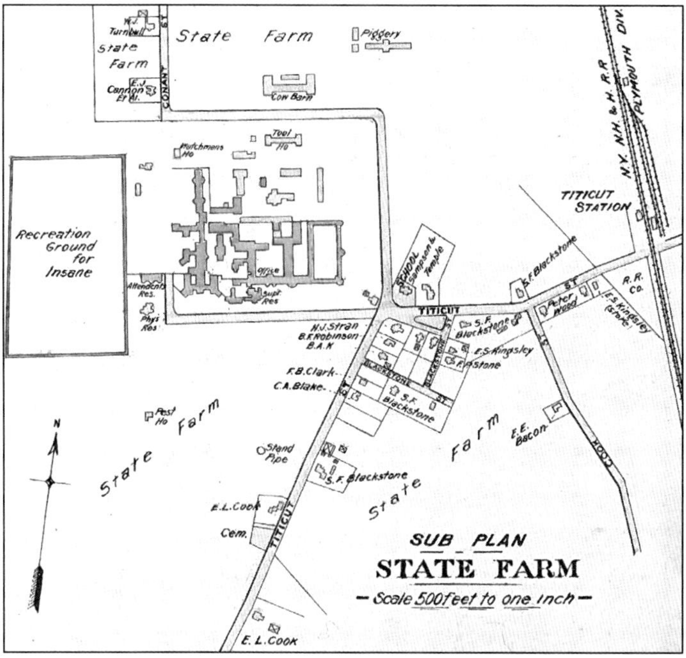


Plan of Bridgewater State Farm. *New Topographical Atlas of Surveys, Plymouth County* (Springfield, MA: L.J. Richards Co., 1903).

## DEFECTIVE DELINQUENTS

In 1911, Massachusetts recognized a new class of criminal, "defective delinquents," who were legally defined as "mentally defective" juveniles convicted of non-capital offenses who were deemed "not a proper subject for the schools for the feeble-minded, or for commitment as an insane person."[137] Many of those categorized as "defective" were developmentally disabled.

Disturbed by an increase in the rates of both insanity and criminality in Massachusetts at the turn of the century, advocates of eugenic criminological theory attributed social problems, including criminality, alcoholism, homelessness and poverty, to inherited biological traits, intelligence and race. The commonwealth's treatment of those it classed as "defective delinquents" was influenced by Dr. Walter E. Fernald, head of the Massachusetts School for the Feeble-Minded (which was later named for him), who believed that the "feeble-minded" should be removed from society in order to prevent individuals deemed as "inferior" or "defective" from reproducing.

From the outset, Superintendent Blackstone at Bridgewater was associated with the development of the defective delinquent concept in Massachusetts, having been named in 1910 to a five-member commission charged with investigating "the question of the increase of criminals, mental defectives, epileptics, degenerates, and allied cases."[138] Recommendations made by the commission included the prohibition of marriage of the mentally ill, alcoholics, habitual criminals and sufferers of venereal diseases and restriction of immigration into the United States. While surgical asexualization of defectives and criminals was not recommended, neither was it ruled out, the commission maintaining that further consideration of its results was warranted. Pertinent to the future development of Bridgewater, the commission insisted that "the mentally defective child, the potential parent of another generation of defectives, can be kept from crime by giving him *permanent* custodial care" (author's italics), and it argued in 1911 for the legal recognition of "defective delinquents" as a dangerous class.[139]

The Massachusetts legislature took up the recommendations and in 1911 authorized eugenic segregation through the establishment of defective delinquent departments at Bridgewater, as well as the two state reformatories. The act sought to permanently remove undesirable individuals—"the mentally defective child, the potential parent of another generation of defectives"—from society and place them in permanent (i.e., lifelong) custodial care. Despite this action, it was not until 1922 that a defective

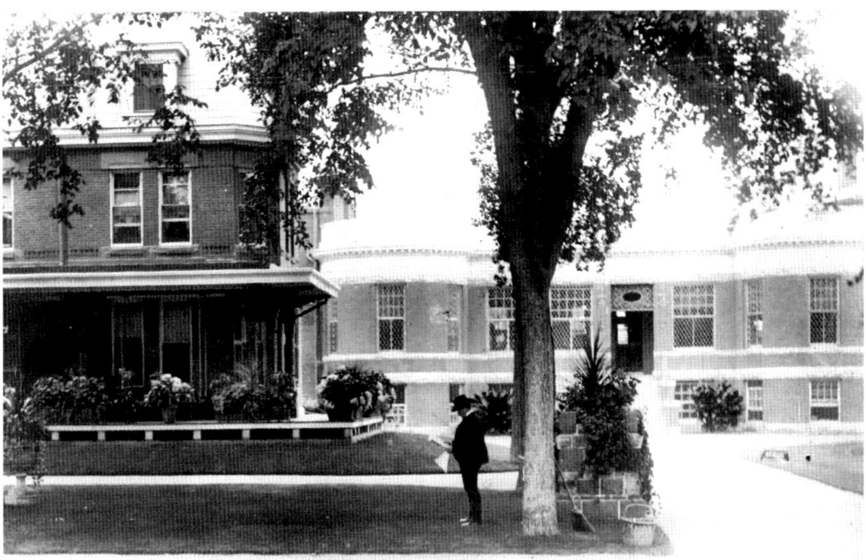

Bridgewater State Farm, administration building and post office with superintendent's residence (*left*), circa 1910. *Author's collection.*

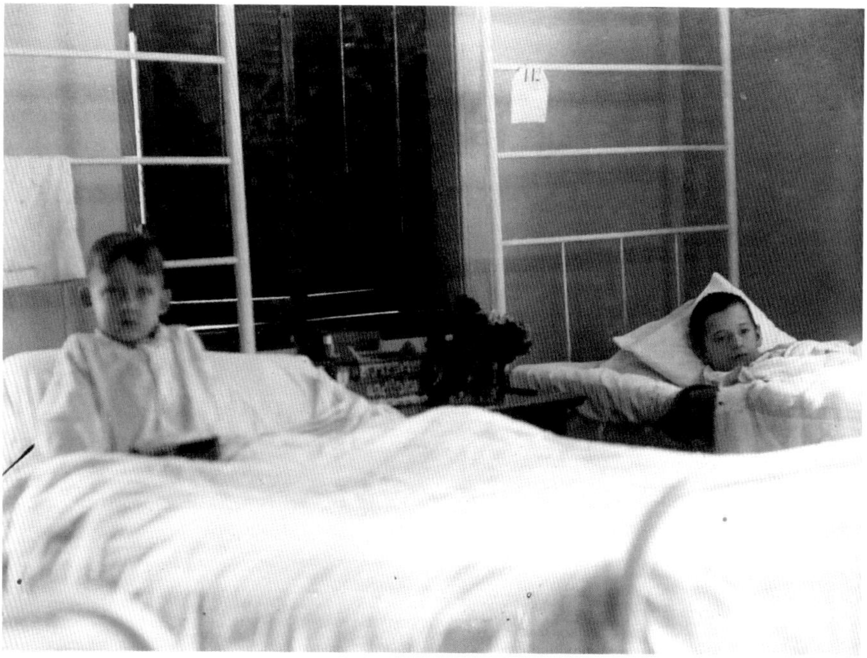

Bridgewater State Farm, children in hospital ward, circa 1905. *Massachusetts State Archives, State Farm (Bridgewater, Mass.), Photographs of facilities and activities [ca. 1900–ca. 1910], HS9.10/973X.*

delinquent department for males was established at Bridgewater, with a corresponding department for females being established in 1926.

Perceived as enlightened progressivism at the time, the defective delinquent department at Bridgewater was charged with providing inmates with medical care to improve their mental conditions, and for years the department and the commonwealth's defective delinquent law were hailed as models of social reform by eugenicist organizations and journals, including *American Breeders Magazine: A Journal of Genetics and Eugenics*, as well as mainstream publications like the *New York Times*.

Ultimately, Massachusetts's defective delinquent law resulted in the incarceration of children, frequently for a lifetime, with over half of those being admitted to Bridgewater as defective delinquents being ages fourteen to twenty. Any hope of reprieve for these individuals was reduced further in 1928, when the law was tightened to permit committal as a defective delinquent upon the first offense should the court feel that the individual had the likelihood to re-offend.

## "DRUNKARDS AND VAGRANTS"

Bridgewater's largest classification, as well as its least controversial, remained the prisoners, primarily alcoholics and homeless individuals. Mixed among them were a small but growing number of drug addicts, convicted on charges relating to heroin, morphine and veronal use or possession.

Initially following World War I, Massachusetts experienced a decline in prison populations, driven by plummeting commitments for drunkenness and vagrancy brought about by increased wages, falling unemployment, implementation of probationary sentencing and the enactment of Prohibition. At Bridgewater, Superintendent Blackstone recognized that the decline in minor offense committals had the effect of emptying the state farm's wards and cells. "The prison problem here is pretty nearly pinched out. Misdemeanor offenses apparently are obsolete and out of date. It would appear that drunkenness by the former standard, that is to say, real, respectable (?), legitimate whiskey boozing, had folded its tents and stolen away….Another year's decline at the same ratio as the last one will find us all putting up the shutters."[140]

The reduction was drastic. For the year ending September 30, 1919, 525 prisoners, 274 paupers and 830 insane constituted Bridgewater's average daily population. Of these numbers, only 73 were women, all confined as prisoners.

While Prohibition following January 1920 contributed to a decline in admissions for drunkenness, a number of developments reversed this trend, and the institution saw increased committals as communities sought to rid themselves of individuals perceived as undesirable or financially burdensome, much as they had done in the past. Crowding at Boston City Hospital, where nearly 3,300 had applied for alcohol-related treatment in 1921, prompted Mayor James M. Curley to announce in May 1922 that cases of persons made ill by cheap liquor would no longer be treated at the hospital but sent to Bridgewater instead. Failure to reopen Norfolk State Hospital as a treatment facility for alcoholics after military use in World War I also contributed to the increased number of alcoholics being remanded to Bridgewater.

During Prohibition and in the years following its 1933 repeal came growing criticism of the manner in which the commonwealth treated chronic alcoholism. Considering mandatory commitment to a prison for drunkenness extreme, in 1936 a group of Massachusetts state senators sponsored legislation allowing those charged with drunkenness to be

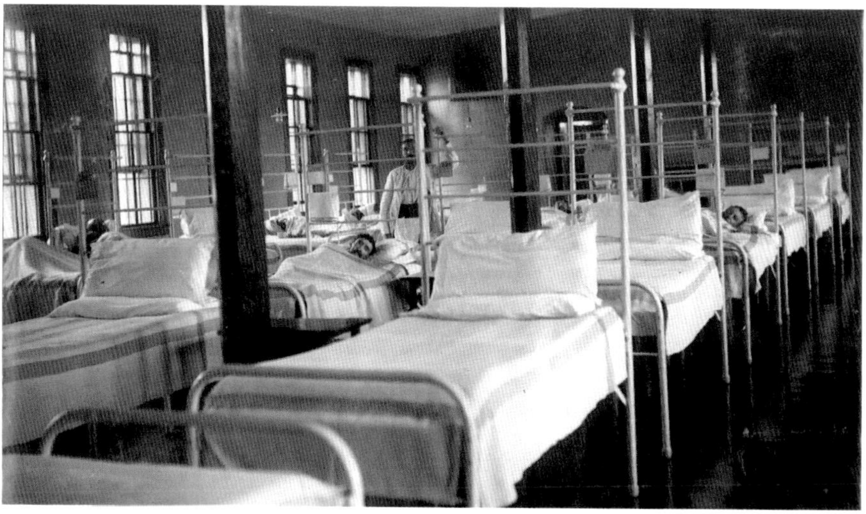

Bridgewater State Farm, men's ward, circa 1905. *Massachusetts State Archives, State Farm (Bridgewater, Mass.), Photographs of facilities and activities [ca. 1900–ca. 1910], HS9.10/973X.*

released upon sobering up. Some senators argued the bill would reduce commonwealth expenditures while granting the "poor drunk" the same privilege as the wealthy, who "can go home in his chauffeured car or taxicab, while the poor one has to stagger home, is arrested and wakes up in Bridgewater."[141]

Senator Arthur W. Hollis of Newton also criticized Massachusetts judges who were "all too free in sending [alcoholics] to Bridgewater."[142] Hollis equated the alcoholic's cycle of committal, release and re-committal to Bridgewater to a merry-go-round. The rate of recidivism remained high as inmates saw repeated periods of incarceration for chronic alcoholism.[143] Ex-prisoners continued to receive little support from the commonwealth following their release, the principal assistance coming in the form of railroad fares to their former homes.

Perhaps not atypical was George Whiting of Haverhill, who was committed to a year at Bridgewater in April 1922 for drunkenness. While one newspaper at the time found Whiting's sixty-two arrests comically unusual, they were neither. Like many ex-inmates, Whiting struggled following his release from Bridgewater. By 1925, he had accrued another eight arrests and was sentenced to his nineteenth term at Bridgewater. Whiting was not alone. John Barry in March 1925 appeared in Attleboro District Court for the fiftieth time and was sentenced to Bridgewater on

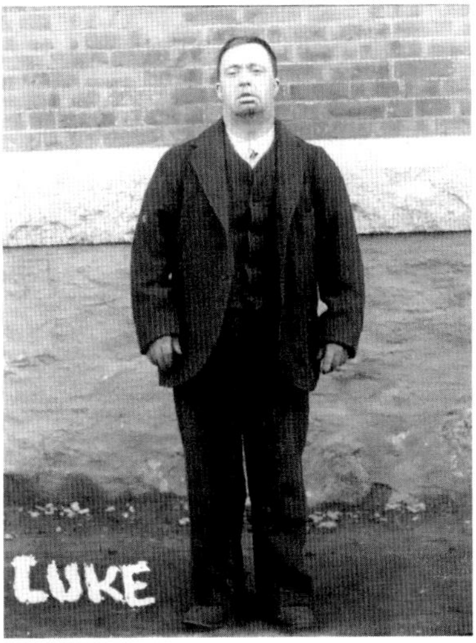


Bridgewater State Farm, inmate tentatively identified by the author as Luke J. Boylan of Taunton, circa 1905. *Massachusetts State Archives, State Farm (Bridgewater, Mass.), Photographs of facilities and activities [ca. 1900–ca. 1910], HS9.10/973X.*

a charge of drunkenness. Leander Bennett similarly had been before the court at Newton some fifty times for drunkenness when he received another Bridgewater sentence on December 28, 1925. William Newmeister of Dalton appeared in district court ninety-six times, having served time at and been paroled from Bridgewater for drunkenness. Salvatore Vitale made his ninetieth appearance in Salem District Court in 1934 on drunkenness charges and was sentenced to the State Farm.

While journalists found such accounts curious news fodder, these tales also reflected Bridgewater's failure to effect any lasting rehabilitation of its alcoholic inmates. In January 1936, James E. Warren (1888–1967), who had been named Bridgewater superintendent two years earlier, testified that hundreds of those convicted for drunkenness were "as regular as the clock in returning to the institution a short time after their release."[144]

Though the 1936 senate bill easing punishment for drunkenness failed to pass, it signaled a willingness to reconsider how the commonwealth treated alcoholics and whether chronic alcoholism should be recognized as a disease rather than a crime, as suggested by Dr. Henry D. Chadwick, state commissioner of public health. In 1937, Chadwick informed the Legislative Committee on Public Welfare that "chronic drunks are now sent to the Bridgewater State Farm, which is under the supervision of the State Department of Correction, left there for a short period to sober up and then let go. These unfortunates are not treated as medical problems." Not only did these individuals go untreated at Bridgewater, but their incarceration sometimes ended tragically, as it did for three inmates who died after drinking wood alcohol–based antifreeze in September 1948.

## CRIMINALLY INSANE

The third classification housed at Bridgewater was the "criminally insane," accommodated at Bridgewater State Hospital, where they composed the institution's most disturbed and potentially violent population. Within this classification were individuals convicted of crimes but found to be insane, those committed from the courts for pre-trial observation and those transferred from the commonwealth's other correctional facilities for observation and confinement. As ultimately recognized by a 1939 legislative report, the term "criminally insane" as applied at Bridgewater was greatly misused, as many patients had never been convicted of a crime and some had never been arrested, having been transferred to Bridgewater from mental health facilities elsewhere in the commonwealth. Despite involvement by the Massachusetts Department of Mental Health (which used the hospital to house its own unmanageable custodial cases), ultimate responsibility for the hospital's operation lay with the Department of Correction, which perforce tended to emphasize punishment and custodial care over rehabilitative treatment.

The criminally insane department also included Bridgewater's most high-profile inmates. Most notorious of all was Jesse Pomeroy, the youngest person to have been convicted of murder in Massachusetts. Found guilty in 1874 for the killing of two children in Boston, fourteen-year-old Pomeroy was sentenced to death by hanging. Following commutation of his sentence to life imprisonment, Pomeroy remained incarcerated at Charlestown state prison until removed to Bridgewater for hospitalization in 1929. Bridgewater superintendent Henry J. Strann (1865–1946), who had previously met Pomeroy, was unimpressed: "He was surly, reticent and unsmiling then, and he is surly, reticent and unsmiling now."[145] Following Pomeroy's death at Bridgewater in September 1932, the sympathy he had elicited during his lifetime was characterized by the *Boston Globe* as "the greatest miscarriage of sentiment in the annals of American crime," the newspaper describing Pomeroy as "a mean, scheming criminal with an inflated idea of [his] own importance."[146]

Representative of patients held at the time at Bridgewater State Hospital were Philip F. Whalen, killer of policeman Andrew B. Cuneo who was committed to Bridgewater in 1921 and was described as "dangerously insane"; George V. Dunham, sentenced to eighteen to twenty years for shooting his sweetheart, Althea B. Knight, at her father's store in Malden on Halloween 1921 and then shooting himself in the head, who was

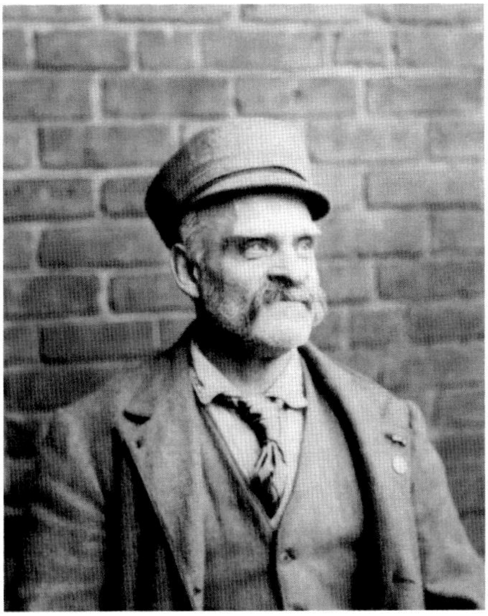

*Left*: Jesse Pomeroy (1859–1932), Massachusetts's longest-serving criminal. Other Bridgewater inmates included world champion boxer George La Blanche (1856–1918) and Boston swindler Cardenio F. King (1867–1913). *Author's collection.*

*Below*: Bridgewater State Farm (Asylum for Insane Criminals), west wing, circa 1900. *Harvard Art Museums/Fogg Museum, Transfer from the Carpenter Center for the Visual Arts, Social Museum Collection, 3.2002.2709.2. Bass Photo. Imaging Department © President and Fellows of Harvard College.*

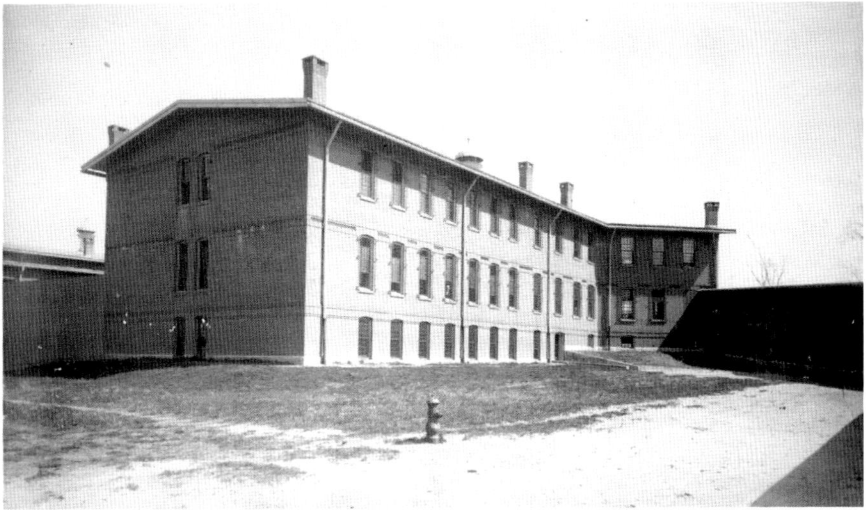

removed from the state prison to Bridgewater for observation after having become so noisy that he kept fellow inmates awake; and Mrs. Ruth E. Compton, who following the July 1933 shooting death of her mother stated, "I thought that mother was walking dead and I was afraid they would bury her alive, so I shot her to keep them from burying her."[147]

## "THEY CANNOT SAY THAT I AM DANGEROUSLY INSANE"

The most high-profile of those remanded to Bridgewater State Hospital during the first half of the twentieth century were Nicola Sacco and Bartolomeo Vanzetti, who in 1921 were convicted of the April 15, 1920 murder of Frederick Parmenter and Alesandro Berardelli at South Braintree. To this day, their trial remains controversial.

Following a thirty-one-day hunger strike, Sacco was committed for observation on April 20, 1923, at the behest of his attorney Fred H. Moore, and he remained at Bridgewater for five months. Sacco found Moore's act of committal unforgivable, later writing his counsel, "Please get out of my case, because you know you are an obstacle to the case.... [What] are you waiting now for? Do you wait until I hang myself." Though a number of alienists declared Sacco of unsound mind, others disagreed, and Moore objected to his client's permanent committal to Bridgewater if ultimately judged insane on the grounds that Bridgewater had been established for the "criminal insane," and as Sacco had not been sentenced and had a pending appeal, he could not be considered criminal.

On January 2, 1925, a warrant was issued authorizing the transfer of Vanzetti from Charlestown State Prison, where he had exhibited signs of mental disturbance. On April 4, 1925, Vanzetti wrote from Bridgewater of being permitted to play ball in the yard, and he later wrote of his memory of the January 24, 1925 solar eclipse when, while reading a book "at the window of my room in the Bridgwater Asilum [*sic*],...the Sun's spectrum colored its pages with rainbow colors."[148] Twelve days following his commitment, Vanzetti sent the following to socialist, reformer and feminist Alice Stone Blackwell:

> *April 16, 1925. Bridgewater Hospital for Criminal Insane*
>
> *DEAR COMRADE BLACKWELL,*
>
> *I bite my tongue 'til now, not to tell you a thing which will make you sorry, but I cannot help but tell it. They took me away from the hospital and brought me in the east north ward, the worst of the wards, for the most dangerous or the punished. While other patients enjoy all day long the sunshine and open air in spacious yards, we have one hour of yard in the morning, and one in the afternoon, and our yard is narrow and shadowy; closing the sight, except to the sky. The door of my room is kept open during*

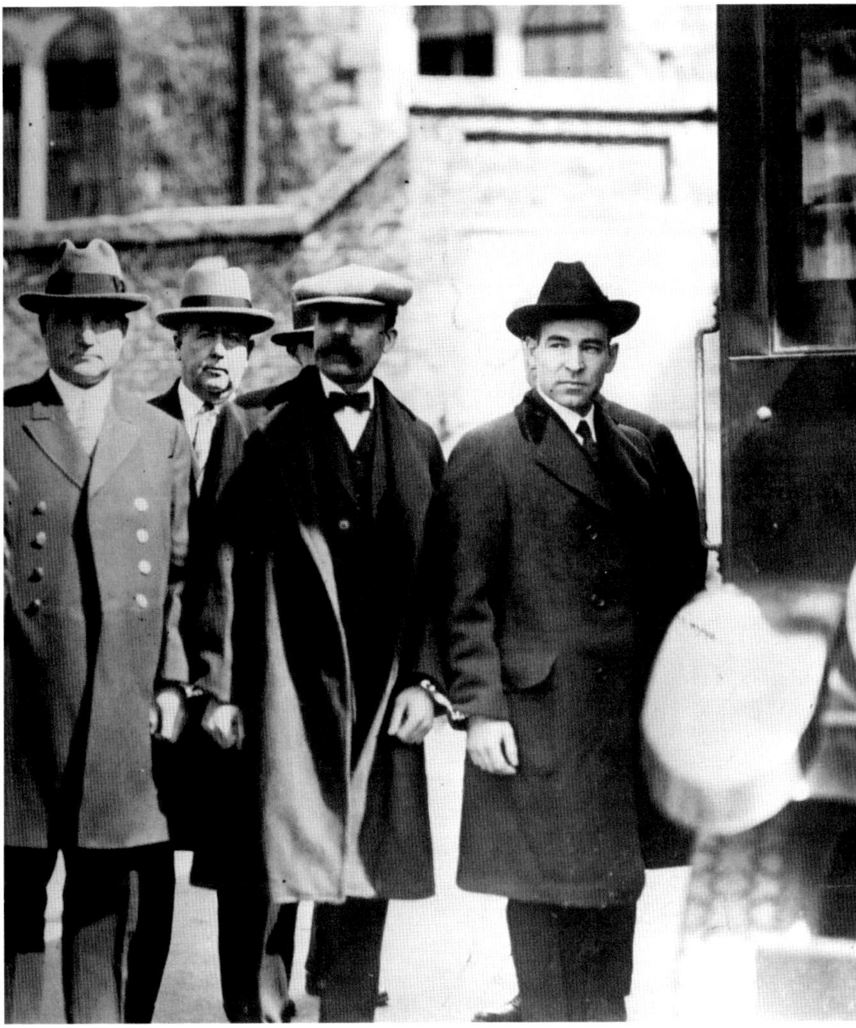

Bartolomeo Vanzetti and Nicola Sacco taken from court, April 9, 1927. Both spent time at Bridgewater. *Courtesy of the Boston Public Library, Leslie Jones Collection.*

*the day, and I have a chair and books in my room. But I stay in because the other prisoners are kept in.*

*Now, they cannot say that I am dangerously insane, nor can they claim that I deserved punishment by my conduct. So they say that in a letter to my sister, I told her that "I wish to go out soon, and get rich quick, and return to Italy." I answered that it is not true, and not knowing if they were saying it for a second end or very uncertain of its truth, I had believed to have*

> *convinced them. But two weeks ago Mr. Thompson* [Vanzetti's counsel] *was here, and they told him the same thing, and said that they cannot give me more liberty because I am a dangerous man. After that, I was declared by the Prison authorities "A model prisoner"; the best one, and after my conduct here, really exemplar.*
>
> *They believe me guilty; they believe my principles to be aberration and insanity; they believe my friends (I mean the comrades and Italians) arch-criminals; they believe, (and told me so) that the Americans in our behalf are fools and cheaters. But, what is worse, they asked me if I believed in God, in the golden rule; if the murderers shall not be punished. If they do not nail me, I will answer.*
>
> *P.S. Yet they are not naturally bad, and they let my door open, give me two cups of milk a day, and the permission to keep books in my room. These are privileges which few are given here. I feel ashamed and my heart aches for them, yet I shall help myself, even when I cannot help others, and appreciate what I receive.*[149]

In another letter written two days earlier to Blackwell, Vanzetti had recorded his thoughts on modern psychiatry as practiced at Bridgewater, seemingly recognizing the inherent conflict between Bridgewater's role as prison and hospital and the contradiction between punishment and rehabilitation.

> *For me, I have already experienced that in* [the] *name of "Psychopathy" may be committed the same, if not more, cruelty, injustice and partiality, as in the name of the law. Psychology is still more subtle and indefinable than law itself. And a doctor may be as mean as* [a] *lawyer or a keeper even more, though, both may be good. We would not have advanced an inch toward justice, progress, liberty or happiness, by simply and only shifting from laws to medicine or psychology, because the real progress represented by the "curing" upon the "punishing" may become, by environment and men's vices, a bloody insult to misfortune and truth. To progress, even a little, we have to destroy a world.*[150]

Found to be sane, Vanzetti was returned to prison. On August 23, 1927, Sacco and Vanzetti were executed in the state prison at Charlestown.

Vanzetti's 1925 letters clearly hint at the duality of Bridgewater's role, and the treatment of the mentally ill in a penal environment became an increasing topic of debate in the following decade. In 1932, a legislative committee

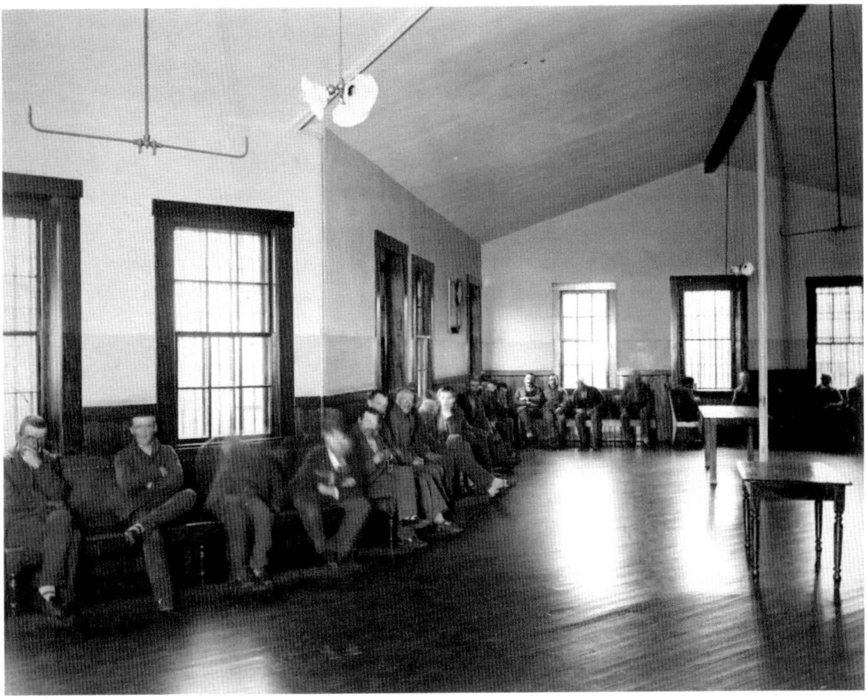

Bridgewater State Farm, asylum department, northwest day room, circa 1900. *Harvard Art Museums/Fogg Museum, Transfer from the Carpenter Center for the Visual Arts, Social Museum Collection, 3.2002.2708.1. Unidentified Artist. Imaging Department © President and Fellows of Harvard College.*

tasked with investigating hospital accommodations for the criminally insane advocated establishment of a separate institution independent of a penal facility where patients might be treated more humanely. "The time has come when it is no longer in conformity with modern standards to run a great hospital for the insane with 938 inmates as an adjunct to a State Farm operated principally for the care of drunkards and vagrants."[151]

The committee found standards of care and accommodation at Bridgewater lower than in state facilities run by the Department of Mental Health, largely due to a lack of medical training. Reports of conditions at Bridgewater were confirmed in May 1935, when Dr. Vernon L. Briggs testified that one patient was confined to an iron cage "like a wild animal" and that correctional officers had transferred convicts from the prison to the insane hospital as punishment. A year later, Briggs excoriated administrators for the "bad and cruel conditions" prevailing at Bridgewater State Hospital, which he described as "not fit for human beings."[152]

Though Superintendent Warren and Correction Commissioner Arthur T. Lyman argued that state hospital patients should be cared for by the Department of Mental Health, they remained under the jurisdiction of the Department of Correction, where

> *they are cared for entirely as prisoners; the problem is necessarily custodial and not medical to the officials there* [at Bridgewater]. *The medical care and treatment is limited to periodic, usually annual, physical and mental examinations, the results of which are recorded in the patient's case record, and such emergency treatment for injuries and intercurrent disease as may be necessary.*
>
> *We find that no attempt is made whatever to use recognized forms of treatment for mental disease as such.*
>
> *There are no hydrotherapy, no occupational therapy, no psychotherapy, and none of the other methods of counteracting or quieting the disturbance of disturbed patients.*[153]

## "It Is Not Such a Bad Job, Being a Farm Hand on the State Farm"

The mingling of multiple classifications within the institution and the "constantly changing population flowing in and ebbing out again" made maintaining order difficult.[154] As in the past, physical labor was relied upon not only to occupy inmates and instill discipline but also to teach them the value of hard work and contribute to their rehabilitation.

"Outdoor work" on the farm remained the principal use for inmate labor. In 1925, ten acres of ground yielded 70,000 ears of sweet corn that were fed to inmates, while an additional 125 acres produced field corn to be ground into meal and ensilage corn to be chopped into winter fodder for a herd of 140 Holstein cattle that produced 1,000 quarts of milk daily for consumption on the farm. Potatoes were the primary crop and were cultivated on 66-plus acres; 12,000 bushels were produced for farm consumption and an additional 9,000 to supply other state institutions, including the state prison at Charlestown, Lakeville Sanatorium, Bridgewater Normal School and Concord Reformatory. Hay was raised by the ton for "several hundred" horses, with 1924's crop from two cuttings aggregating 525 tons. Over 50

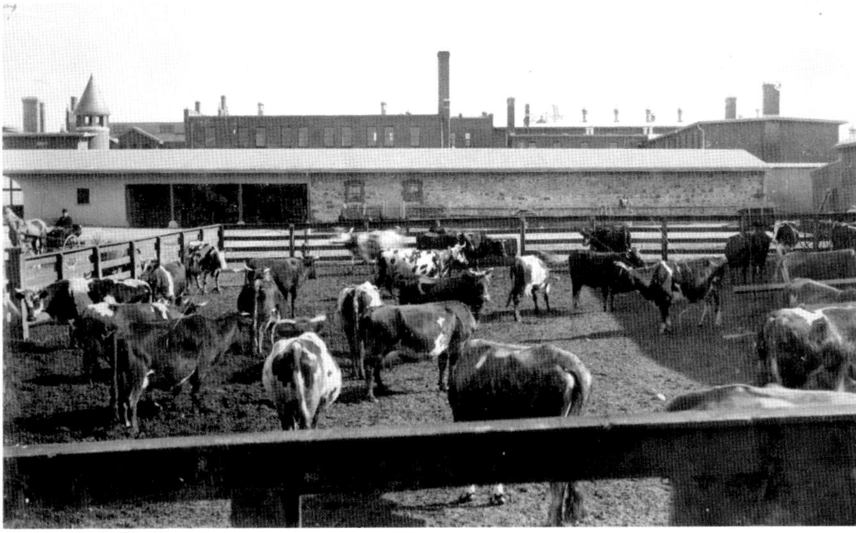

Bridgewater State Farm, stock yard, circa 1903. *Harvard Art Museums/Fogg Museum, Transfer from the Carpenter Center for the Visual Arts, Social Museum Collection, 3.2002.882.4. Bass Photo. Imaging Department © President and Fellows of Harvard College.*

acres of beans, 4 acres of peas, 5 acres of summer and winter squash, an acre of pole beans and 4 acres of cabbage contributed to the total 1,200 acres under cultivation. So strong was the belief in the value of "outdoor work" that the state hospital included a walled garden where a large variety of vegetables, melons and fruits was raised.

A laudatory article appearing in the *Boston Globe* in 1925 little recognized the realities of life at Bridgewater, instead painting an idealized view of the farm where "individuals come in, broken down and almost out, or convicted of criminal tendencies, and they leave hardened up by healthy labor in the open air, three husky meals a day and regular hours, and enforced good behavior." Head farmer Charles O. Bearse told readers, "It is not such a bad job, being a farm hand on the State Farm; you get three meals a day, a place to sleep, a dollar when you leave, and a man to watch you by day and another one to watch you by night. Where could one do better?"[155] Not everyone agreed, and life at Bridgewater was reputed to be hard. In February 1929, when John Williams was sentenced in Superior Criminal Court to a fifteen-month term at the State Farm on six counts of breaking and entering, he complained that farm work at Bridgewater was too difficult. Judge Lummus sentenced him to the House of Correction instead. Similarly, Victor Demoranville, unemployed and homeless in the depths of the Depression, desperately sought to have himself sentenced to a state institution for care, telling New Bedford police in 1934 that he would plead guilty to vagrancy charges only if they would see that he was not sent to Bridgewater.

Predictably, enforcing labor on the farm was challenging. "The farm labor for all this acreage includes 200 inmates of the institution, more or less unreliable who have to be watched constantly, whose work is of a variable quality."[156] Attorney Joseph W. Keith in 1931 called the defective delinquents "a dead load, as they can do nothing productive."[157] (Contrary to these characterizations, inmates were commended for their actions during a September 1925 blaze attributed to spontaneous combustion that destroyed a series of barns, two hundred tons of hay and eight hundred tons of ensilage, as well as badly damaging four concrete silos. According to Correction Commissioner Bates, "They all turned to and helped in this critical hour and not a man attempted to escape."[158] In November 1930, prisoners similarly formed a bucket brigade to quell a fire in the home of Fred B. Turner on Titicut Street.)

For those inmates unable to engage in outdoor work, weaving, furniture making, tailoring or other tasks in one of the farm's workshops was assigned. The few female prisoners were put to work at housekeeping and later performed laundry work for the Lakeville Sanatorium. Trustworthy

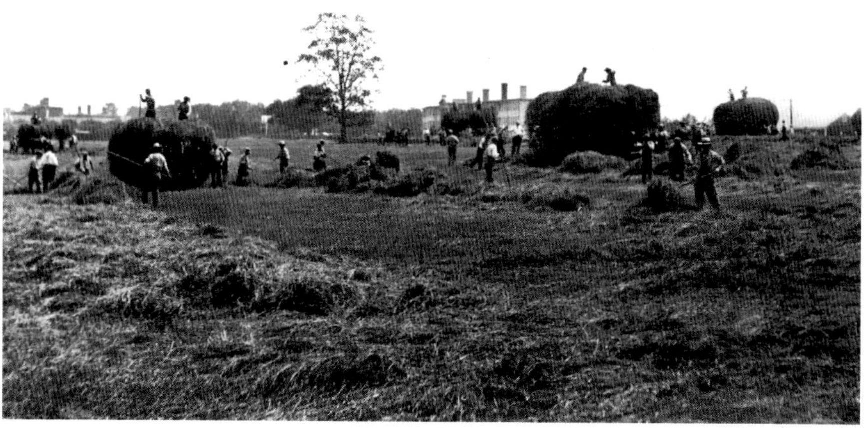

Bridgewater State Farm, haying, circa 1912. Thirty years earlier in 1880, the farm included one hundred acres of hay and seventy acres of mown grassland. *Author's collection.*

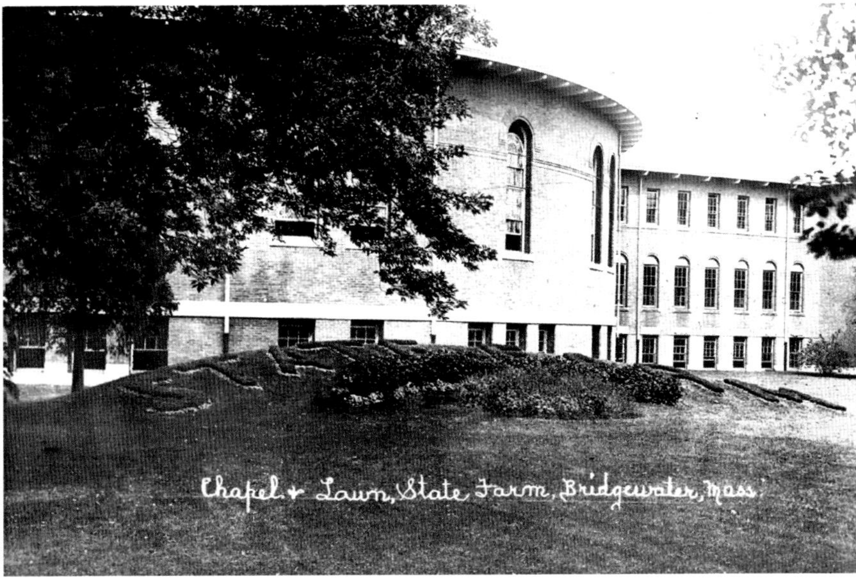


Bridgewater State Farm, chapel and floral "State Farm" display, circa 1910. *Author's collection.*

inmates known as "trusties" performed work about the institution and off the farm, though this outside work was sometimes controversial. In 1924, following a devastating fire at the Bridgewater Normal School, union carpenters challenged use of State Farm labor at the school though the inmates were engaged solely in removing debris and salvaging brick and other material.

Entertainment was provided on a limited basis. Hospital patients in 1919, for instance, engaged in outdoor sports and baseball games during the summer and enjoyed movies in the colder months. Holidays were celebrated on a limited basis. At Thanksgiving 1927 as part of their holiday dinner, the inmates had chicken for the first time in more than twenty years, followed by movies. Mother's Day 1936 was observed with services in the chapel, musical numbers and singing under the auspices of the Salvation Army. Christmas 1938 was celebrated with roast chicken, religious services and entertainment.

## Escape

As in the past, forced incarceration prompted many inmates to escape. Some resorted to suicide, including Arthur Tatro of New Bedford, confined for larceny, who hanged himself in his cell on January 23, 1923, and George Willette, who threw himself under a delivery truck. Eighty-two-year-old John Mack, an inmate of Tewksbury State Infirmary who killed four other inmates there with a mail-order pistol and was subsequently committed to Bridgewater State Hospital, hanged himself in July 1942 with an improvised noose.

Escapes remained a fact of State Farm life. The increased number of dangerous criminals housed at Bridgewater, however, made past breakouts appear almost comical, and fears in neighboring communities were heightened whenever inmates managed to escape. On January 7, 1920, three criminally insane inmates made their way out, followed three months later by George Lewis, an infirmary patient committed from Barnstable on April 5, 1920, who broke an iron guard, climbed out a window and disappeared over the roofs. Later that year, on October 16, 1920, two trusties, William Wood and Flora Black, escaped while working at the home of assistant superintendent Arthur Wood. On April 18, 1921, convicted murderer Joseph Rogers, sentenced to life in May 1916, adjudged insane and transferred to the State Farm in 1919, used boards and a table to climb over the wall and escape into the woods. Joseph Thompson escaped by clambering over a wall by means of a rope fashioned from his bed clothing on August 16, 1921. John Stollers escaped in May 1922 before being caught at West Bridgewater after having set fire to a henhouse in an effort to keep warm. Three escaped in the early evening of November 24, 1923, and swam across the Taunton River east of the institution near Auburn Street. One, Henry Long, was believed to have drowned, and though State Farm officials dragged the river, no body was recovered. Two prisoners being treated for drug addiction in the hospital, Manning Haley and Arthur Galbin, escaped on May 15, 1925, as did two youths who fled on August 19, 1928. Crippled inmate Walter Perry escaped on October 11, 1929, from the hospital ward using a rope made from bedsheets. Thomas J. Gildea, sentenced to twenty to thirty years for armed robbery, escaped on May 6, 1935, by sawing through the bars of his cell window in the criminally insane ward. At the time, Gildea was clad only in his underwear, his uniform having been used to create a dummy left in his bed to fool attendants. A posse of sixty prison attendants flushed the surrounding fields and woods in search of Gildea, without success. (He ultimately was recaptured at Roxbury a few days later.)

A number of those who escaped slipped away from transfer officers while being transported to Bridgewater, including George Chaisson, who eluded his guard at Worcester's Union Station in March 1928, and John J. Doyle, who similarly fled from his guard at South Station, Boston, in March 1931. Both had been sentenced for drunkenness.

Admittedly, while many attempted escapes were thwarted and those who did succeed were most often captured quickly, some escapees remained at large for extended periods of time. Joseph Luzinski of Peabody escaped in spring 1929 and was not recaptured until October 1929.

## "The Ever-Lurking Menace"

Given that many Bridgewater patients and inmates were not reconciled to being there, guards faced continual danger, as noted in a 1935 newspaper that reminded readers that "murderous assault by one of the crazed inmates of the hospital, many of whom were committed to the institution after they had committed murderous acts and been adjudged insane, is the ever-lurking menace for the attendants."[159] Guards at Bridgewater remained unarmed and were constantly vulnerable, their exposure to potential danger aggravated by understaffing during the first half of the twentieth century, when there was about one guard for every ten inmates. Not only was the danger inherent in the position a deterrent to potential guards, but low wages were also a factor in dissuading qualified applicants. In early 1936, nine individuals eligible for the position with a $1,080 annual salary declined in the belief that a better position might be offered later. Additionally, Bridgewater attendants were classified as guards, which carried a lower pay grade than correctional officers. Prior to 1942, Bridgewater guards were paid on average $16.10 a week, though after the 1942 New Year's Day riot they received $33 weekly, on par with state prison guards. In 1943, in an effort aimed in part at improving the lot of those employed on the farm, State Farm employees were classed as civil servants, while attendants and guards were reclassified as correctional officers.

Increased wages, however, were little compensation for the daily dangers faced by guards, who had to remain vigilant for signs of violence that might erupt at any time. And it did. On July 22, 1920, as they were being marched

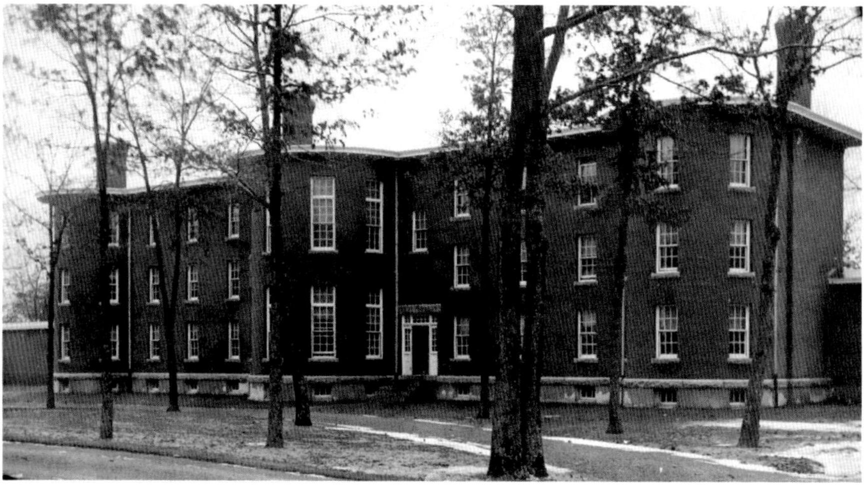

Bridgewater State Farm, male attendants' residence, circa 1903, housed twelve in six double rooms and eighteen in single rooms and included a reading and billiard room. The basement had shower baths and space for a bowling alley. *Harvard Art Museums/Fogg Museum, Transfer from the Carpenter Center for the Visual Arts, Social Museum Collection, 3.2002.2686.4. Unidentified Artist. Imaging Department © President and Fellows of Harvard College.*

from the dining hall to the dangerous ward, inmates Lloyd Kingdom and Antonio Disrest attacked guards Edwin Kingsley, William Garnier and Fred Bowles, slashing and stabbing the men. Stealing keys from a fourth attendant, Fred Shattuck, the two attempted to release prisoners from the violent wards. Before they could do so, Kingdom was shot and killed, prompting Disrest to surrender. The episode, though contained, was magnified by the coincidental escape of five criminally insane inmates from the Maine State Insane Hospital that same day. Disrest remained problematic; in December 1920, he stabbed guard John McDonald in the abdomen with splintered wood he had fashioned into a weapon. A riot call was sounded, and Disrest was subdued with ammonia gas.

Even more horrific was the deadly February 13, 1928 attack on night watchman Wilfred Gerrior and night supervisor Eugene E. Amlaw by inmate James Melton, "a criminally insane person of the most vicious type."[160] Melton, an inmate at the state hospital for twenty years, slipped through the transom with a post from his bed, brutally clubbing and strangling the men and injuring two others before releasing four additional inmates. Like several guards, Gerrior had previously known violence at the hands of inmates. Twice before the fatal attack, Gerrior had been subjected to violent behavior, and on another occasion his son Clifford,

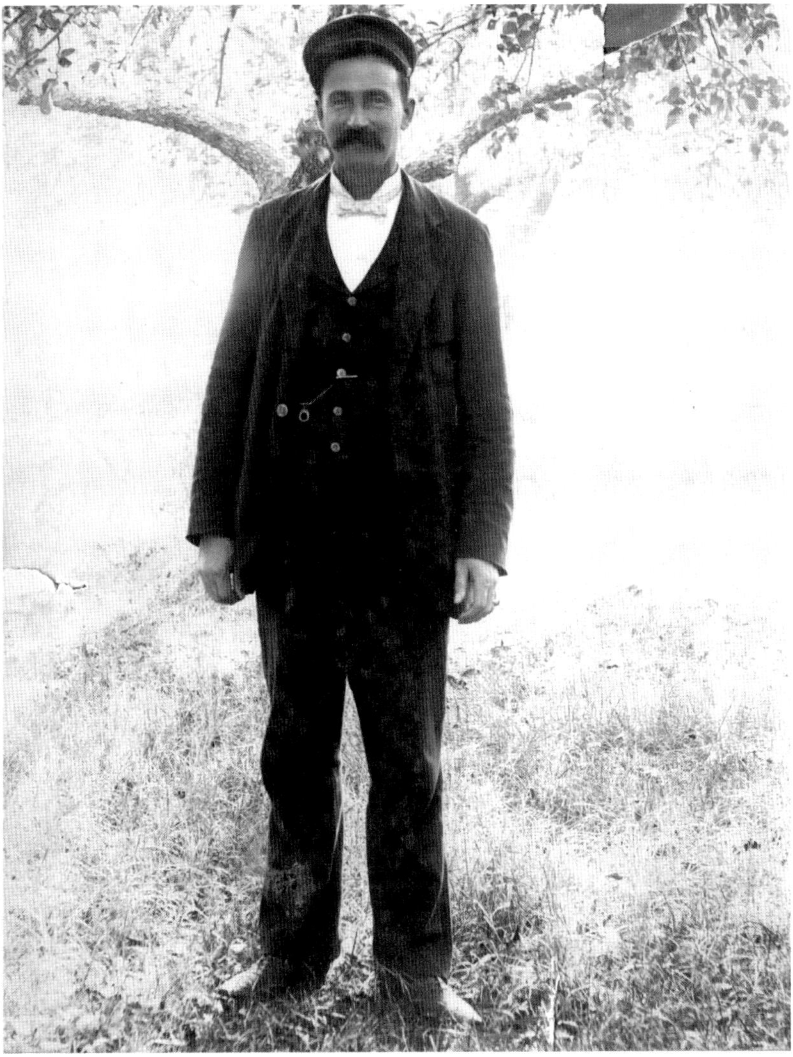

Bridgewater State Farm, unidentified attendant, circa 1900. *Massachusetts State Archives, State Farm (Bridgewater, Mass.), Photographs of facilities and activities [ca. 1900–ca. 1910], HS9.10/973X.*

who was visiting Gerrior at the hospital, was dragged into a cell by an insane inmate who attempted to strangle him.

Following the 1928 incident, although the legislature appropriated funds for additional night guards at Bridgewater, their presence did not always guarantee safety. On July 21, 1935, guard Frederick H. Dean was killed when he was caught unawares by an inmate in the hospital who dealt Dean a fatal blow to the head. In late April 1952, guards Everett Jenkins and Sydney Canfield were beaten by a prisoner, as was reform officer Margaret Waldron in February 1953. Even off-duty guards were subject to attack, as evidenced by an assault on James W. Spear made by two former inmates in fall 1930 at Brockton.

Violence was not directed solely at correctional officers. On November 11, 1931, criminally insane inmate Joseph E. Bamforth fatally attacked his thirteen-year-old daughter Irene while she was visiting, dragging her into a closet and attacking her with a hammer he had concealed in his uniform.[161] Confined to the state hospital after having been declared insane following the double axe murder of his wife and mother-in-law at Haverhill in January 1919, Bamforth had subsequently earned a reputation for being harmless, acquiring the status of "trusty." He justified the murder of his daughter on the grounds that "I thought the little thing would be better off in heaven with her mother."[162]

Though the guard on duty at the time of Irene Bamforth's murder was later characterized as stone deaf and elderly, Massachusetts Correction commissioner Stearns blamed the killing not on an individual but on the generally poor situation at Bridgewater. Stearns used the opportunity to advocate for a separate institution for the criminal insane with proper financing, professional staff and public support. "The care of the criminal insane is a medical problem. It should have a separate institution, proper financial backing, high-grade staff and generous public support. Bridgewater has never had this. It has been repeatedly tossed upon the Department of Mental Diseases, then upon the Board of Charity and last upon the Department of Correction."[163] Dr. William T. Hanson (1880–1950), medical director of the Hospital for the Criminal Insane, emphasized the immediate need for ten additional guards and was supported by the Executive Committee on Public Welfare, an indication that staffing increases following the 1928 killing of Gerrior and Amlaw had had little substantive impact in raising the level of safety within the institution.

Inmates, however, were not the only perpetrators of violence; there were instances, admittedly rare, of refractory inmates being maltreated by guards. William G. Register, a criminally insane inmate, died on February 5, 1935, after a violent scuffle with three guards. Register was known to be a dangerous inmate who on six previous occasions had attacked officers and attendants in the hospital. Though Dr. Hanson accused the guards of mauling Register and requested their dismissal, Superintendent Warren refused and was supported by Correction Commissioner Lyman, who attributed the death to an "error of judgement in the excitement of the moment."[164] A similar incident occurred in December 1952 when criminally insane inmate Robert Leonard died following a struggle with an officer, Louis J. Bonaparte, who subsequently was tried for manslaughter.

## "Administration Has Been Inefficient and Imprudent"

In addition to increased violence within the institution, the State Farm attracted attention for alleged mismanagement and malfeasance under the administration of Henry J. Strann, who had succeeded Blackstone as superintendent in 1922. In 1930, head farmer Charles O. Bearse and Frederick E. Standish, head of the motor equipment department, were accused of stealing potatoes and reselling the produce at Middleborough and elsewhere, delivered in State Farm trucks by State Farm prisoners. Bearse in June 1931 pleaded guilty to conspiracy and larceny indictments and was sentenced to a year in the Plymouth County House of Correction, followed by Standish, who received nine months. After Standish implicated Superintendent Strann in the scheme, the State Commission on Administration and Finance conducted an intensive investigation, which, although it cleared Strann of any criminal wrongdoing, was highly critical of his lack of oversight. The commission found that 97 tons of hay and 130 tons of cement could not be accounted for, while coke, fresh beef, milk, pigs, calves and gasoline had all been given away or exchanged. Additionally, though the institution was legally permitted to sell unclaimed bodies to the commonwealth's medical schools for twelve dollars, it was found that Martin Pratt, the elderly man engaged in transporting the corpses, was pocketing the funds. (Pratt was dismissed in June 1932.)

The commission concluded that Strann's administration over the past several years had "been inefficient and imprudent."[165] It recommended Strann's dismissal and appointment of a medically trained superintendent, attributing some of Bridgewater's problems to a lack of professional qualifications among its administrators. Strann was relieved of his duties on July 28, 1931, and replaced as interim superintendent by Dr. Hanson. Hanson declined an offer of the superintendency, which instead went to New Bedford fruit and produce dealer and former alderman Robert C. Sherman, who was appointed in December 1931 in place of medically trained

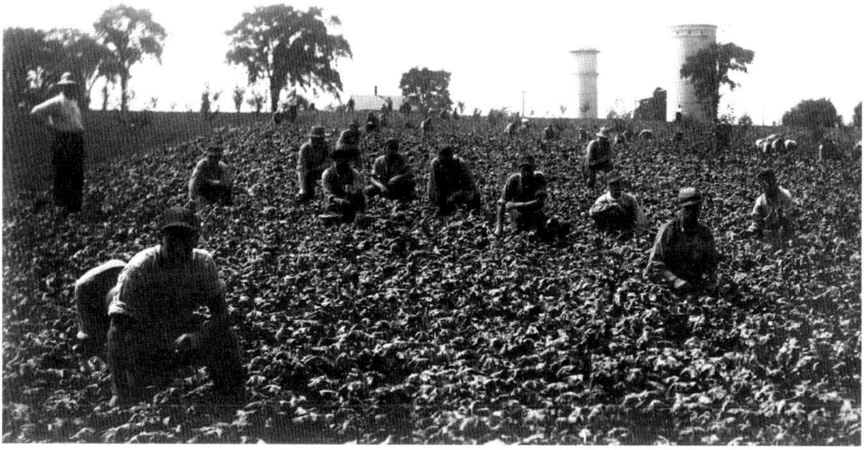

Bridgewater State Farm, potato fields, circa 1912. *Author's collection.*

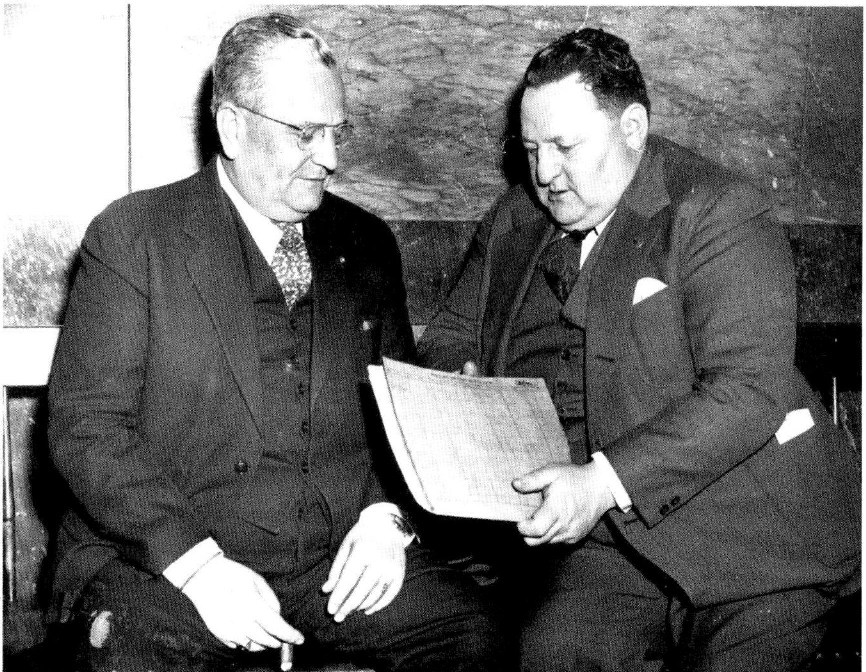

State Farm superintendent James Warren and Massachusetts assistant attorney general Conde Brodbine confer at a March 12, 1946 parole and defective delinquents' hearing. *Press photo.*

professionals who had been recommended. Sherman himself resigned on December 1, 1933, under mysterious circumstances and was succeeded by James E. Warren, a Lawrence automobile and insurance salesman and Massachusetts state senator since 1928, despite repeated calls from various experts that a medical professional be named to head the institution.

## "A Cesspool of Depravity and Degeneracy"

The investigation and subsequent dismissal of Superintendent Strann was part of a larger campaign to improve conditions within the commonwealth's correctional institutions, which had come under fire in early 1931, by which time Bridgewater had acquired a reputation as the worst among them. James H. Brennan, a member of the Governor's Council who had investigated conditions in the prisons in 1931, likened the Norfolk Prison Camp to a country club while characterizing Bridgewater as a "Hell Hole." Brennan deemed Bridgewater "a cesspool of depravity and degeneracy where hundreds of unfortunates have never been given a chance. The State Prison at Charlestown is by comparison a paradise."[166]

Despite the administrative mismanagement prevalent at Bridgewater during the 1930s, investigations concluded that harsh treatment of inmates or an absence of discipline did not exist on a wide scale. Deteriorating conditions were instead attributed to the mixed classification system and the lack of coordinated efforts to rehabilitate inmates.

Inmate Wilfred E. Besner, who transferred to Bridgewater in the mid-1930s, characterized it as "a bad prison. The food was often spoiled and we were treated without consideration. Morale was at rock bottom and there was constant unrest. There was little recreation." Unmentioned by Besner was a 1936 statewide spinal meningitis outbreak that originated at the State Farm and ultimately killed sixteen throughout the commonwealth, including an eleven-year-old girl whose father, a police sergeant, had earlier arrested a drunken man who had been released from Bridgewater with the disease.

The atmosphere described by Besner was indicative of an institution that was overwhelmed. By 1932, Bridgewater was operating as the second-largest correctional facility in Massachusetts, with 270 employees caring for a population of some 2,489 inmates composed of 964 male prisoners, 80 female prisoners, 112 male paupers, 945 male insane, 289 male defective

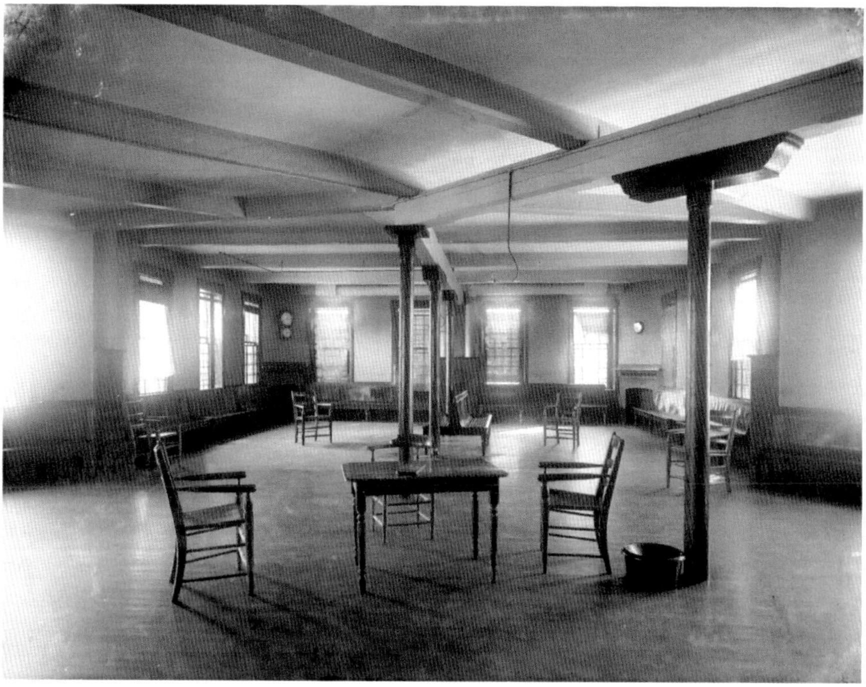

Bridgewater State Farm, day room, west wing, first floor, circa 1900. *Harvard Art Museums/ Fogg Museum, Transfer from the Carpenter Center for the Visual Arts, Social Museum Collection, 3.2002.2709.4. Bass Photo. Imaging Department © President and Fellows of Harvard College.*

delinquents, 83 female defective delinquents and 16 male drug addicts. Rather than looking to reform its residents and prepare them for a future life outside prison, it was all Bridgewater could do to provide permanent custodial care for the individuals residing there.

## "Better Than the State Farm"

Throughout the 1930s, media scrutiny of worsening conditions at Bridgewater focused principally on the state hospital, with little attention given to the prison and less to the defective delinquent department, which continued to be upheld as an exemplary institution. Some dissented from this view. Dr. Hanson, who twice acted as superintendent, opposed treating defective delinquents in penal institutions and advocated a more

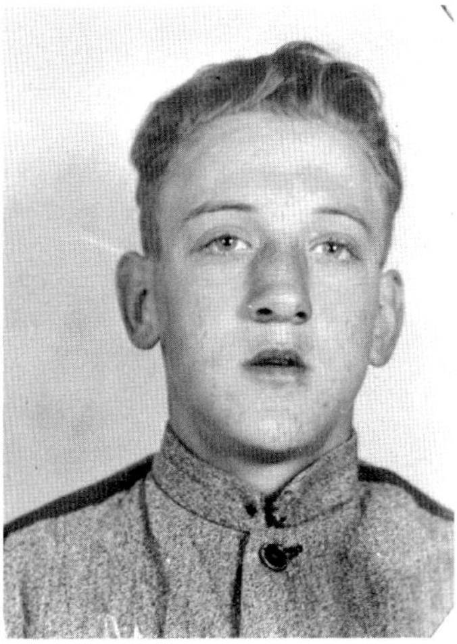

Donald Millard, prison record photograph, October 7, 1938. *Courtesy of the Boston Public Library, Leslie Jones Collection.*

compassionate approach. He remained powerless, however, to alter the medical establishment's entrenched views on the matter, which were shared by several of the commonwealth's most prestigious academic institutions, including Harvard, Smith and Boston University, and influential physicians like Fernald.

Joining with other progressives at the time, Hanson argued that Bridgewater inmates would be better served by the Department of Mental Health rather than the Department of Correction: "I still feel that the Defective Delinquent is a mental problem and that this department should be under the jurisdiction of the Department for Mental Diseases....I feel that a school established for defective delinquents would be much more appropriate than an institution for defective delinquents under jail conditions."[167]

Indefinite incarceration under the "jail conditions" mentioned by Hanson was the reality for many defective delinquents who were dischargeable in one of only two ways, either through parole or through discharge by court order, their confinement justified on the grounds that they might relapse if released. In 1933, the consequence of this policy was acknowledged when it was stated that "the [defective delinquent] department has difficulty in getting rid of cases wrongly diagnosed."[168] Worse than the logistics of the situation was the injustice of it, an issue acknowledged some twenty years later by Massachusetts Superior Court judge Charles A. Rome, who recognized that committal "as a defective delinquent to the state farm...is practically equivalent to commitment for life."[169]

At Bridgewater, defective delinquents were known disparagingly as "DDs" or "blue boys," the latter term derived from the color of the prison-made military-style uniforms that consisted of gray-blue tunics, pants with a single dark blue stripe and visor-less caps. Derided by Superintendent Strann as "mentally deficient" and "morally blunted," the boys were confined in the prison department's Tower Building (1897) and Beacon Street (1912), the latter so named for its resemblance to the bow-fronted row houses and apartment blocks of Boston. Rising each day at 6:30

a.m., they breakfasted and then took part in military drills intended to instill discipline, obedience and moral and social responsibility. Following this, the inmates worked for six hours, ate lunch and engaged in exercise before supper. At 5:00 p.m., they were confined to their cells, with lights extinguished at 8:00 p.m. Any infractions resulted in immediate loss of privileges, while subsequent violations resulted in solitary confinement as punishment. Though the *Boston Globe* reassured readers that "the solitary cells are not dungeons," it contradicted itself when it reported that the cells remained "in total darkness" and were furnished solely with "a bed of planks." Officers and administrators at Bridgewater held little hope that the "defective delinquents" could be either rehabilitated or prepared for a role in society so rarely made an effort to do so. Meanwhile, most Massachusetts residents remained unaware of the defective delinquents' existence, and those who did know of them were generally unsympathetic, including the *Boston Globe*, which ran a feature article in 1934 that was alternately mocking and glib in tone. The *Globe* nonetheless revealed the sad condition of the defective delinquents, many of whom had simply been abandoned by their families and society, when it reported their habit of adorning their rooms:

> *Almost every cot is decorated with pictures, laid on the bed and leaned against the pillow. Centerpiece of one design is a card reading, "Merry Christmas from Somebody." Many have religious pictures, surrounded by pictures of movie queens, or snapshots of scenes of people, or picture postcards. As the beds are made up each morning, these decorative schemes have to be renewed daily.*[170]

Among those "delinquents" arguing against what they considered to be their unlawful incarceration were Ernest Valley of Boston, twenty, and Leon E. Benoit of Dracut, twenty-two, who fled from the defective delinquent department on October 27, 1931, by concealing themselves in a milk truck. Captured in central New York, the pair disputed their re-committal to Bridgewater, contending that they were not mentally deficient and their detention was unjust. Dr. Hanson disagreed regarding the pair's first claim, testifying that although they "spoke intelligently they still were defective."[171] In early February 1932, the two again escaped, this time during their arraignment at Plymouth Superior Court, where Benoit made another passionate plea not to be returned to Bridgewater. Handcuffed together while being escorted from the courthouse, Benoit slipped free, and the two

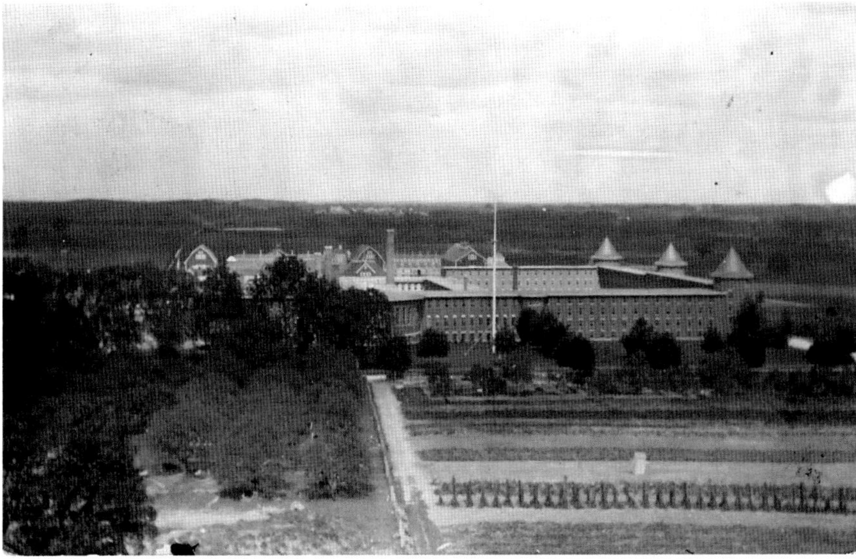

Bridgewater State Farm looking north from the water tower, circa 1900, showing the orchard, garden, prison and farm. The Tower Building is at right. *Author's collection.*

dashed in separate directions through the center of Plymouth, with shots being fired by their pursuers.

While Valley and Benoit were unsuccessful in avoiding incarceration at Bridgewater, their claims began to raise doubts about the propriety and legality of indefinitely sentencing developmentally disabled misdemeanants to Bridgewater and other state institutions. Councilor James H. Brennan in January 1932 cited an example of an inmate in the defective delinquent department who had been confined for eight years simply for having broken into a summer cottage. As head of a three-member investigative committee in 1932, Brennan witnessed at Bridgewater the "wholesale condemnation of young men for what amounts practically to a life sentence," a practice that he deemed a "fiendish injustice." Brennan argued that inmates should be reexamined by impartial parties, and he criticized "the mania for mental examination of prisoners [that] has so far over-reached itself that many young men, otherwise completely normal mentally, who fail in certain specified psychopathic tests, are adjudged by these alienists to be defective and are clapped into the State Farm without any hope of release."[172]

Despite Brennan's impassioned arguments, he remained in the minority, and the failure to address problems within the defective delinquent department resulted in the most serious disturbance ever to have occurred

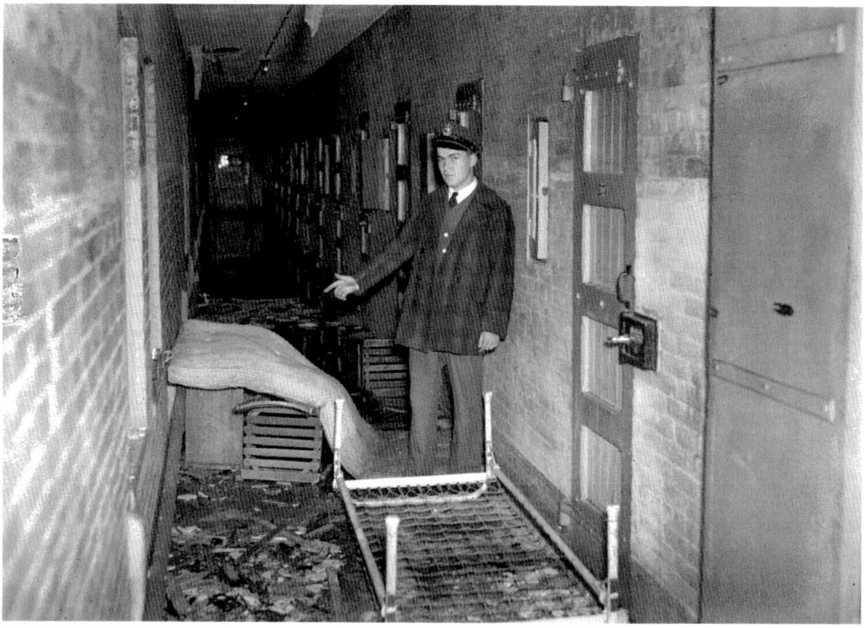

*Above*: Fourth-floor corridor, south tower, following the attempted escape of three defective delinquents on January 1, 1942. *Courtesy of the Boston Public Library, Leslie Jones Collection.*

*Opposite, top*: Guard John Rollins displays the tool cabinet from which chisels used to attack guards were taken. *Courtesy of the Boston Public Library, Leslie Jones Collection.*

*Opposite, bottom*: Massachusetts state troopers John H. Bucklye and Raymond J. Moran with Sergeant Joseph Fratas at the State Farm, January 1942. *Courtesy of the Boston Public Library, Leslie Jones Collection.*

at the farm when, on New Year's Day 1942, fourteen inmates conspired to escape. Though ultimately only three did so, the subsequent rampage they went on that day ended in the brutal slaying of three guards: George H. Landry, Howard V. Murphy and Franklin L. Weston. Two of the boys were later convicted of Landry's murder, and both wrote letters criticizing conditions in the facility and making allegations about "guards protecting favorites among the prisoners, and about prisoners buying favors from guards" that prompted a subsequent investigation. Tellingly, nineteen-year-old Donald Millard's final words prior to his execution were "this is better than the state farm." Though hyperbolic, Millard's statement was indicative of at least one inmate's view of the injustice of the situation, the meaning of the prospect of a lifetime of imprisonment and just how deplorable conditions in the prison had become.

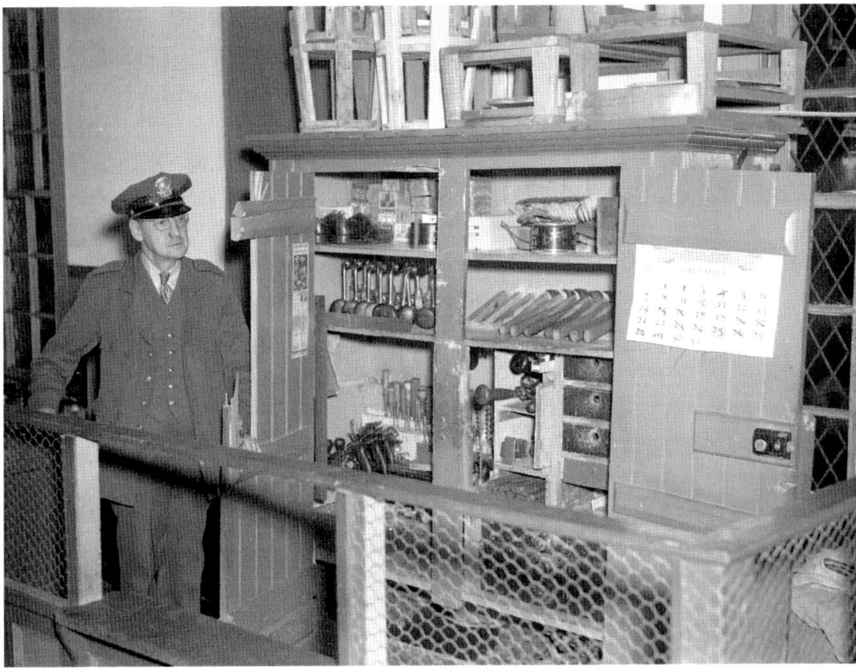

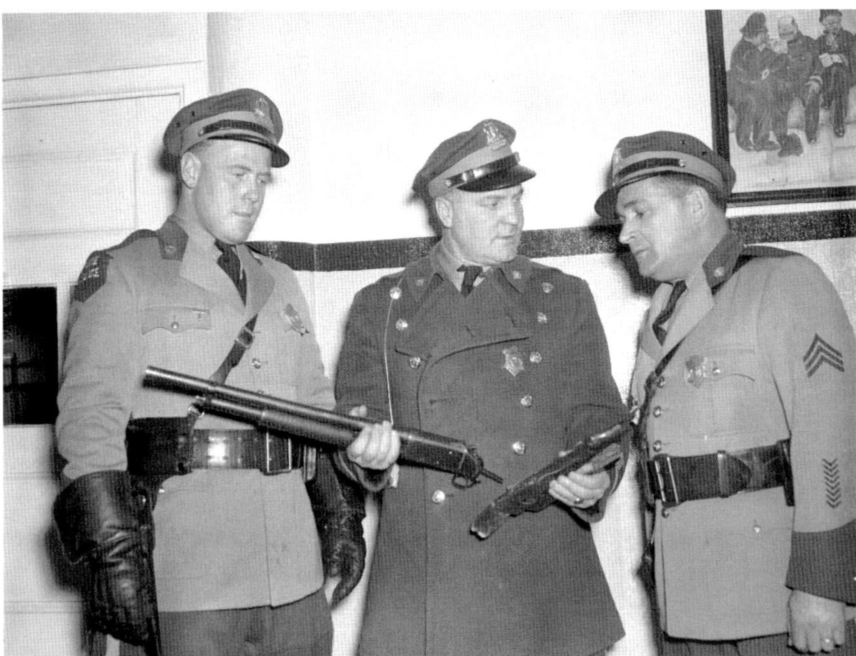

Overcrowding of inmates, poor living conditions and understaffing partially attributable to the war were all blamed for the tragic turn of events. At the time, Bridgewater housed 2,526 total inmates, among whom were 545 defective delinquents jailed in a wing built to accommodate only 399. Seriously undermanned (there were then 55 vacancies at the State Farm), a total of 18 guards were on duty on New Year's Day, with only 4 on the night shift. In part to alleviate the situation, four months later, a secret pre-dawn convoy carrying 150 defective delinquents left Bridgewater for the reformatory at Concord, the largest mass prisoner transfer in the commonwealth's history.

## "A JAIL INSTEAD OF A CLINIC"

While the savage killing of three guards horrified the commonwealth, it also focused attention on the plight of "defective delinquents" and others at Bridgewater, with increased attention being given to the numerous cases of inmates who had been placed in permanent custodial care. Once more, the failure to provide a rigid classification system and corresponding treatment resurrected questions as to whether Bridgewater was positioned to deal with mental health issues.[173]

In 1929, four years after questions first had been raised regarding Bridgewater's ability to effect patient rehabilitation, Commissioner of Correction Stearns sought to revolutionize rehabilitative practice in Massachusetts's penal institutions by providing individualized treatment of inmates. "The basis of the plan," wrote the *New York Times* in describing Stearns's proposal, "is a system of classification which will carry out the single principle of modern penology, the individualization of treatment."[174] Yet a survey of Bridgewater conducted in the mid-1940s, fifteen years following roll-out of the initiative, revealed that Bridgewater had not implemented it and remained ill equipped to do so.

> *Individual treatment cannot be accomplished at the State Farm due to the fact that there are no facilities for diagnostic work, nor room for the segregation of the various types. At the present time the legally criminal and non-criminal, the young and old, the violent, the hardened criminal type, the low grade imbecile…and the diagnosed sex deviates are mixed together; and due to the fact that facilities are lacking, no proper classification program is in existence or can be put into effect.*[175]

Governor Joseph B. Ely a decade earlier had similarly criticized Bridgewater's continuing mixed classifications, which hindered administration and impeded rehabilitation efforts, complaining of Bridgewater, "There are 1,000 prisoners, 950 insane, 397 defective delinquents, 138 paupers and nine drug addicts. They've got everything down there."[176] Experts agreed that the larger number of classifications existing in a single institution complicated management and exponentially increased costs. Calls for the establishment of a separate institution for the criminally insane, including the transfer of this class from Bridgewater, were raised once more in the interest of providing proper medical care but went unheeded.

While the 1940 survey reemphasized the need for segregation of the various classifications and better treatment for them, other questions arose at the time regarding the legality of the incarceration of many of Bridgewater's inmates, some of whom had been confined for years without ever having been charged or convicted of a crime, having been examined or having had a public hearing.

As early as 1925, questions had been raised concerning the legitimacy of some inmates' sentences. In February of that year, the *Boston Globe* reported the story of Ben and Tom Butler, who were physically disabled and had been cared for at the Quincy city farm following the loss of their parents. In 1924, the pair was removed to Bridgewater without a hearing, the city indicating that they had been sent as medical charity cases. Though Quincy officials eventually secured the Butlers' release, "many people wondered how it was possible to send the pair to the State Farm without a court hearing."[177] Citizens of the commonwealth learned, however, that it was possible as they became aware beginning in the mid-1940s of a growing number of inmates incarcerated at Bridgewater without due process.

In June 1944, thirty-four-year-old Joseph T. Barros secured his release from Bridgewater. Having contracted infantile paralysis as a baby, he was placed in a succession of state institutions before being sentenced indefinitely to Bridgewater as a defective delinquent at age twenty-three. The interest of Commissioner Lyman and the attention of Bridgewater officials over the course of ten years helped rehabilitate Barros, who "is neither defective nor delinquent and never has been." Upon Barros's release, the *Boston Globe* called him "the near mistake of society," overlooking the fact that he had been imprisoned for eleven years without cause. Though some sought to have Barros's record expunged through a gubernatorial pardon, Lyman acknowledged that Barros, ironically, could not be pardoned: "As Joseph

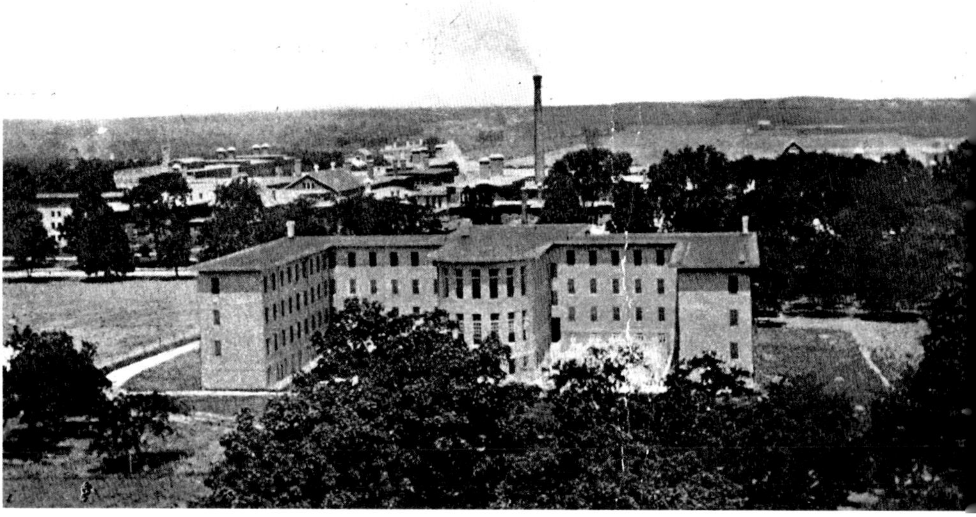

Barros was never found guilty of any crime there is no offense from which he might be pardoned."[178] John J. Perry, sentenced as a defective delinquent to Bridgewater at fourteen for a criminal attack on a Cambridge girl, was released in January 1945 on the grounds that anyone charged with a crime punishable by death or life imprisonment could not be sentenced as a defective delinquent without trial.

These and other cases encouraged Brookline selectman and former head of the Massachusetts Parole Board Reuben L. Lurie in 1946 to advocate for persons illegally confined at Bridgewater for whom "no finger has been turned in any office to examine why they are there....Without classification, men and boys are mixed together—defective delinquents and all. It is a jail instead of the clinic it should be. We have given the defective delinquents nothing but confinement, idleness, a poor staff to supervise them in many cases and politically appointed supervisors with little experience." Lurie criticized the judiciary, noting that "there are very few judges who have ever been to Bridgewater to see the place where they have ordered the accused confined."[179] At the time, it was estimated that some 350 men and women were being held illegally in the state institutions, including Bridgewater, which in 1946 the former warden of the notorious Sing Sing prison called a "disgrace."

Due to pressure from Lurie and others, as well as the publicity around the issue, on July 1, 1947, the commonwealth enacted a law requiring immediate psychiatric examination of all individuals committed in

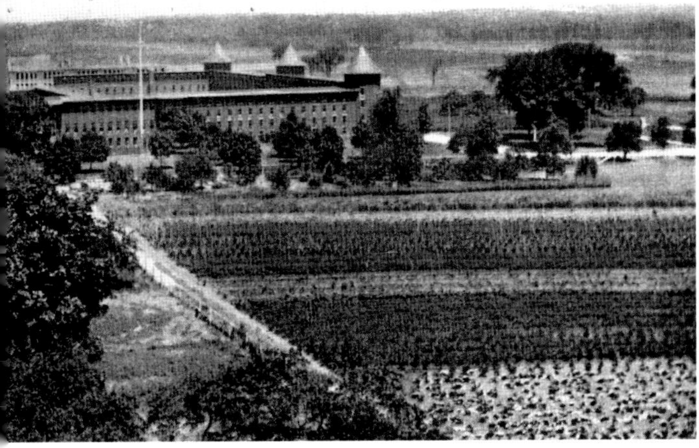

Panorama showing how large the State Farm had grown by 1910. The women's prison opened in 1909 appears in the left foreground. *Author's collection.*

state institutions as defective delinquents, a step originally proposed by Councilor Brennan in 1932. Those found not to be mentally defective were ordered to be released.[180]

A growing number of defective delinquents like Wilfred E. Besner successfully secured their freedom in the wake of this action. Besner had passed through a string of state institutions before being transferred in 1935 as a seventeen-year-old to Bridgewater as a defective delinquent on the grounds of having been refractory while in state care. "My one set of ragged clothes was taken from me and replaced with prison garb, and I was thrown into the company of hardened crooks, alcoholics, and sex offenders….I had never been arrested. No one had ever told me I was charged with a crime. I had no hearing and no judge sentenced me. How could this happen in Massachusetts, cradle of liberty?" Besner asked in 1953. After eighteen years of imprisonment, he was released in May 1953, at which time Judge Felix Forte of the Brockton Superior Court emphasized that Besner had been imprisoned without due process and without the benefit of a trial by jury.[181] Attorney Jack J. Moss similarly argued that Massachusetts's defective delinquent law was unconstitutional, as it permitted committal for the equivalent of a life sentence without the right of appeal or opportunity for release.

By 1953, the defective delinquent department had been largely discredited as a cruel institution in which numerous inmates were held in violation of their constitutional rights, committed without hearing and offered no

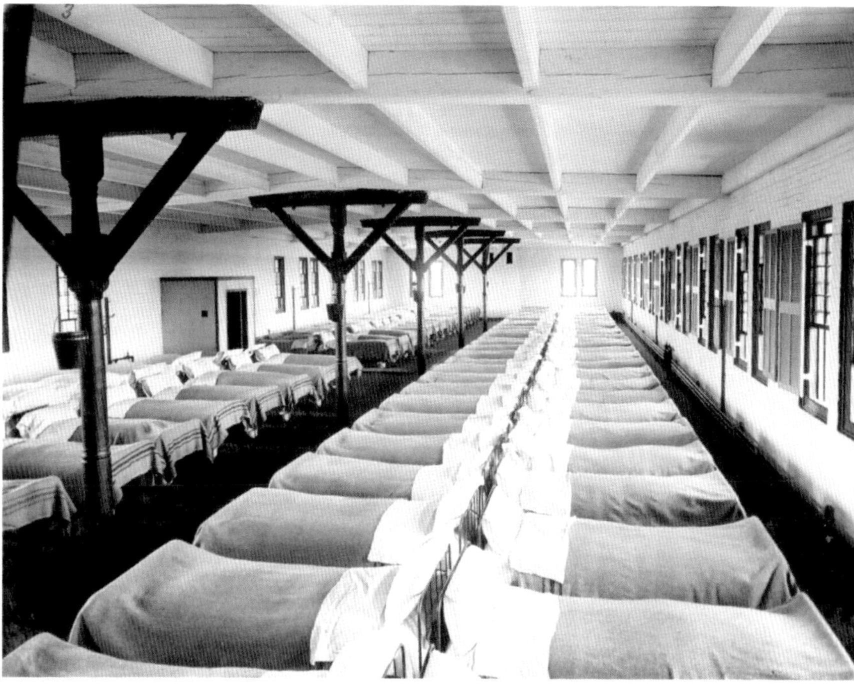

Bridgewater State Farm, prison dormitory, circa 1903. *Harvard Art Museums/Fogg Museum, Transfer from the Carpenter Center for the Visual Arts, Social Museum Collection, 3.2002.2710.3. Bass Photo. Imaging Department © President and Fellows of Harvard College.*

opportunity for release. Most lawmakers had accepted that two-thirds of the commonwealth's defective delinquents were being held illegally but grappled with how to balance the rights of the individual with the public's safety. Some argued that it would be calamitous to release them back into society, as many were mentally ill, and several recalled the case of Howard Long, who, following release from the Bridgewater defective delinquent department in October 1935, had subsequently murdered two New Hampshire boys in attempted sexual assaults. Penologists, criminal justice experts and legislators blamed the morass surrounding the defective delinquent situation on Massachusetts's several laws that were described as "confusing, contradictory and partially unconstitutional."[182] While efforts were made to clarify them, they remained largely in place until 1970, when the law was overturned and the defective delinquent department at Bridgewater abolished.

Chapter 6

# "A Hospital or a Stable?"

## Massachusetts Correctional Institution–Bridgewater, 1955–87

Though the situation of Bridgewater's defective delinquents began to see relief in the mid-twentieth century, criticism of conditions at the institution and the continuing plight of many of its other inmates mounted following 1955, despite a reorganization of the commonwealth's penal system in that year. While Bridgewater authorities were generally considered to be competent (as had not been the case in the 1930s), they were hampered in their efforts to stem deteriorating conditions because of limited funding and public apathy. The efforts of Superintendent Charles W. Gaughan and others to shed greater light on the state of Bridgewater in order to effect positive change encouraged a growing debate in the press, a development discouraged by Correction Commissioner John A. Gavin. The public's right to know, however, overruled Gavin's qualmishness that he shared with other top commonwealth officials, which Bridgewater critics attributed to a desire to keep the institution's shameful conditions secret. With public disclosure of these conditions, Bridgewater came to be regarded as among the worst penal institutions in the nation. Allegations of unlawful incarceration, abuse, the lack of medical treatment and deteriorating buildings that housed inmates in the meanest accommodations created public outrage and initiated remedial efforts in the courts to improve conditions. Though the crumbling physical plant was drastically improved, being replaced in part after 1974, charges of wrongful incarceration and allegations of mistreatment and abuse lingered throughout the era.

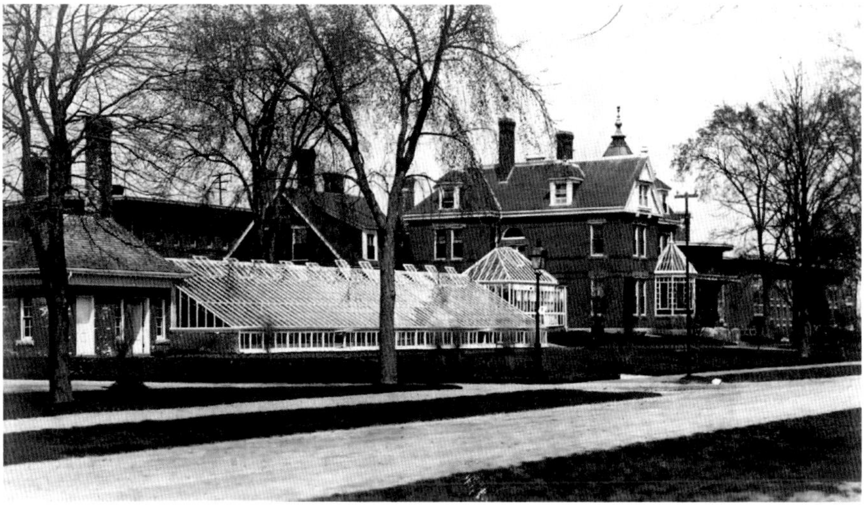

Bridgewater State Farm, greenhouses and superintendent's residence, circa 1910. The image indicates the high physical standard the facility once maintained. *Author's collection.*

## "A Hopeless Bastille"

In the wake of a January 1955 riot at Charlestown State Prison, an investigative committee headed by Tufts University president Dr. Nils Y. Wessel characterized the commonwealth's penal system as deplorable and recommended sweeping changes, including the establishment of a genuine classification system for prisoners and practical training programs for correctional officers and prison staff. Based on the report, the commonwealth's correctional facilities were reorganized, at which time the State Farm officially became the Massachusetts Correctional Institution (MCI)–Bridgewater, a nomenclatural change that underscored its role as a prison.[183]

Though reorganization was intended to establish "modern correctional practices," institutional roles remained largely unchanged.[184] The admittance of vagrants, state charges and aged or infirm convicts to Bridgewater was ended, leaving alcohol- and drug-dependent inmates to compose the majority of those confined in the prison there. Though the 1955 study committee recommended an alternative to imprisonment for alcoholism in the form of community treatment centers, the 1,200-bed prison department at Bridgewater remained filled with alcoholics, an unsurprising statistic given that two-thirds of those sentenced to correctional institutions in

Massachusetts in 1954 were sentenced for drunkenness, many still for terms of up to two years.

By far the greatest legislative concern and media attention was reserved for Bridgewater State Hospital, where 800 to 900 criminally insane individuals were confined in less than ideal conditions. "A shortage of personnel and the daily routine for patients leave much to be desired," noted the Wessel Committee report. "Patients are fed at 7:30 a.m., 11:30 a.m. and at 4:30 p.m., after which they are locked in their rooms or in the wards. No recreational program is available for the evening. Some patients' rooms are lacking in lights so that the patient cannot even read."[185] The lack of adequate medical treatment was also cited, a situation later exacerbated by the precipitous increase in the annual number of patients admitted for psychiatric observation, which skyrocketed from 137 in 1957 to 454 in 1966.

Increasingly, it was recognized that simple reorganization of the commonwealth's penal system would not be sufficient to remedy conditions at Bridgewater. A flurry of postwar plans for the commonwealth's prisons that variously considered improvement, replacement or expansion of Bridgewater's aging facilities went unrealized, and in 1958, when Governor Foster Furcolo requested $4.2 million for prison improvements in the commonwealth, he called Bridgewater State Hospital a "hopeless

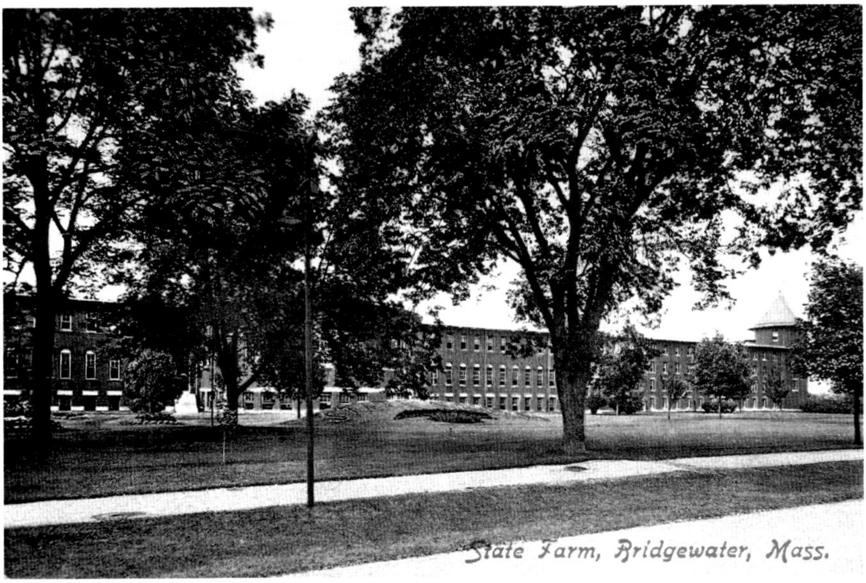


Bridgewater State Farm, prison department, circa 1910. The complex depicted on this picture postcard predated 1897 and was much outdated by the 1950s. *Author's collection.*

bastille," indicating the grim character of hospital accommodations.[186] While proposals for new hospital facilities at Bridgewater were made throughout the 1960s, it was not until 1974 that a new state hospital there was finally opened.

Adding to growing concerns over the level and quality of treatment at Bridgewater State Hospital was the facility's management by the Department of Correction, which had limited experience in the provision of psychiatric care in contrast to the Department of Mental Health. Senator Leslie B. Cutler of Needham and others argued that because of this administrative arrangement, inmates at Bridgewater were not being rehabilitated but merely confined. In December 1934, Commissioner of Correction Lyman had called for the Department of Mental Diseases to assume oversight of the hospital, and in April 1959, a similar proposal by Furcolo to transfer authority to the Department of Mental Health was made, but both were defeated by the legislature.

## "Forgotten Men"

The consequences for patients of the simmering disagreement between the Departments of Correction and Mental Health over which of the two should have jurisdiction over the state hospital and how care should be managed came to public attention through a 1963 *Boston Globe* exposé of some 240 Bridgewater State Hospital patients it termed "forgotten men." Confined an average of thirty years, these men had been convicted of petty crimes such as drunkenness, vagrancy, walking on railroad tracks and taking coins out of gas meters, and their sentences had long since expired. Others had never been convicted of any crime but had been confined by their families to one of the commonwealth's mental hospitals, where they had committed an offense that prompted their removal to Bridgewater as "dangerous."

Often cited was an inmate identified only as "Kippy," sentenced in 1938 for a two-year term on a charge of drunkenness after painting his horse to resemble a zebra. He remained jailed for the remainder of his life and died at Bridgewater in 1967. Another inmate, reported the *Globe*, had "been there for 62 years. Arrested in 1901 as a vagrant, he's now 86 years old and paralyzed in both legs. Old, crippled and many of them senile, they are still judged in need of the strictest confinement the commonwealth

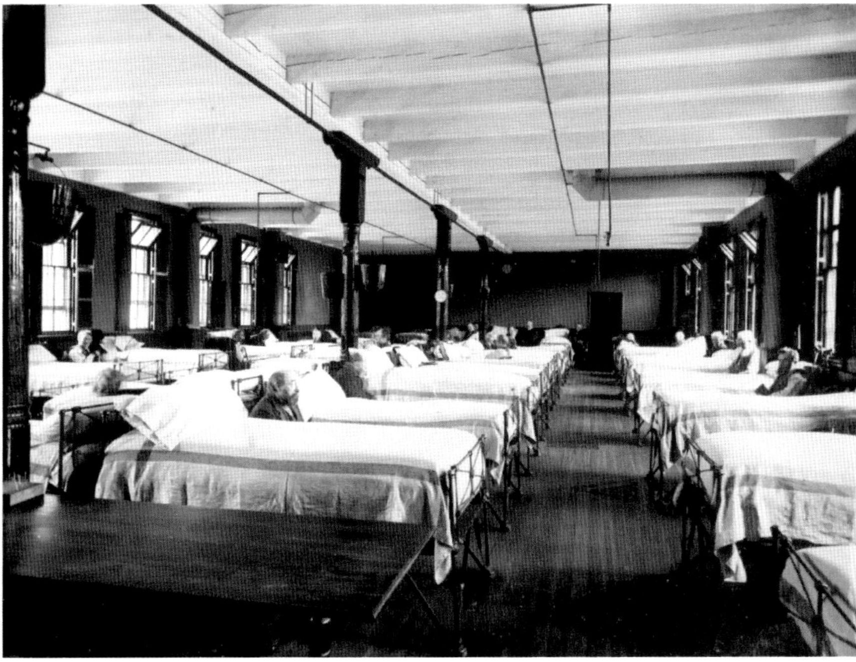

"Forgotten men" of an earlier generation. Bridgewater State Farm, infirmary, "Old Men's Ward," circa 1900. *Harvard Art Museums/Fogg Museum, Transfer from the Carpenter Center for the Visual Arts, Social Museum Collection, 3.2002.2711/4. Bass Photo. Imaging Department © President and Fellows of Harvard College.*

can provide. For many years they have been pawns in the shoving contest between the Corrections Dept. and the Mental Health Dept. The feud is still on."[187]

Correction Commissioner George McGrath, frustrated by what he saw as a lack of action on the part of the mental health department, criticized that department's inaction in relieving Bridgewater of mentally ill individuals no longer deemed dangerous, as well as its past treatment of Bridgewater "as a dumping ground for anyone whom the mental hospitals couldn't handle."[188]

At Bridgewater, Superintendent Gaughan, who had succeeded James E. Warren in 1959, was vexed by the politicking surrounding the matter. "I don't want to be in charge of any institution where this is going on year after year while bureaucrats here at the State House quibble over legal phraseology. We are asking you, out of pure humanitarianism to help these men."[189] In years to come, Gaughan would emerge as one of the most visible advocates for the inmates he was tasked with jailing, arguing that the plight of Bridgewater's "forgotten men" be considered on compassionate grounds.

He described them as "poor, burned out old men [who] have to mingle with 150 insane murderers....When arrested, some of them talked gibberish. The judge committed them to Bridgewater. It's as simple as that in most cases."[190] Without vocational occupation, they remained idle. "They are simply vegetating, waiting to die."[191] Commissioner McGrath concurred, insisting, "We want Bridgewater to be a truly therapeutic institution—not something hidden away in some dark corner of the state with a stone curtain around it."[192] Ultimately, mediation by Lieutenant Governor Francis X. Bellotti led to a resolution and an agreement by the Department of Mental Health to accept up to twelve transfers a month of senile inmates from Bridgewater.

In late 1967, the matter of whether some hospital patients were being illegally confined was raised when carnival worker Robert Rohrer petitioned for discharge on the grounds that he had been denied counsel prior to having been confined indefinitely at Bridgewater in 1963 on a vagrancy charge. The Supreme Judicial Court upheld Rohrer's claim and questioned the constitutionality of the state law that permitted the superintendent to issue warrants for indefinite committals of individuals sent merely for temporary observation.

In response, Attorney General Elliot Richardson initiated the Bridgewater Release Project, which determined that some 300 patients, or nearly 50 percent of the hospital population, were unlawfully

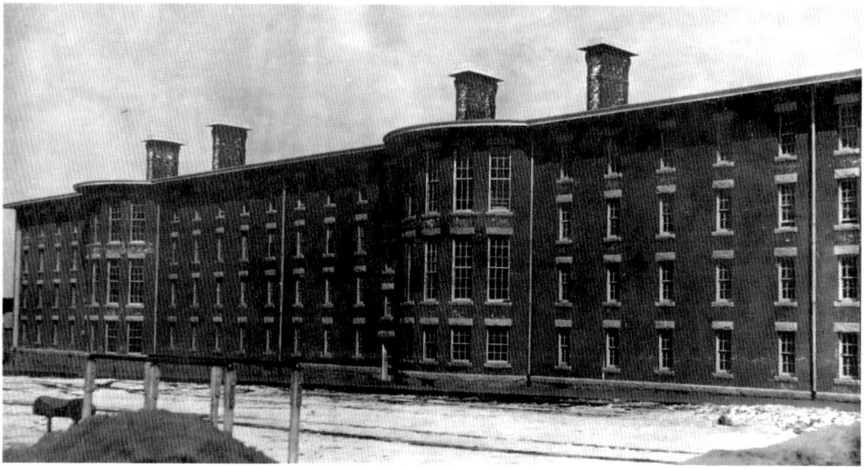

Bridgewater State Farm, wing of asylum for insane criminals, circa 1900, with accommodation for 140 patients in single rooms with day rooms and a hospital ward. *Harvard Art Museums/Fogg Museum, Transfer from the Carpenter Center for the Visual Arts, Social Museum Collection, 3.2002.2686.1. Unidentified Artist. Imaging Department © President and Fellows of Harvard College.*

confined. Hearings were subsequently held for 113 patients, all of whom were determined to have been illegally confined; 2 were discharged, 96 were committed to Department of Mental Health hospitals, 4 were recommitted to Bridgewater as dangerously ill, 8 remained at Bridgewater at their own request and 3 were committed to Veterans' Administration hospitals. "The vast number of transfers and discharges benefited not only the patients involved in the hearings," Richardson later wrote, "but also the remaining patients at Bridgewater, due to the salutary effect upon the staff–patient ratio there. It was a particularly gratifying experience to be involved in providing hearings for these 'forgotten men,' some of whom had been held unlawfully for many decades."[193]

## "The Boston Strangler"

Drawn into the growing debate over conditions at Bridgewater was the institution's most notorious inmate, Albert DeSalvo, the "Boston Strangler." Arrested on November 6, 1964, and committed to Bridgewater State Hospital for observation for the "Green Man" sexual assaults, DeSalvo was later transferred to Cambridge Prison before being recommitted to Bridgewater in February 1965. It was at Bridgewater the following month that DeSalvo confessed to the strangulation deaths of thirteen women between 1962 and 1964 in Boston. DeSalvo later withdrew his confession but was ultimately sentenced to life imprisonment in 1967 on ten counts of assault and burglary. He was never tried for the strangling deaths.

During the early morning of February 24, 1967, DeSalvo escaped from a locked cell on the third floor of an infirmary building, in the company of two other inmates. The men were presumed to have reached through the peepholes in their antiquated cell doors and used a fabricated key to open them before escaping through an unfinished elevator shaft and scaling a twelve-foot wall by means of scaffolding. They fled across open fields, leaving footprints in the freshly fallen snow and rolled blankets on their cots to simulate the form of sleeping bodies. Shortly afterward, DeSalvo contacted his attorney to turn himself in. He was subsequently sentenced to Walpole State Prison, where he was stabbed to death in his cell in 1973.

DeSalvo later claimed that the escape was intended to draw attention to conditions at Bridgewater. While successful in this, the investigation it prompted focused principally on security. State Senator John Conte of

Worcester alleged that security at Bridgewater was lax, with easily removable windows and some locks dating from the nineteenth century. A candid Gaughan agreed, describing it as "mental and not prison security" and telling the media that "we're holding murderers in a hen coop."[194] Commissioner Gavin proposed a plan to raze and replace the buildings at a cost of $32 million but got nowhere. DeSalvo's attorney, the ever controversial F. Lee Bailey, agreed, stating that the complex "should be leveled and I'd be happy to do it with my own plane."[195]

## "The State's Crime of the Century"

At this same time, living conditions inside Bridgewater State Hospital also came under scrutiny. A 1966 examination by the *Boston Globe* remarked that "somewhere between the emotional limits of horror and haven is the State Hospital for the Criminally Insane at Bridgewater."[196] Mental health commissioner Harry C. Solomon disparaged conditions there after the *Globe* documented "the most barbaric security practices."[197] F. Lee Bailey referred to Bridgewater as an "animal farm and garbage bin."[198] The *Globe* was only minimally less judgmental, asking in January 1967 whether Bridgewater was "a hospital or a stable?"[199]

Criticisms of Bridgewater were rooted in the absence of genuine psychiatric treatment as well as degrading living conditions resulting from a failure to modernize the nineteenth-century plant. A legislative investigation that followed the December 1966 suicide of inmate Domenic E. Rosati found outdated and decaying buildings, an inadequate hospital and recreational and kitchen facilities that failed to meet minimum sanitation requirements. Hay-drying equipment was used in the hospital to heat three wards after the heating system failed, while in several buildings the heat was turned on in the fall and left unadjusted until the spring due to the lack of a single thermostat in the entire complex. The hospital lacked proper medical or recreational facilities, though recreation rooms had been constructed in former coal bins and hallways "dank with dampness and permeated with odors from decades of forgotten men."[200] Most damning of all was the disclosure that 1,200 cells were without flush toilets or running water. Patients were expected to relieve themselves in a bucket, which they emptied once daily. Superintendent Gaughan, fiscally constrained to do anything about these conditions, confessed in 1967, "I

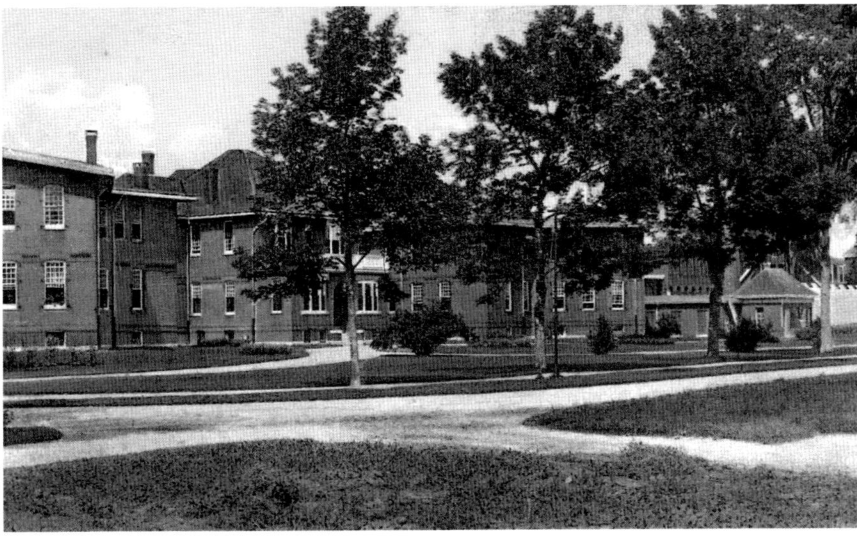

Bridgewater State Farm, asylum department, picture postcard, circa 1909. These buildings remained in use for patients as Bridgewater State Hospital until 1974. *Author's collection.*

can't accept any longer the responsibility for the upkeep of buildings in such disrepair. We can't keep these buildings about our head much longer. Every one of them has to be rebuilt."[201]

Equally disturbing were revelations regarding the quality and level of treatment provided in the hospital. Superior Court judge Henry H. Chmielinski testified that treatment and observation facilities at Bridgewater belonged "somewhere in the 17th or 18th century."[202] Medicine often went unadministered on the nurse's day off, and the hospital was understaffed, with two of four medical psychiatric positions being vacant. Commissioner Solomon urged radical action by the legislature, in the absence of which "Bridgewater will always be a problem."[203]

Not only were the conditions at Bridgewater perceived as a moral wrong, they also came to be challenged as a legal wrong. Martin Fay, chief counsel for the legislative committee investigating the needs and operations of the commonwealth's penal institutions, termed Bridgewater "the state's crime of the century."[204] In 1966 and 1967, the condition of 630 mental patients held at Bridgewater was found to be "cruel, inhuman and barbarous." The deprivation of adequate medical treatment, largely due to a lack of professionally trained treatment specialists, was deemed a violation of patients' civil rights, constitutive of cruel and unusual punishment.

This finding reflected growing acceptance of the "right to treatment" concept originated in 1960 by Dr. Morton Birnbaum, who asserted that mentally ill persons had a legal right to medical treatment.[205] In January 1967, when attorneys sought to transfer one patient from Bridgewater to a mental hospital, they argued that Bridgewater's failure to provide proper treatment was criminal and uncivil. In Bridgewater's care, the attorneys argued, their client was "becoming more withdrawn all the time and if he stays there will become nothing more than a vegetable."[206] Similar reports of prisoners confined to cells ceaselessly pacing in circles seemingly corroborated their claims.

President of the Massachusetts Bar Association attorney Paul A. Tamburello of Pittsfield argued that the physical conditions themselves were unconstitutional, maintaining that the commonwealth "must bow its head in shame over Bridgewater State Hospital until the physical facilities are corrected or abandoned." Describing the facilities as "deplorable," Tamburello wrote that men "live, eat and sleep under degrading conditions that do violence to our elemental concepts of decency" and insisted that the rights of all were being violated. "It has been held that, when elemental decency in confinement of prisoners has been abandoned by permitting conditions of a shocking and debased nature to prevail, the courts must properly intervene to restore primal roles of civilized community in accord with the Federal Constitution."[207]

## *Titicut Follies*

While the critical press attention Bridgewater received in 1966 and 1967 was largely confined to Massachusetts, a controversial documentary film, *Titicut Follies*, brought conditions within the institution to national attention, provoking a constitutional debate juxtaposing First and Fourth Amendment rights of free speech and individual privacy. While important in this regard, *Titicut Follies* was also significant for further raising awareness of conditions within the facility and in creating demand for reform.

Though Superintendent Gaughan approved filming as part of his effort to publicize conditions within the hospital, permission was subsequently revoked by Gaughan's immediate superior, State Commissioner of Correction John A. Gavin, who had earlier looked to minimize criticism of the institution. Intercession by then Lieutenant Governor Elliot Richardson

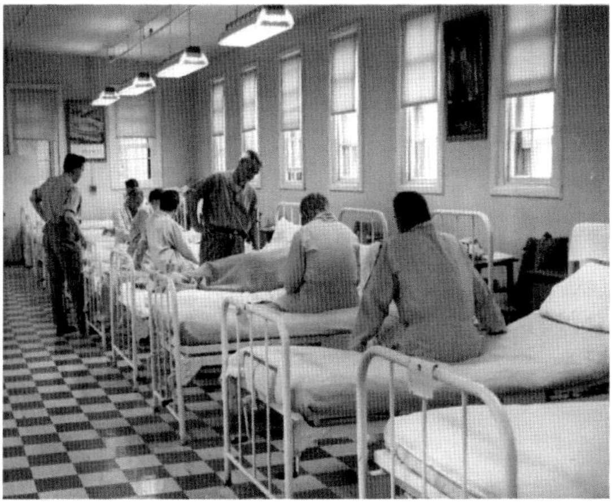

Bridgewater State Hospital Infirmary, 1966. *Courtesy of www.asylumprojects.org.*

and state representative Katherine Kane and a 1966 opinion by Senator Edward M. Brooke, then Massachusetts attorney general, that the film might be made if the rights of the inmates were protected led Gavin to rescind his refusal. Cambridge filmmaker and attorney Frederick Wiseman was subsequently permitted free access to the facility, with the exception of the Massachusetts Treatment Center for the sexually dangerous, which had been established at Bridgewater in the late 1950s and whose director, Harry Kozol, strongly objected to filming there without explicit written consent of the patients.

Filmed over twenty-nine days between April 22 and June 29, 1966, the documentary depicted scenes of humiliation, mistreatment and nudity, including the force feeding of an inmate, a patient being bullied by guards and another being questioned about abnormal sexual practices. These brutal episodes were intercut with pathetic scenes of the institution's annual musical revue, *Titicut Follies*, from which the film took its title. Democratic state representative Robert L. Cawley later described the film as "an exploitation of human misery."[208]

After viewing the completed film in 1967 with its unflinching portrayal of inmate life, Richardson claimed that Wiseman had "double-crossed" the commonwealth by exhibiting the film contrary to an oral agreement that its showing would be contingent upon approval by the commonwealth. The film was immediately banned in Massachusetts through a temporary restraining order on the grounds that it violated the privacy of the sixty-two patients depicted. "We had the responsibility to protect their rights," Richardson told reporter Roger Goodrich.

*The very simple and clear issue presented is the issue of individual rights and this is the basis on which I have taken action in the light of Attorney General Brooke's opinion given to Commissioner Gavin at his request when the question of allowing the film to be made first came up. In that opinion Attorney General Brooks said that the film could be within the discretion of the commissioner to allow if, but only if, individuals who were not competent to give their consent to having it made were not shown and if other individuals who were competent to understand the implications of the film were able intelligently to give waivers and did give waivers.*[209]

Wiseman contended that Massachusetts officials wished to hide the true conditions at Bridgewater, which had become an embarrassment to the commonwealth. "The state has a conflict of interest. It asserts that it wants to protect the inmates' privacy rights, but it really doesn't want the public to know how these people are treated."[210]

On January 4, 1968, Superior Court judge Harry Kalus issued an injunction against further showings of *Titicut Follies* in Massachusetts. The injunction was upheld on an appeal in 1969 by the Massachusetts Supreme Judicial Court, which ruled that the film constituted a "massive unrestrained invasion of the intimate lives of the patients at the institution." Viewing by specialized professional audiences was permitted, however, in recognition of the film's clinical value.[211] Meanwhile, efforts to ban the film outside Massachusetts were unsuccessful.

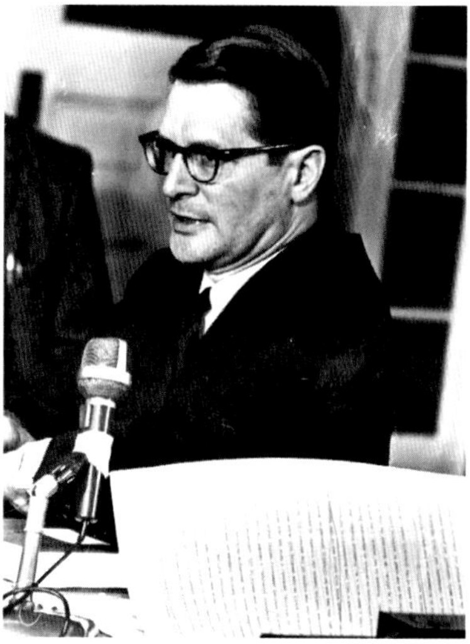

Massachusetts attorney general Elliot Richardson answers questions before the *Titicut Follies* hearing, November 1967. *Author's collection.*

*Titicut Follies* became noteworthy as the only American film ever to have been censored for reasons other than obscenity or national security concerns, while the court's decision marked Massachusetts's first recognition of an individual's right to privacy. Twice in 1970, the United States Supreme Court refused to hear the case, while Wiseman argued that the commonwealth's ban was a far greater threat to civil liberties than any infringement on inmate rights. Years later, reminiscing on the failure of the film to provoke immediate improvements, Wiseman remarked, "Ah, 'Titicut Follies.' It was all so simple then—make a film, show a situation and produce instant change. But then I continued through life and began to realize the untidiness of it all, the enormous complexity of people and the places they work and live in."[212]

## "The Worst Place I Have Visited"

If *Titicut Follies* did not bring about the sweeping social change Wiseman, Gaughan and others had hoped for, it nonetheless kept media attention focused on Bridgewater, intensifying scrutiny and fueling demands for improvements. Journalist and academic Bruce Jackson's 1968 *New York Times* examination of American prison conditions included a scathing indictment of Bridgewater:

> *Even now Massachusetts has one of the most wretched institutions in the country, the Correctional Institution at Bridgewater, designed to handle the "criminally insane." Fred Wiseman's portrayal of this place in "Titicut Follies" did not exaggerate; it is the worst place I have visited, North or South. I remember one building in particular with row upon row of door-lined corridors, and board floors and brick walls. Every few feet there was a wooden door braced shut by a beam and a Judas-hole to peek through. Some of the rooms had a bed and a pan, none had running water, some had nothing at all but a naked man wrapped in an army blanket.*[213]

While the media focused nearly exclusively on Bridgewater State Hospital during this period, conditions were no better in the treatment center where sexually dangerous persons were housed. In 1971, former inmate Arthur H. DeBour refuted a characterization of the treatment center as having "the most intensive treatment given in any institution in the world, public or private." DeBour described the conditions as execrable and noted the lack of any type of treatment or rehabilitative training: "Men committed to the Treatment Center are there to be helped. Yet they are forced to live in far worse conditions than men such as myself who are in prisons to be punished."[214]

In 1971, a citizens' committee named by Governor Francis W. Sargent to investigate the need for prison reform found conditions at Bridgewater unchanged since 1966. The group described the Departmental Segregation

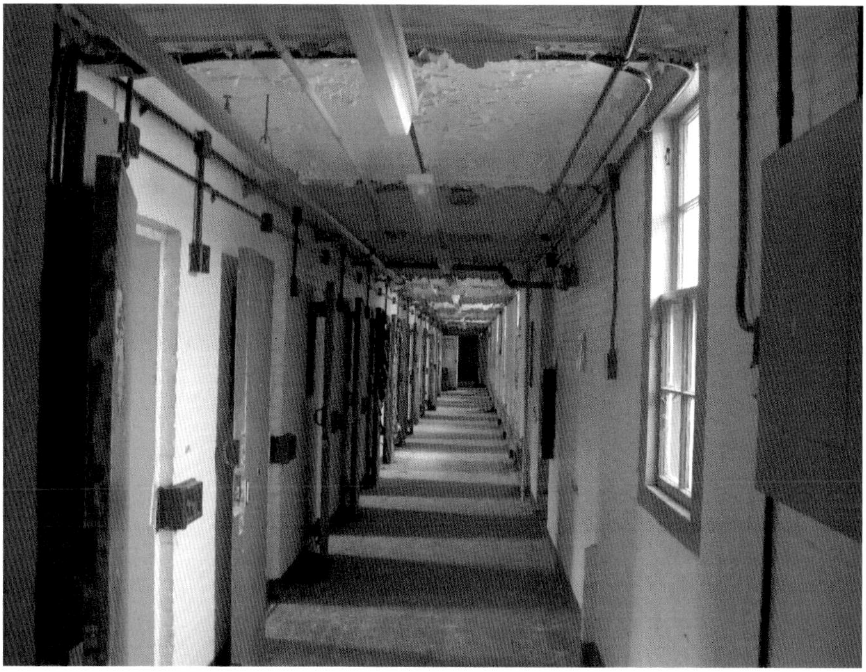

Bridgewater State Hospital, 2009, following its abandonment several years earlier. *Courtesy of www.asylumprojects.org.*

Unit, where unruly, disruptive, assaultive and dangerous inmates were sequestered, as a "medieval chamber of horrors" and a "filthy hole" furnished solely with a bed and a pot.[215] Inmates were confined to cells for twenty-three and a half hours with no toilets or running water. They were shaved and showered twice weekly and were denied radios and smoking privileges due to the fire hazard of the cells' wooden floors. Due to the committee's findings, the segregation unit, which committee member Judge Harry J. Elam described as "the worst of Bridgewater," was closed in 1972.[216]

Also at this time, changing social attitudes toward delinquency, alcoholism and homelessness brought improvement and radically altered Bridgewater's population. The defective delinquent department, long considered a failure, was statutorily abolished in 1970. In 1971, Massachusetts's Alcoholism Treatment and Rehabilitation Law decriminalized public intoxication and defined alcoholism as a "medically diagnosable disease," resulting in the reduction of Bridgewater's prison population to those who had been civilly committed for alcohol- and drug-related issues. The law also mandated that those committed to Bridgewater for treatment be housed and treated separately from convicted criminals.[217] The following year, homelessness was similarly decriminalized when vagrancy statutes were overturned as constitutionally vague and too arbitrarily enforced.

Ultimately, the prison department was superseded by new facilities. The Southeast Correction Center (SECC), opened in 1976 under separate administration, reduced crowding in the prison and segregated the prison population from that of the hospital. The SECC operated until 2002, when its role was assumed by the Old Colony Correction Center (OCCC), which opened in 1987 and operates today as a medium-security prison. In 2002, at the time the SECC closed, its addiction programs and services were transferred to the reorganized Massachusetts Alcohol and Substance Abuse Center.

## "They're Suing Us Right and Left"

Despite improvements within the prison department, court-based remediation efforts continued to focus on the state hospital and the treatment center as patients brought forward a number of legal suits, prompting a beleaguered Superintendent Gaughan to remark in 1975, "They're suing us right and left for thousands of dollars and it isn't necessary."[218]

In February 1968, the Massachusetts Supreme Judicial Court ruled in *John W. Nason v. Superintendent of Bridgewater State Hospital* that the institution had violated the civil rights of a mentally ill patient by withholding reasonable treatment from him.[219] The court found that "Bridgewater affords less adequate treatment than any other state hospital and we conclude that its staff and facilities still require substantial improvement before they will be able to provide fully suitable treatment to the patient."[220] The landmark ruling established a right to effective mental health treatment in Massachusetts.

Lack of work, job training programs and educational facilities; poor sanitary conditions; and inadequate medical care at the treatment center were similarly challenged in 1972 as unconstitutional.[221] A year prior, the absence of vocational opportunities had been criticized by the Sargent Committee, which noted that "there was a tremendous amount of idleness, lots of fellows just hanging around. It seemed like a complete waste of time."[222] In part, the limited opportunities were due to a reduction in farm work, which had once been the primary means of occupation. Neither Superintendent Gaughan nor Correction Commissioner Frank Hall disputed the findings, and in 1974 U.S. District Court judge Charles E. Wyzanski placed operation of the treatment center under the Department of Mental Health, ordered that the physical plant be improved and work programs and avocational activities be provided, prohibited sequestration (solitary confinement) for either punishment or discipline and mandated the establishment of rules and regulations to govern the daily operation of the center.

Poor physical conditions within the treatment center were also challenged in a 1972 class action lawsuit that contended that "grossly inadequate heating" leading to illness and discomfort constituted cruel and unusual punishment.[223] In 1974, in response to a similar suit brought by 151 addiction center inmates alleging that their constitutional rights had been violated by unsanitary conditions, inadequate heating and inoperable shower facilities, Federal Magistrate Willie J. Davis found that conditions in the older part of the facility did constitute cruel and unusual punishment. "The majority of inmates must wait until after they have eaten before they have an opportunity to clean themselves. The inmates must also empty their chamber pots before breakfast and quite often must take breakfast without seeing soap and water, even after handling excrement."[224]

The level of psychiatric treatment provided by Bridgewater State Hospital, which had not improved substantially since the 1968 Nason ruling, prompted still another action in 1974, resulting in an April 1975 finding by Davis that Bridgewater's failure to provide minimally adequate treatment constituted a violation of patients' rights. Davis found that "the only thing done for the patients (at the hospital) is the administration of drugs…prescribed by doctors without sufficient medical knowledge to do so. They are simply being maintained and controlled. They rarely, if ever, see a psychiatrist, are given heavy medication to keep them quiet, sit around all day with nothing to do and receive no individual course of treatment."[225] New admissions were usually prescribed drugs without knowledge of their clinical history, and Dr. A. Louis McGarry, director of the Mental Health Department's Division of Legal Medicine, estimated that 90 to 95 percent of patients at the hospital were daily sedated with 300 to 400 milligrams of Thorazine. Patient Thomas J. Swift testified that "crowd control is the only treatment that is given, there is no individual treatment."[226] Attorney James M. Pool argued that Bridgewater was a "dumping ground" where, without treatment, inmates were essentially sentenced for life; he attributed the situation in part to the difficulty in attracting qualified medical personnel due to low pay and lack of affiliation with any medical school.[227]

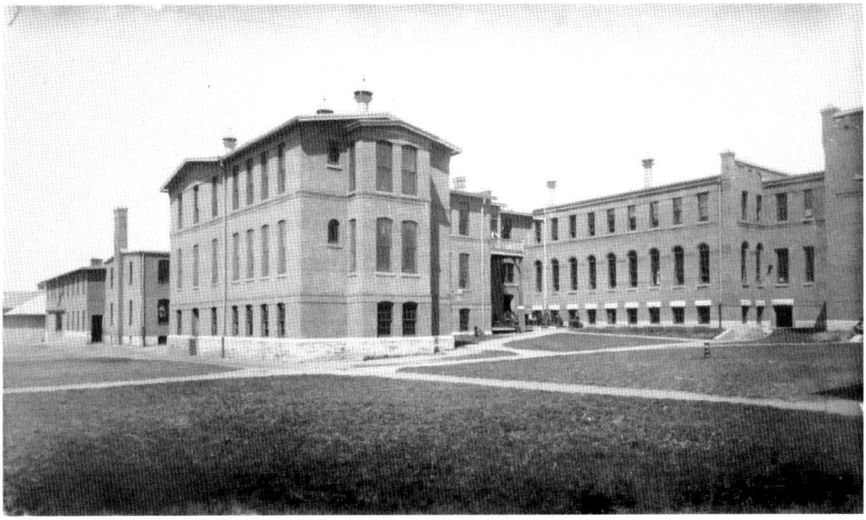

Bridgewater State Farm, hospital buildings, circa 1900. *Harvard Art Museums/Fogg Museum, Transfer from the Carpenter Center for the Visual Arts, Social Museum Collection, 3.2002.2711/1. Bass Photo. Imaging Department © President and Fellows of Harvard College.*

While previous committees and courts had absolved Bridgewater's administrators from responsibility for these conditions, Davis was less sparing, acknowledging that though Gaughan and Commissioner Hall were not directly responsible for the poor conditions that persisted, they still had a duty to those confined: "If mere custodial care for the patients at Bridgewater is violative of the Constitution, then the fact that the defendants are unable to improve conditions because of the lack of funds is no excuse."[228] Though Davis's criticism was understandable, it was still a harsh judgement, particularly on Gaughan, who for a decade had fought assiduously to bring public attention to the conditions at Bridgewater. Gaughan was clearly dissatisfied with the situation and recognized that administrative difficulties at Bridgewater State Hospital were in large part due to its control by the Department of Correction, which exempted it from the higher standards required by the commonwealth of its psychiatric hospitals. He labeled Bridgewater "a bastard institution" under jurisdiction of the Department of Correction with psychiatric services furnished by the Department of Mental Health.[229] Edward V. Keating, clerk of Suffolk Superior Court, suggested that the remedy was to transfer control of Bridgewater to the Department of Mental Health, arguing that a new facility alone was not sufficient to remedy issues there.

## "No More Warehousing of Human Beings"

Improvements at Bridgewater during the early 1970s occurred in response to court-ordered action. In 1974, a new $10 million, 450-bed replacement hospital opened with a campus-style arrangement of eight buildings, providing for modern facilities that permitted treatment of groups of up to 48 patients. At the time construction was announced, Superintendent Gaughan promised, "We'll have no more warehousing of human beings." In 1975 and 1976, installation of chemical toilets in the older part of the institution was undertaken, and plans for a new $5 million treatment center to hold 120 to 150 sexually dangerous persons were announced. Most promisingly, in 1975, Bridgewater contracted with McLean Hospital, the psychiatric training hospital for Harvard University, for the provision of mental health services. The subsequent dramatic reversal in the quality of treatment provided at Bridgewater State Hospital led the *Boston Globe*, long critical of the institution, to characterize it in 1980 as among the commonwealth's best mental health facilities.

Ironically, improvements in the level of psychiatric services provided by Bridgewater were accompanied by an overall decline in conditions, and by 1985, the hospital was "beset by severe overcrowding, allegations of brutality and charges that scores of inmates are being sent there inappropriately and left to languish without adequate care," long-standing complaints that continued uninterrupted.[230] The new hospital, designed to hold some three hundred, by mid-decade was housing five hundred patients.

Overcrowding at Bridgewater was the result of a number of factors. Deinstitutionalization throughout the commonwealth left fewer alternatives for mentally ill individuals requiring some level of security, who were consequently placed in the criminal justice system. The suddenly high reputation of Bridgewater's mental health services made the hospital more appealing than other institutions and led to increased admissions, though it was cynicism on the part of the *Boston Globe* when it suggested that overcrowding was due to district and superior court judges remanding individuals there for pre-trial evaluation because "they apparently like the Harvard Medical School touch they get from the McLean staff better than the report they might get from a less prestigious state mental hospital staff."[231]

An increase in the number of individuals convicted of petty offenses such as vagrancy and trespassing also swelled Bridgewater's population, as the commonwealth's lack of a suitable medium-security facility left few options for judges despite a state law that mandated that mentally ill patients who were not judged dangerous were entitled to treatment at a facility other than a maximum-security penal institution like Bridgewater.

Given the pettiness of their offenses, many patients were deemed "inappropriate admissions," individuals who were in need of psychological help but not within the confines of a maximum-security institution. "Officials said one man was admitted for 40-day observation for failing to put the correct change in a toll booth." Dr. William S. James, the hospital's medical director, estimated that over a quarter of those admitted to Bridgewater each year for pre-trial observation did not warrant confinement at Bridgewater, while McLean representatives determined that two-thirds of Bridgewater committals were "inappropriate."[232] Similarly, a 1979 review completed by state hospital staff concluded that half of the patients did not belong there and that some 60 or more of the 370 patients were not dangerous and should be housed at a medium-security facility. Dr. Robert A. Fein, deputy medical director at Bridgewater, testified that anywhere from 400 to 600 of the 1,100 patients admitted between July 1978 and June 1979 had been inappropriately admitted to Bridgewater.

James saw a more sinister aspect to the increase and argued that the rise in commitments was due to the historic practice of sentencing unwanted individuals to Bridgewater. "Many of the people ending up in Bridgewater today are people who are not terribly popular with the courts or their communities. The truth of the matter is they need help. They do not belong here but no one else wants anything to do with them."

## Screw: A Guard's View of Bridgewater State Hospital

Renewed allegations of abuse at the institution came in 1981 with the publication of a book by former correctional officer Thomas Ryan titled *Screw: A Guard's View of Bridgewater State Hospital*, which stated that correctional officers had beaten patients, withheld food and toilet privileges as punishment, taunted inmates, written false reports and were otherwise abusive toward patients. While Gaughan and the president of the Bridgewater guards' union refuted these charges, many critics saw in them a need for better training, an issue that had been regularly advocated over the previous decades. Ryan also perceived a larger moral imperative, writing, "Bridgewater insults our common humanity….Bridgewater is the bottom line for our society and for all of us. It is not a special hell for an isolated group of people, different from the rest of humanity, but a place where anyone of us can end up under the right amount of pressure at a given moment."[233]

Allegations made in the book seemingly confirmed legal claims made against the institution, including a 1982 class action that alleged that patients had been restrained or placed in seclusion without medical approval and that new arrivals were stripped to their underwear and placed in solitary confinement in bare cells. Two years later, an agreement filed in U.S. District Court prohibited sequestration for nonmedical reasons except as authorized by the superintendent in consultation with the chief psychiatrist, restricted the use of physical restraints, required the provision of weather-appropriate clothing, prohibited the stripping of patients for reasons other than self-protection and mandated institution of a grievance procedure.

While this agreement called for comprehensive changes in how patients were treated, the courts also made it clear that improvements had been made at Bridgewater. In his ruling in a 1985 suit, U.S. District judge Andrew A. Caffrey found that confinement of civilly committed mentally ill patients with the criminally committed was not a violation of patients' constitutional rights, that the use of seclusion and restraints at Bridgewater was not excessive or arbitrarily imposed and that the care provided was adequate and at times extraordinary. While Caffrey found that incidents of abuse and mistreatment had occurred, they had been isolated and addressed at the time, and the standard of treatment had improved since 1982.[234] The following year, the First Circuit Court of Appeals upheld Caffrey's decision.[235] Though the appellate court recognized that "the level of care at Bridgewater can be a matter of legitimate and deeply felt differences," it stressed that the question was whether such care met a constitutionally mandated *minimum* and found that it did. The ruling was controversial, eliciting a sharp editorial reply from the *Boston Phoenix*, which characterized the decision as uncivilized.[236]

Chapter 7

# "Recoil, Reform, Repeat"

## Massachusetts Correctional Complex–Bridgewater, 1987–2017

Though not all critics of the institution may have agreed, by 1987, MCI-Bridgewater appeared to have turned itself around. At Bridgewater State Hospital, which had been the most troubled of the institution's units, staffing had increased and the quality of mental health services offered had improved so greatly that they were considered superior to those provided by the commonwealth's other mental health institutions. Modern prison facilities with their own administrators had opened, and the state hospital was also placed under separate administration in that same year. In April 1990, the existence of MCI-Bridgewater as a commonly administered entity was effectively terminated when the Massachusetts Treatment Center was made a separate facility, the fourth at Bridgewater under its own superintendent. Since that time, the several units have been collectively known as the Bridgewater Correctional Complex.

In 1986 and 1987, however, a string of unexplained deaths over the course of eighteen months at the state hospital, including three possible suicides of sequestered patients and one who died while in restraint, triggered a state investigation and placed the hospital back in the public eye, where it has since remained. Following these deaths, a group of patients filed suit alleging that their rights had been violated by inadequate care, understaffing and overcrowding and that the commonwealth had been negligent in permitting abuse and sequestration of patients. Suffolk Superior Court judge James P. Lynch Jr. concluded that Bridgewater's patients required greater medical attention and found that they had frequently and carelessly been placed in solitary confinement and restrained, contrary to a 1985 law restricting use of sequestration and restraints, and he ordered immediate compliance.[237]

The 1987 investigation and ruling revived long-standing issues. Once more, the lingering question of whether the hospital should be administered by the Department of Correction or the Department of Mental Health was raised. Though it was classified as a correctional institution under Massachusetts law, Secretary of Human Services Philip Johnston's investigative committee acknowledged that Bridgewater differed "significantly from other state correctional facilities in its character, population and purpose. Indeed, in these respects, Bridgewater is substantially more closely akin to Department of Mental Health facilities with the additional complicating factor of Bridgewater's special safety and security needs." Another finding was that the mixed classification system persisted. "Clearly, the 'mixed' nature of the Bridgewater patient population, whose commonality lies both in their need to be hospitalized and in society's need to isolate the dangerous mentally ill individuals, distinguishes Bridgewater in both orientation and purpose from traditional correctional and mental health institutions."[238] The historic portrayal of Bridgewater as a "dumping ground' for unwanted patients was resurrected when the 1987 report characterized Bridgewater as the "end of the line" and "facility of last resort." To this was added a new criticism that challenged the practice of confining civilly and criminally committed individuals in common at Bridgewater State Hospital.

Changes were promised following the investigation. In October 1987, an emergency bill funding the hire of 186 new full-time staff members and installation of video monitoring equipment was approved, and immediate compliance with sequestration and restraint laws was advocated. Secretary Johnston told a national audience on ABC's *Nightline* on August 25, 1987, that "the policy of our administration is that civil commitments will not and should not be sent to Bridgewater State Hospital" and later assured that the practice of sending mentally ill persons who had not been convicted of a crime to Bridgewater would be ended following March 1989, as would sequestration of new admissions and strip searches of patients.[239]

Many questioned the level of substantive change made at Bridgewater State Hospital following 1987, and ABC *Nightline* host Ted Koppel asked in a follow-up report in 1989 "why insane people who have committed no crime are still being housed in what is supposed to be a facility for the criminally insane." Massachusetts was (and remains) one of only two states to permit joint confinement of the civilly and criminally committed in a common facility.

While contemporaneous improvements within the treatment center demonstrated the Department of Correction's ability to operate that facility consistent with patient rights and goals of treatment, they also highlighted the lack of corresponding developments within the state hospital.[240] In February 1997, a thirty-eight-year-old patient died after being placed in restraint following an attack on an officer. The commonwealth later reached a settlement with the patient's family. In 2003, administrators agreed to reduce reliance on sequestration and physical restraint in order to secure national accreditation as a mental health care provider, which had been sought since 1997. The death of patient Joshua K. Messier, who died in 2009 while being restrained during a schizophrenic attack, and additional deaths under similar circumstances in 2010 and 2013 once more raised questions about the use of restraint to calm and control patients, as well as the level of training provided to correctional officers. Debate has since raged over the events surrounding Messier's death. Three officers involved have been indicted on manslaughter charges, while the head of the Massachusetts Corrections Officers Federated Union attributed ongoing issues at Bridgewater to "failures in leadership, training and policy development" on the part of the commonwealth.[241]

The *Boston Globe* reported that despite the circumstances surrounding these deaths, the use of physical restraint increased 27 percent through the end of 2013. A report by the Disability Law Center in 2014 concluded that what it saw as an excessive use of restraint and sequestration was "symptomatic of a more fundamental problem:...patients with serious mental illness are being held and 'treated' within a correctional facility rather than within a mental health facility."[242]

Prompted by these reports, as well as a threat to Bridgewater's accreditation and another lawsuit, Governor Deval Patrick in July 2014 proposed a reform package calling for better training to reduce the use of sequestration and restraints, the hiring of additional full-time mental health clinicians, physical upgrades and the creation of de-escalation rooms and the relocation of many mentally ill patients to less restrictive facilities. The proposal was stymied by the legislature, citing a budget shortfall and disagreement over how best to solve Bridgewater's problems.

Since then, Bridgewater has continued in its same pattern of crisis-instigated response or, as the headline of the November 20, 2016 *Boston Globe* put it, "recoil, reform, repeat."[243] On April 8, 2016, a mentally ill patient committed suicide while confined to his cell, prompting one newspaper to refer to Bridgewater State Hospital as a "moral stain."[244] Most recently, Governor Charlie Baker has called for sweeping changes to remedy long-standing issues at the hospital. In his 2017 State of the Commonwealth address, Baker announced:

> *For decades, mental health advocates have urged the Commonwealth to redesign the way it serves those who are committed to Bridgewater State Hospital. Little has changed, and the results, in many cases, have been disastrous for all involved.*
>
> *We propose to do two things to address this longstanding and unacceptable situation.*
>
> *First, move Corrections Officers out of the hospital. And instead deploy them outside the facility to provide security.*
>
> *Second, the size and scale of the clinical program offered inside the hospital will be significantly expanded. This reform will not come cheap, as spending on clinical services will increase by $37 million. It's the right thing to do and we ask the legislature to support it.*[245]

Consistent with the governor's proposals, the commonwealth in January 2017 contracted with Correct Care Solutions, a behavioral healthcare provider and acknowledged leader in the reduction of seclusion and restraint, for the provision of clinical care at Bridgewater State Hospital. Included as part of the services provided will be individualized treatment plans, a change first advocated for the hospital in 1929; enhanced and ongoing training; and limitation of contact with patients by correctional officers, who will be dedicated to providing perimeter security.

It will remain up to the commonwealth to determine where Bridgewater goes from here.

# Afterword

In 1864, when the State Board of Charities labeled the Bridgewater State Almshouse as among "the most severely criticized, and the least agreeable to the philanthropist of all our public institutions," little did it realize this characterization would remain applicable for the next century and a half. Throughout much of its history, the Bridgewater correctional complex and particularly its most public unit, Bridgewater State Hospital, has continually been troubled by challenges that have persisted from the outset.

The commonwealth's failure to maintain a clear mandate for Bridgewater or to create proper custodial classification of its inmates nearly immediately confounded Bridgewater's role and hampered its effective operation. As early as 1870, it was recognized as a penal institution in all but name, yet despite this, mentally ill individuals in need of care that only the commonwealth's mental hospitals were equipped to provide were admitted to Bridgewater, which also continued to fulfill a role as a pauper institution. Commingling of the criminal, the poor, the mentally disturbed, the aged, the ill and the infirm at Bridgewater made it a challenge to administer the institution or to effectively rehabilitate its inmates. Issues arose, as well, from the admixture of civilly and criminally committed individuals. While the asylum at Worcester recognized the difficulties arising from the mixing of these two classes, its subsequent transfer of the criminal insane to Bridgewater merely shifted the problem there, which in time was recognized not only as an administrative concern but a constitutional one as well. Remarkably, Massachusetts remains one of only two states to operate a forensic psychiatric hospital under the control of its Department of Correction.

Inability to consistently staff Bridgewater historically compromised the level of mental healthcare and vocational training programs provided, contributing at times to violence and abuse directed at both inmates and officers and limiting the institution's ability to effect substantial rehabilitation and lower recidivism rates. Since the mid-twentieth-century development of the "right to treatment" concept, attorneys and courts have tackled treatment concerns as civil rights issues as well. Closely related is the matter of staff and officer training in the institution, where, notably, the first administrators were valued more for their farming knowledge than their sociological, penological or medical expertise. Since that time, the institution has continually been challenged to raise its level of professionalism, level of staffing and quality of training.

Periodic abusive treatment and violence remains a historical reality. Grievances including the failure to provide proper clothing and the denial of a right of appeal to the superintendent first noted in the nineteenth century have remained persistent, resurfacing in litigation as late as 1982. The use of sequestration and physical restraint to control inmates likely dates back to the establishment of the institution, when "exemplary punishment" was prescribed for the lazy, the refractory and the disobedient. Former officers in 1877, 1913 and 1981 publicized allegations of maltreatment of inmates by fellow officers. The use of sequestration as a punitive response was confirmed during investigations in 1877, and physical restraint led to inmate deaths in 1912 and 1952, but it was not until the 1980s that the use of both was procedurally restricted and statutorily defined. Despite the restraining deaths of inmates in 1997, 2009, 2010 and 2013, a report by the Prisoners' Legal Services in early 2017 alleged that sequestration and restraint of the mentally ill was still occurring, in possible violation of state law and departmental procedures.

Also considered at times as "cruel and unusual" have been the accommodations provided. From the start, the physical plant was shoddily constructed, and when the original almshouse was replaced in 1883, it was built to the lowest habitable standard. The mindset of "good enough" prevailed throughout much of the century, resulting in a failure to modernize the facility such that conditions by the mid-twentieth century were among the worst in the nation.

What improvements have come to Bridgewater over the course of time have largely been the product of crisis-instigated investigations and court orders. Highly publicized investigations in 1858, 1870, 1874, 1877, 1931, 1933, 1942, 1967 and 1987 followed in the wake of unaccounted deaths, deplorable living conditions or allegations of maladministration and resulted in remedial efforts by the legislature and the courts.

Perhaps Bridgewater's most tragic historic aspect has been the persistent stigmatization of its residents—the poor, the homeless, the mentally ill, the developmentally disabled, the addicted and the criminal—as society's unwanted, undesirable and forgettable. Equally terrible has been the consequent perception and use of Bridgewater as a "dumping ground" where these unfortunate individuals were sent, many of them permanently and without due process. Though on the whole legislators, administrators, officers and doctors within the institution have had and continue to have the best intentions, not until this view of Bridgewater's patients and inmates is changed and Bridgewater is regarded as a rehabilitative rather than a punitive institution will the commonwealth overcome the issues that have troubled the institution from the start. Then may Bridgewater become the exemplar of the commonwealth's public welfare that it once sought to be.

# Notes

## *Abbreviations*

*BDA* *Boston Daily Advertiser*
*BG* *Boston Globe*
*BP* *Boston Post*
BPC Report of the Massachusetts Board of Prison Commissioners
BSC Report of the Massachusetts Board of State Charities
CP Report of the Massachusetts Commissioners of Prisons
MBP Report of the Massachusetts Bureau of Prisons
*MG* *Middleboro Gazette*
MPL Middleborough Public Library
*NG* *Namasket Gazette*
*NYT* *New York Times*
*OCM* *Old Colony Memorial*
SAB Report of the Inspectors of the State Almshouse at Bridgewater
SAM Report of the Inspectors of the State Almshouse at Monson
SAT Report of the Inspectors of the State Almshouse at Tewksbury
SFB Report of the Trustees of the State Farm at Bridgewater
SWB Report of the Inspectors of the State Workhouse at Bridgewater/ Report of the Trustees of the State Workhouse at Bridgewater

## *Introduction*

1. Sanborn, "Poor-Laws of New England," 486, 487. See BSC, October 1864, 236–45 for an overview of poor law development in Massachusetts to 1854.
2. Quincy in BSC, October 1864, 239.
3. *An Act in Relation to Paupers Having No Settlement in This Commonwealth*, 1852 Mass. Acts 275.

## *Chapter 1*

4. Quoted by Hollis M. Blackstone in *Bridgewater Book*, 37. 1852 Mass. Acts 275, appropriated $100,000 for construction of the commonwealth's three almshouses.
5. SAB, December 1856, 4.
6. *Report of the Working Group on Bridgewater State Hospital*, August 10, 1987, 9. Superintendent Blackstone, in an impatient 1886 letter complaining about poor telephone service at the State Farm, described its location as "4 miles back in the country." Letter, Hollis M. Blackstone to Mr. Hatch, General Manager of the Southeastern Massachusetts Telephone Company, June 28, 1886, Massachusetts State Archives, State Farm (Bridgewater, MA), State Workhouse/State Farm superintendent letter books, 1883–1912, HS9.10/2525X, Box 1: 1883–1891, vol. 1, 291, 292.
7. *Report of the Inspectors of the State Almshouse, at Monson, for the Year Ending December 31, 1854.* Blackstone maintained that the wood-frame construction was necessitated by the "meagre appropriation for the great undertaking" (Blackstone, *Bridgewater Book*, 37). SAT, 1854, 9.
8. Blackstone, *Bridgewater Book*, 38.
9. SAB, October 1860, 5.
10. Ibid., October 1859, 14 and October 1864, 16.
11. *NG*, "State Alms House at Titicut," August 13, 1855, 3.
12. 1852 Mass. Acts 275; *An Act in Relation to State Charitable and Correctional Institutions*, 1863 Mass. Acts 240; *An Act to Create a State Board of Health, Lunacy and Charity*, 1879 Mass. Acts 291; *An Act to Establish a State Board of Health*, 1886 Mass. Acts 101; *An Act to Establish a State Board of Insanity*, 1898 Mass. Acts 433.
13. SAB, October 1858, 3; SFB, December 1908, 11.
14. SAT, December 1854, 4.

15. John O'Connor, *The Workhouses of Ireland: The Fate of Ireland's Poor* (Dublin: Anvil Books, 1995) and numerous other sources document the negative Irish view of workhouses.
16. SAB, January 1855, 11–22.
17. *MG*, "North Middleboro," April 21, 1905, 4. See also Creedon Papers, MPL, "Climate Too Severe."
18. *BP*, "Naturalized Voters in Massachusetts," February 15, 1859.
19. BSC, October 1864, 298. In 1866, the Tewksbury almshouse began officially accepting "pauper insane," and it is often stated to have been the first in the state to do so, though in fact for years prior to this date the state's almshouses had been informally accepting mentally disturbed inmates.
20. SAT, 1856, 5.
21. SAB, October 1861, 5. In 1873, Bridgewater's chaplain recommended classification of lunatics into "well disposed" and "incorrigible"; see report for 1873.
22. SAB, October 1863, 4.
23. Pride, *Short History of Tewksbury*, 56.
24. SAB, October 1857, 10.
25. Ibid., October 1858, 12; *An Act in Relation to the State Almshouses*, 1858 Mass. Acts 168.
26. Physician's Report in SAB, January 1856, 15. The second most common reason for hospitalization was childbirth, euphemistically referred to as "parturition."
27. Ibid., 21. Not until 1895 did Massachusetts establish the nation's first state tubercular hospital at Rutland.
28. SAB, October 1857, 11.
29. Senate Doc. No. 2, 1858 in BSC, October 1864, 293.
30. *An Act Providing for the Classification of State Paupers*, 1855 Mass. Acts 412.
31. BSC, October 1864, 307.
32. Ibid., 305.
33. Ibid., 294, 304, 305.
34. Ibid., xxvi, 297.
35. Ibid., xxv.
36. SAB, October 1860, 4; October 1864, 6; October 1866, 5.
37. Ibid., January 1856, 5.
38. SAM, 1854.
39. The description of inmate life is taken from "Rules and Regulations of the State Almshouse, Monson" in SAM, 1854.

40. SAT, 1855, 15.
41. BSC, October 1964, 305.
42. *Morning Journal* [Halifax, NS], December 17, 1855, 2.
43. *BP*, "Massachusetts Legislature," January 8, 1859; see also BSC, October 1864, 247.
44. *BP*, "Massachusetts Legislature," January 14, 1859.
45. BSC, October 1864, 285.

## *Chapter 2*

46. Bullock in *BP Supplement*, "Massachusetts Legislature," January 4, 1868, 1.
47. Sanborn, "Poor-Law Administration," 11.
48. Bullock in *BP*, "The Governor's Messagc," January 5, 1867, 4; Blackstone, *Bridgewater Book*, 37.
49. *BP*, "Boston Post Court Record," November 17, 1869, 3; *BP*, November 27, 1869, 4; *BP*, "Chelsea," December 2, 1869, 3.
50. CP, January 1873, 33.
51. Senate Report No. 110, 1870, quoted in *Bridgewater Correctional Complex*, 1.
52. Blackstone, *Bridgewater Book*, 37.
53. *BP*, "Outrageous, If True," May 3, 1872, 3.
54. Blackstone, *Bridgewater Book*, 38.

## *Chapter 3*

55. *An Act to Abolish the State Almshouses at Bridgewater and Monson*, 1872 Mass. Acts 45.
56. Ibid. On January 9, 1873, a convoy of thirty-six criminals and paupers with sentences ranging from six months to two years were transferred from Tewksbury to Bridgewater. In March, an additional thirty-six were transferred to Bridgewater from Tewksbury.
57. BSC, October 1876, 152–53.
58. *OCM*, "County and Elsewhere," July 26, 1883, 4.
59. SWB, September 30, 1879, 4.
60. *BG*, "Malden," March 14, 1881.
61. SWB, September 30, 1878, 4.
62. *BG*, "A Rumored Murder," May 27, 1874, 2.
63. Ibid., "The Other Side," May 7, 1877, 5.

64. Ibid., "The Bridgewater Workhouse," July 20, 1877, 2.
65. Ibid., "That Investigation," October 27, 1877.
66. BSC, January 1878, 215.
67. Ibid., lii. Again in 1883, allegations of systematic cruelty, including beatings, failure to clothe some inmates properly and withholding food, were levied against the workhouse, this time by John McGrath, a former inmate released for good behavior. One officer was allegedly known as the "John L. Sullivan" of Bridgewater due to the beatings he meted out to prisoners.
68. *An Act Concerning Vagrants and Vagabonds*, 1866 Mass. Acts 235.
69. *BG*, "On the Tramp," January 28, 1879.
70. Ibid. Ironically, the *Globe* article was carried immediately above another reflecting a more compassionate approach to vagrancy, reporting conversion of the Mayhew schoolhouse on Hawkins Street in Boston to a lodging place "for homeless wanderers" where vagrants could voluntarily find a bed and work without the harshness of the workhouse.
71. *An Act for the Protection of the People of the Commonwealth against Tramps*, 1880 Mass. Acts 257.
72. *BG*, "Returned in Poverty," November 24, 1885, 3
73. Fields, *Letters of Sarah Orne Jewett*, 13.
74. *BG*, "On the Tramp," January 28, 1879.
75. Ibid., "State Workhouse Burned," July 8, 1883, 1.
76. *BDA*, "City and Suburbs," July 16, 1885, 8.
77. *BG*, "Alcoholic Poisoning," July 31, 1891, 1. In a letter to J. White Belcher of the board of trustees, dated July 27, 1891, Blackstone elaborated on the circumstances surrounding the incident following the death of twenty-four-year-old inmate James Rice on July 26: "The wood alcohol or alcoline is used in paint shops in place of alcohol for cutting shellac and varnish and is known to be very poisonous by all who use it. Rice had a companion, Walter C. Chamberlain who was taken sick this morning and confessed they had stolen wood alcohol from the paint shop and drank it.…I regret sincerely the sad accident. Our painters (inmates) have been using this article for several years and we have not felt any uneasiness about such use of it, particularly since the Mass. Reformatory cases of poisoning about a year ago." Chamberlain subsequently died of alcohol poisoning on July 28. Letter, Hollis M. Blackstone to J. White Belcher, Board of Trustees, July 27, 1891, Massachusetts State Archives, State Farm (Bridgewater, MA), State Workhouse/State Farm superintendent letter books, 1883–1912, HS9.10/2525X, Box 1: 1883–91, vol. 4, 470, 471.

78. SWB, October 1878, 3.
79. *BG*, "The State Workhouse," July 18, 1877, 3.
80. *BP*, "Massachusetts Legislature," January 8, 1859.
81. *NYT*, "A Work-House Burned," July 8, 1883. Other reports state that the fire was not discovered until 9:30 a.m. (*BG*, "The Workhouse on Fire," July 7, 1883.)
82. *NYT*, "A Work-House Burned," July 8, 1883.
83. *BG*, "State Workhouse Burned," July 8, 1883, 1.
84. *NYT*, "A Work-House Burned," July 8, 1883; *NYT*, "An Incendiary Sentenced," October 25, 1883.
85. *Oil City* [PA] *Derrick*, "Fire Record," July 9, 1883. The *Lowell Sun* gives a slightly different version of Gilmore's statement, recording, "I have carried a match for one year to accomplish it; I shoved a lot of straw up a ventilator flue and tampered with the steam pumps, and I am glad the damn place is in ashes." (*Lowell Sun*, "Burning of the State Workhouse at Bridgewater," July 14, 1883, 1.)
86. *Report of the Special Committee of the Seventy-Seventh General Assembly of Ohio*, 12.
87. Whitehill, "Making of an Architectural Masterpiece: The Boston Public Library," 14. In Clough's defense are his designs for the original B.M.C. Durfee High School at Fall River (1886) and the Suffolk County Courthouse at Boston.

## *Chapter 4*

88. *An Act to Establish a State Board of Health*, 1886 Mass. Acts 101, §5; *An Act to Provide a Building for the Chronic Insane at the State Workhouse at Bridgewater*, 1886 Mass. Acts 219.
89. *Resolve Providing for the Erection of New Buildings at the State Farm at Bridgewater*, 1888 Mass. Resolves 89, and *An Act in Further Addition to the Several Acts Making Appropriations for Expenses Authorized the Present Year, and for Certain Other Expenses Authorized by Law*, 1888 Mass. Acts 413 authorized expenditure of up to $30,000 for these buildings.
90. *An Act to Provide for the Removal of Prisoners from the State Prison in Boston to the State Farm in Bridgewater*, 1890 Mass. Acts 180.
91. Blackstone, *Bridgewater Book*, 38; *An Act to Change the Name of the State Workhouse at Bridgewater*, 1887 Mass. Acts 264; see also SWB, October 1886, 7.
92. Blackstone, *Bridgewater Book*, 37.

93. Letter, Hollis M. Blackstone to F.B. Sanborn, Honorable Prison Committee, November 4, 1889, Massachusetts State Archives, State Farm (Bridgewater, MA), State Workhouse/State Farm superintendent letter books, 1883–1912, HS9.10/2525X, Box 1: 1883–91, vol. 3, 333.
94. SFB, October 1896.
95. *BG*, "New Bedford," February 21, 1897, 2.
96. Blackstone, *Bridgewater Book*, 38.
97. *An Act to Establish an Asylum for Insane Criminals at Bridgewater and to Regulate Commitments and Removals to the Same*, 1895 Mass. Acts 390 established the "Asylum for Insane Criminals at Bridgewater." *An Act to Revise and Codify the Laws Relating to Insane Persons*, 1909 Mass. Acts 504, §98; SFB, December 1912, 9.
98. SFB, October 1896, 40.
99. *BP*, "The Pratt Case," September 29, 1894, 6.
100. *Lewiston Daily Sun*, "'Had to Do Queer Things to Fool the Doctors,'" November 24, 1911, 1.
101. Ernest B. Emerson, "Hospital Report" in SFB, December 1912, 41.
102. *MG*, "North Middleboro," January 26, 1894, 1.
103. Such high numbers of admissions for drunkenness and vagrancy were not unusual for the time. In 1908, the *New York Times* reported that drunkenness and vagrancy convictions had accounted for 43 percent of jail, prison and workhouse commitments nationally in 1904. *NYT*, "The Growing Problem of the American Tramp," June 14, 1908, SM10.
104. SFB, October 1898, 10.
105. *BG*, "Board Says Judges Disregard Mentality," August 31, 1915, 10.
106. *BG*, "Strong Order," June 4, 1903, 7. See also *NYT*, "Crusade against 'Jags' in Boston," June 15, 1903.
107. *MG*, "North Middleboro," July 21, 1905, 1; *MG*, August 18, 1905, 1; *MG*, February 2, 1906, 1.
108. SFB, December 1910, 21, 22.
109. Ibid., 22, 23.
110. Ibid., December 1911, 12.
111. Cabot, "Relation of Alcohol to Arteriosclerosis," 137.
112. *Cambridge Tribune*.
113. *MG*, "North Middleboro," February 17, 1905, 1.
114. *Report of the Members of the Royal Commission on the Care and Control of the Feeble-Minded*, VII, 70, 71.
115. *Report of the Special Committee of the Seventy-Seventh General Assembly of Ohio*, 12.

116. Massachusetts State Archives, State Farm (Bridgewater, MA), daily schedules and diaries, 1911–53, HS9.10/2532X, Box 1: 1911–23, vol. 1 (1911).
117. Creedon Papers, MPL, "State Farm Hay Cut Covers 1100 Acres of Land"; Creedon Papers, MPL, "Cut 450 Tons of Hay."
118. SFB, 1916, 15; BPC, January 1911, 165.
119. *NYT*, "The Growing Problem of the American Tramp," June 14, 1908, SM10. The *Times* did acknowledge that conditions at Bridgewater were "far better than in most correctional institutions."
120. *MG*, "North Middleboro," April 21, 1905, 1.
121. Ibid., April 17, 1891, 1.
122. *Fitchburg Daily Sentinel*, "Patients' Lives Are Gambled On," November 10, 1913, 10.
123. McLean, *Reply to the Plymouth County Grand Jury Report.*
124. *MG*, "North Middleboro," July 6, 1894, 1.
125. SFB, October 1888, 14.
126. Letter, Hollis M. Blackstone to George Washburn, Esq., August 16, 1889, Massachusetts State Archives, State Farm (Bridgewater, MA), State Workhouse/State Farm superintendent letter books, 1883–1912, HS9.10/2525X, Box 1: 1883–91, vol. 3, 257.
127. Ibid., October 13, 1893, 1; *BG*, "Insane Man at Large," May 9, 1890, 7; *MG*, "North Middleboro," September 1, 1893, 1; *MG*, October 27, 1893, 1; Creedon Papers, MPL, "Their Liberty Brief," November 1, 1902; *MG*, "North Middleboro," February 17, 1905, 1; Creedon Papers, MPL, "In Automobile"; *MG*, "North Middleboro," April 28, 1905, 1; *MG*, August 4, 1905, 1; *MG*, August 11, 1905, 1; *MG*, September 1, 1905, 1; Letter, Hollis M. Blackstone to George Washburn, Esq., August 16, 1889, Massachusetts State Archives, State Farm (Bridgewater, MA), State Workhouse/State Farm superintendent letter books, 1883–1912, HS9.10/2525X, Box 1: 1883–91, vol. 3, 257.
128. *MG*, "North Middleboro," July 28, 1893, 1.
129. Ibid., September 22, 1905, 1.
130. SFB, October 1905, 17; Creedon Papers, MPL, "For Drink Victims" and "Know About Francis."
131. *MG*, "North Middleboro," November 18, 1898, 1.
132. Ibid., November 10, 1905, 1.
133. *Brockton Enterprise*, "Sentence Pleased Him," September 27, 1910, 10.
134. *Odon* [IN] *Journal*, "Pardoned, Stays in Prison," June 18, 1909.

## *Chapter 5*

135. *An Act Relative to the Management of the State Farm at Bridgewater and to the Release of Inmates Therefrom*, 1919 Mass. Acts 199. The commitment and discharge of insane patients not under sentence at Bridgewater State Hospital was supervised until 1916 by the Board of Insanity, the Commission on Mental Diseases (1916–19) and the Department of Mental Diseases (after 1919). *An Act Relative to the Commitment of Insane Persons to the Bridgewater State Hospital and the Transfer or Discharge of Inmates Thereof*, 1923 Mass. Acts 467 confirmed that the state hospital would remain under the jurisdiction of the Department of Correction and control of the superintendent of the State Farm.
136. Stearns in *BG*, Louis M. Lyons, "The Doctor Gives His Diagnosis After Three Years in Our Prisons," December 4, 1932, B1.
137. *An Act to Provide for the Maintenance at the Reformatory for Women, the Massachusetts Reformatory and the State Farm of Departments for Defective Delinquents*, 1911 Mass. Acts 595.
138. *Report of the Commission to Investigate the Question of the Increase of Criminals*.
139. Kirkbride, "Review of Two Investigations on the Defective Delinquent," 167; *Report of the Commission to Investigate the Question of the Increase of Criminals*, 50. The commission also advocated more stringent gun control as a means to reduce crime.
140. MBP, January 1920, 88.
141. *BG*, "Bill Favoring 'Drunks' Lost," January 30, 1936, 15.
142. Ibid.
143. Since this time, recidivism rates at Bridgewater have declined sharply. Massachusetts Department of Correction Research intern Linda Druker in 1978 calculated the recidivism rate for the period 1971 and 1975 to be 27 percent, consistent with the commonwealth's other correctional facilities during the same years. Druker, *Analysis of Recidivism*.
144. Warren in *BG*, "Unrest Laid to Parole Board," January 4, 1936, 1.
145. *NYT*, "After 53 Years Behind Bars, Massachusetts Lifer Continues to Sulk in Country," August 2, 1929, 11.
146. *BG*, "Records Show Jesse Pomeroy Never Did Deserve Sympathy," October 2, 1932, A57.
147. Ibid., "Slayer of Cuneo Found Insane," August 30, 1921, 16; *NYT*, "Woman Kills Mother," July 29, 1933, 26.
148. Bartolomeo Vanzetti typed letter (copy) to Gertrude L. Winslow, March 23, 1927, Boston Public Library, Rare Books Department.

149. Bartolomeo Vanzetti typed letter (copy) to Alice Stone Blackwell, April 16, 1925, Boston Public Library, Rare Books Department.
150. Bartolomeo Vanzetti typed letter (copy) to Alice Stone Blackwell, April 14, 1925, Boston Public Library, Rare Books Department.
151. *BG*, "Make Report on Criminal Insane," December 11, 1932, A2
152. *BG*, "Dr. Briggs Urges New Hospital for the Insane," May 20, 1936, 12.
153. *Report of the Special Commission Established to Study the Whole Matter of the Mentally Diseased*, 92.
154. Ibid.
155. Ibid. Bearse's assessment was reflective of the period when reformers viewed the State Farm as a progressive institution. In 1921, the *Radcliffe News* had praised the State Farm. "The State farms offer to the prisoners a wholesome out-of-door life, and stress the fact that a prison is rather a reforming and uplifting influence than a place of punishment." (*Radcliffe News* (Cambridge, MA), "State vs. County Prisons," January 7, 1921, 2.)
156. Ibid.
157. *BG*, "Pension for Strann Urged by Residents," November 5, 1931, 29.
158. Ibid., "Caused $30,000 Fire at Bridgewater Farm," September 24, 1925, A21.
159. Ibid., "Insane Patient Slays Keeper," July 22, 1935, 19.
160. Ibid., "Murders in Asylum Blamed on Melton," February 14, 1928, 17.
161. *Lebanon* [PA] *Daily News*, November 13, 1931.
162. *BG*, "Denies Any Blame for Insane Killing," November 14, 1931, 12.
163. Ibid.
164. Ibid., "Lyman Starts Inquiry on Death," February 7, 1935, 1.
165. Ibid., "Audit of State Farm Hits at Lax Methods," June 27, 1931, 19.
166. Ibid., "One 'Country Club,' Other 'Hell Hole,'" January 12, 1932, 15.
167. Hanson in Robinson, "Institutions for Defective Delinquents," *Journal of Criminal Law & Criminology*, 396.
168. Ibid., 393.
169. *BG*, "Illegal Prisoner 32 Years Wins Release on Own Writ," n.d.; *Berkshire Evening Eagle* [Pittsfield, MA], March 26, 1953.
170. *BG*, "State's Strangest Battalion March with Wooden Guns," November 18, 1934, B2.
171. Ibid., "Two Held after Escape from Bridgewater Farm," November 10, 1931, 19.
172. Ibid., "Brennan Denounces State Farm System," June 2, 1932, 9.
173. Ibid., "Some Inmates Held 'Illegally,' Lurie Says of Bridgewater Farm," October 30, 1946, 1.

174. *NYT*, "Crime Cure Sought in Bay State Jails," October 13, 1929, N1.
175. *BG*, "'Defective Delinquent' Law Was Changed in Bay State," March 25, 1947, 14.
176. Ibid., "Ely Backs Stearns for Prison Changes," February 13, 1931, 42.
177. Ibid., "'Tom' and 'Ben' Are Reunited at Quincy," February 9, 1925, 6.
178. Ibid., "Justice Comes to Joe Barros," June 4, 1944, D1.
179. Ibid., "Some Inmates Held 'Illegally,' Lurie Says of Bridgewater Farm," October 30, 1946, 1.
180. *An Act Further Regulating the Commitment and Parole of Defective Delinquents and Drug Addicts*, 1947 Mass. Acts 684.
181. Wilfred E. Besner, "I Spent 30 Years in Jail…without a Trial!" *American Weekly*, December 13, 1953, 4–5.
182. *BG*, Paul Craigue, "Two Out of Three Illegally Committed in Massachusetts," August 16, 1953, C44.

## *Chapter 6*

183. *An Act Relative to the Penal and Reformatory Institutions of the Commonwealth*, 1955 Mass. Acts 770.
184. *Report of the Governor's Committee on Jails and Houses of Correction*, Commonwealth of Massachusetts Senate, June 1965, 5; *An Act Relative to the Commitment and Care of the Mentally Ill, Epileptics, Alcoholics and Drug Addicts*, 1956 Mass. Acts 589.
185. *BG*, "Prison for Its Sake Alone, Makes Hardened Criminals, Report Says," June 9, 1955, 2.
186. Ibid., "Furcolo Asks 44 Million to End Prison Firetraps," August 19, 1958, 1.
187. Ibid., "Imprisoned…Forgotten," February 20, 1963, 1.
188. Ibid.
189. Ibid.
190. Ibid.
191. Robert V. Leary, "Story to Be Aired Today of Long-Forgotten Men," *BG*, February 21, 1963, 1.
192. Ibid., "These Are Nice Old Guys," February 22, 1963, 1.
193. *Report of the Attorney General for the Year Ending June 30, 1968*, Commonwealth of Massachusetts, 1968, 21.
194. *NYT*, "'Boston Strangler' Flees Mental Institution," February 25, 1967, 1.
195. Bailey in *BG*, "Cruel, Barbarous, Illegal, Insanitary," January 21, 1967, 1.

196. Jean Dietz, "Horror or Haven," *BG*, June 19, 1966, 2.
197. Ibid., Solomon.
198. John H. Fenton, "Reform Is Urged in Mental Health," *NYT*, January 29, 1967, 43.
199. Ray Richard, "A Hospital or a Stable?" *BG*, January 15, 1967, 1.
200. Ibid.
201. Ibid.
202. Fenton, "Reform Is Urged in Mental Health," 43.
203. Ibid.
204. Richard, "A Hospital or a Stable?" 1.
205. Birnbaum, "Right to Treatment," 499+. *Estelle v. Gamble*, 429 U.S. 97 (1976) affirmed a prisoner's right to medical treatment under the Eighth Amendment and ruled, "A prisoner must allege acts or omissions sufficiently harmful to evidence deliberate indifference to serious medical needs." *Ruiz v. Estelle*, 503 F. Supp. 1265 (S.D. Tex 1980) subsequently set forth the constitutionally acceptable minimum for mental health treatment. The Massachusetts Supreme Judicial Court has similarly read Article 26 of the Massachusetts Declaration of Rights, which prohibits cruel and unusual punishment, to require a minimum level of mental health treatment for prisoners. See *Goodman v. Commissioner of Correction*, 629 N.E.2d 1321 (1994).
206. *BG*, "Bridgewater Patient's Shift Sought," January 19, 1967, 4.
207. *BG*, "Report Says Bridgewater Breaks Law," February 22, 1967, 1.
208. *NYT*, "The Screen: 'Titicut Follies' Observes Life in a Modern Bedlam," October 4, 1967, 38; *NYT*, "Film Stirs Furor in Massachusetts," October 18, 1967, 40.
209. Boston Public Library, WHDH Film Collection, Boston TV News Digital Library.
210. *NYT*, "Judge Proposes Compromise on Banned Film," September 30, 1989, 24.
211. *NYT*, "'Titicut' Is Barred to Bay State Public," June 25, 1969, 41; *Commonwealth v. Wiseman* 356 Mass. 251, 249 N.E.2d 610 (1969).
212. Paul Wilkes, "Documentarian Offers Viewers a Challenge," *NYT*, June 19, 1988, H31. On July 29, 1991, the commonwealth finally lifted its ban on the film, which has since entered the national cultural consciousness and most recently has been developed into a ballet.
213. Bruce Jackson, "Our Prisons Are Criminal," *NYT*, September 22, 1968, 258+.
214. *BG*, "A Prisoner Speaks Up," August 27, 1971, 16.

215. Ibid., "Sargent Urged to Visit State Prison Facilities," November 29, 1971, 36; *BG*, "Probers Disturbed: Bridgewater Unit 'Filthy,'" October 16, 1971, 6.
216. *BG*, "Probers Disturbed: Bridgewater Unit 'Filthy,'" October 16, 1971, 6.
217. *An Act Establishing a Comprehensive Program for the Treatment and Rehabilitation of Intoxicated Persons and Alcoholics and Abolishing the Crime of Public Intoxication*, 1971 Mass. Acts 1076.
218. *BG*, "Improvements Planned at Bridgewater in Response to Court Actions by Inmates," June 15, 1975, 25.
219. *John W. Nason v. Superintendent of Bridgewater State Hospital*, 353 Mass. 604.
220. *Nashua Telegraph*, "Court Contends Hospital Violated Patient's Rights," February 7, 1968, 32.
221. *Williams v. Lesiak*, 566 F.2d 1167 (1st Cir. 1977); *Williams v. Lesiak*, 822 F.2d 1223 (1st Cir. 1987); *King v. Greenblatt*, 53 F. Supp. 2d 117 (D. Mass. 1999).
222. *BG*, "Probers Disturbed: Bridgewater Unit 'Filthy,'" October 16, 1971, 6.
223. *Rozecki v. Gaughan*, 459 F.2d 6 (1972).
224. *Bel v. Hall*, 392 F. Supp. 274 (D. Mass. 1975); *BG*, "Court Condemns Bridgewater Unit," September 19, 1974, 1.
225. *BG*, "Treatment at Bridgewater State Hospital Virtually Nonexistent, Study Finds," April 12, 1975, 3.
226. Ibid., "Inmates, Governor's Aide Testify," December 4, 1974, 3.
227. Ibid., "Treatment at Bridgewater State Hospital Virtually Nonexistent," April 12, 1975, 3.
228. Ibid.
229. Ibid., "The 'Forgotten Women' of Bridgewater," May 20, 1973, 1.
230. Ibid., "Hospital for Insane Beset by Problems," May 27, 1985, 1.
231. Ibid., "Men Who Don't Need Bridgewater…," September 9, 1979, A4.
232. Jean Dietz, "State Planning Inmate Transfers from Bridgewater," *BG*, July 23, 1980, 35.
233. Ryan, *Screw*, 155.
234. *Doe by Roe v. Gaughan*, 617 F. Supp. 1477 (1985); *BG*, "Suit Filed for Noncriminal Bridgewater Patient," January 20, 1985, 41.
235. *Doe v. Gaughan* 808 F.2d 871 (1986).
236. *Boston Phoenix*, "Brief Cases: Trouble over Bridgewater," January 13, 1987, 3.

## *Chapter 7*

237. M.G.L. c. 123, §21.
238. Report of the Working Group on Bridgewater State Hospital, August 10, 1987, 3, 4.
239. *An Act Making Appropriations for the Fiscal Year Ending June Thirtieth, Nineteen Hundred and Eighty-Eight to Provide for Supplementing Certain Existing Appropriations and for Certain Other Activities and Projects*, 1988 Mass. Acts 1, §5 required the commissioner of mental health to file a plan to cease transfers of individuals "who neither are serving a criminal sentence nor have a criminal charge pending against them nor are awaiting sentence" to Bridgewater by March 31, 1989, and to transfer all those individuals who had previously been transferred to Bridgewater to mental health facilities elsewhere in the commonwealth. See Philip W. Johnston, Secretary, and Edward M. Murphy, Commissioner, "The Plan as Required by Section 5 of Chapter 1 of the Acts of 1988 by the Commissioner of Mental Health to the House Ways and Senate Committees on Ways and Means," April 25, 1988.
240. *King v. Greenblatt*, 53 F. Supp. 2d 117 (D. Mass. 1999).
241. *BG*, "Guards Fired in Man's Death," September 27, 2014, A1.
242. Ibid., "Scathing Study Cites Bridgewater Practices," July 13, 2014, A1.
243. Ibid., "Recoil, Reform, Repeat," November 20, 2016, K1.
244. Yvonne Abraham, "It's Time to Fix Bridgewater State Hospital," *BG*, April 20, 2016.
245. Massachusetts Governor Charlie Baker, State of the Commonwealth Address, January 2017.

# Select Bibliography

## *Archival Sources*

Boston Public Library
Massachusetts State Archives
Massachusetts State Library
Middleborough Public Library

## *Official Reports*

Annual Reports of the Inspectors of the State Almshouse at Bridgewater, 1854–72.
Annual Reports of the Inspectors of the State Almshouse at Monson, 1854–63.
Annual Reports of the Inspectors of the State Almshouse at Tewksbury, 1854–63.
Annual Reports of the Inspectors of the State Workhouse at Bridgewater, 1873–78.
Annual Reports of the Massachusetts Board of Prison Commissioners, 1902–16.
Annual Reports of the Massachusetts Board of State Charities, 1863–89.
Annual Reports of the Massachusetts Bureau of Prisons, 1917–55.
Annual Reports of the Massachusetts Commissioners of Prisons, 1872–1901.

Annual Reports of the Trustees of the State Farm at Bridgewater, 1886–1955.

Annual Reports of the Trustees of the State Workhouse at Bridgewater, 1879–86.

Reports of the Massachusetts Attorney General, 1854–1955.

*The Bridgewater Correctional Complex, 1855–1987: A Policy Report of the Senate Committee on Ways and Means.* Patricia McGovern, Chairwoman. Massachusetts Senate, November 1987.

Druker, Linda. *An Analysis of Recidivism among Residents Released from MCI Bridgewater during 1971–1975.* April 1978. Publication #10, 358-25-250-4-78-CR.

Farrington, Faye, and Christopher Mackey. *Population Trends at MCI-Bridgewater, 1969–1974.* Massachusetts Department of Correction, Division of Research and Planning, November 1974.

Mudd, John, et al. *Report of the Working Group on Bridgewater State Hospital.* August 10, 1987.

"The Plan as Required by Section 5 of Chapter 1 of the Acts of 1988 by the Commissioner of Mental Health to the House Ways and Senate Committees on Ways and Means." April 25, 1988.

*Report of the Commission to Investigate the Question of the Increase of Criminals, Mental Defectives, Epileptics and Degenerates.* Boston, January 1911.

*Report of the Members of the Royal Commission on the Care and Control of the Feeble-Minded upon their Visit to American Institutions.* London: Royal Commission on the Care and Control of the Feeble-Minded, 1908.

*Report of the Special Commission Established to Study the Whole Matter of the Mentally Diseased in Their Relation to the Commonwealth, Including All Phases of Work of the Department of Mental Diseases.* Boston: Commonwealth of Massachusetts, March 1, 1939.

*Report of the Special Committee of the Seventy-Seventh General Assembly of Ohio Appointed to Investigate Penitentiary Buildings, Management and Convict Labor.* Columbus: State of Ohio, 1908.

Urban, Kimberly M. *A Chronology of the Correctional Facility at Bridgewater.* December 1987.

## *Newspapers*

*Boston Daily Advertiser*, Boston, MA
*Boston Globe*, Boston, MA
*Boston Herald*, Boston, MA
*Boston Phoenix*, Boston, MA
*Boston Post*, Boston, MA
*Bridgewater Independent*, Bridgewater, MA
*Middleboro Gazette*, Middleborough, MA
*Namasket Gazette*, Middleborough, MA
*New York Times*, New York, NY
*Old Colony Memorial*, Plymouth, MA

## *Books and Periodicals*

Anderson, Carolyn. "The Conundrum of Competing Rights in TITICUT FOLLIES." *Journal of the University Film Association* 33, no. 1 (Winter 1981): 15–22.

Anderson, Carolyn, and Thomas W. Benson. *Documentary Dilemmas: Frederick Wiseman's* Titicut Follies. Carbondale: Southern Illinois University Press, 1991.

Birnbaum, Morton "Right to Treatment." *American Bar Association Journal* 46, no. 5 (May 1960): 499+.

*The Bridgewater Book.* Boston: George H. Ellis, printer, 1899.

Cabot, Richard C. "The Relation of Alcohol to Arteriosclerosis." *Transactions of the Section on Practice of Medicine of the American Medical Association* (June 1904): 137.

Fields, Annie, ed. *Letters of Sarah Orne Jewett.* Boston: Houghton Mifflin Company, 1911.

George, Charles E. "Sterilization of Criminals, Idiots and Insane." *Central Law Journal* 75, no. 5 (August 2, 1912): 91–95.

Kirkbride, Franklin B. "A Review of Two Investigations on the Defective Delinquent," *The Survey* (New York: The Charity Organization Society) 16 (April 1911): 167.

McLean, H.J. *A Reply to the Plymouth County Grand Jury Report on the Bridgewater State Hospital.* N.p.: privately printed, 1914.

Pride, Edward W. *A Short History of Tewksbury.* Tewksbury, MA: Tewksbury Village Improvement Association, 1888.

Robinson, Louis. "Institutions for Defective Delinquents." *Journal of Criminal Law & Criminology* 24 (1933): 352.

Ryan, Thomas. *Screw: A Guard's View of Bridgewater State Hospital*. Boston: South End Press, 1981.

Sanborn, F.B. "Poor-Law Administration in New England." *North American Review* 114, no. 234 (January 1872).

———. "The Poor-Laws of New England." *North American Review* 106, no. 219 (April 1868): 486, 487.

Whitehill, W.M. "The Making of an Architectural Masterpiece: The Boston Public Library." *American Art Journal* 2, no. 2 (Autumn 1970): 14.

# Index

## C



## D

## E



## F



## G



## H



## J



## K

## L



## M



## N



## O



## P

# W

# About the Author

Historian Michael J. Maddigan has been engaged in research, writing and historic preservation for over thirty years. He is the author of twelve previous books, including *Nemasket River Herring: A History*; *Images of America: Middleborough*; *Onset and Point Independence*; *Spiritualist Onset: Talking with the Dead by the Sea*; and *Muttock: Middleborough's Revolutionary Village*. His work is carried in the *Middleboro Gazette*, for which he has written over five hundred historical columns; is featured on the blog Recollecting Nemasket; and has appeared in numerous publications.

A native of Middleborough, Massachusetts, he is the founder of Recollecting Nemasket, a small publishing press devoted to the history of southeastern Massachusetts. A graduate of Stonehill College, he holds a master of arts degree from the Maxwell School of Citizenship and Public Affairs at Syracuse University. He currently serves as the chairman of the Middleborough Historical Commission and as a commissioner was responsible for listing South Middleborough on the National Register of Historic Places. He makes his home in a renovated 1863 woolen mill. To learn more about Mike's work, visit www.recollectingnemasket.com.